COMMUNITY POLICING

This project, conducted by the Police Executive Research Forum (PERF), was supported by The Annie E. Casey Foundation. Points of view or opinions contained in this document are those of the authors and do not necessarily reflect the official position or policies of PERF or The Annie E. Casey Foundation.

Police Executive Research Forum
Washington, DC 20036
United States of America

November 2004

ISBN: 1-878734-82-2

Library of Congress: 2004116837

Cover design by Nelson Design Group
Interior layout by Cynthia Stock

COMMUNITY POLICING

THE PAST, PRESENT, AND FUTURE

Edited by

Lorie Fridell and Mary Ann Wycoff

THE ANNIE E. CASEY FOUNDATION
and
POLICE EXECUTIVE RESEARCH FORUM
Washington, D.C.

Contents

PART III. THE FUTURE OF COMMUNITY POLICING

Foreword

I t is quite appropriate that The Annie E. Casey Foundation and the Police Executive Research Forum (PERF) have come together to produce this book on the past, present, and future of community policing. The mission of The Annie E. Casey Foundation is to improve the lives of disadvantaged youth and their families—particularly those in distressed areas. PERF's mission is to improve policing services to all individuals. These missions intersect at community policing, which brings police and communities together to solve neighborhood problems and improve the quality of life there. While there are many factors and entities at work that determine the welfare of America's children and families, certainly community policing is a significant one. With this mutual concern for communities plagued by violence, disorder, and fear, we have joined forces to produce this book to demonstrate the importance of community policing and reflect on its development, current status, and prospects for the future.

There has been tremendous speculation about the future of community policing. Can it flourish in agencies that are still in the early stages of implementation? In agencies that have demonstrated their commitment to community policing, can it be sustained and even advanced beyond current models when there are so many challenges facing innovative policing professionals? This book addresses these important questions. The authors provide valuable information on the implementation of community policing as well as informed opinions about what community policing may one day become. These national experts and leaders in policing speak out on critical issues and evaluate a decade of survey data. Their sometimes-disparate views reveal the many obstacles that must be overcome for community policing to meet its full potential.

Among those obstacles are the demands created by ongoing terrorist threats and the organizational and cultural barriers to successful implementation of community policing principles. Several chapters evaluate the impact of September 11, 2001, on law enforcement. Some observers are concerned that the nation's focus on antiterrorist activities will be the death knell for community policing. This book assesses how new demands on police related to homeland security will affect community policing; and it underscores the very real contribution that community policing has made and will make to advance U.S. security interests. Among the many other factors the authors discuss are officer training, organizational changes in police agencies, new performance measures, management-union issues, and police-citizen partnerships.

Part I describes the community policing model. While attempts during the past decade to develop a single definition of community policing have been controversial, consensus has emerged on three elements common to any community policing effort. These elements form the main themes of Chapter 1 written by Lorie Fridell. Mary Ann Wycoff then highlights best practices in community policing (Chapter 2), warning that the visible accomplishments of community engagement and problem solving will not be sustained without organizational transformation. In Chapter 3, Edward Flynn argues that community policing is fundamentally just "good policing" and he reminds us—through reflections on his own experiences in law enforcement from line officer to leader—of the great transformation from traditional to community policing.

Part II examines how community policing principles are reflected in policing practices and assesses whether community policing is "rhetoric or reality." To conduct this assessment, PERF staff drew upon information obtained through national surveys of law enforcement agencies in 1992, 1997, and 2002. The data were used to report not only the extent to which agencies identify as *community policing agencies,* but also the specific manifestations of that orientation in terms of activities, training, and reorganization. Because the three surveys were similar in content and implemented at three different times over a period of ten years, the reader can chronicle changes in community policing implementation in the United States for that decade. In the 2002 survey, law enforcement agencies added information about the impact of the terrorist threat on community policing, as well as how community policing practices help police address that threat. Lorie Fridell, in Chapter 4, discusses the results from the three surveys. In Chapter 5, Gary Cordner outlines the strengths and weaknesses of the survey data and highlights the aspects of community policing that have been most successfully implemented, as well as those features that agency executives need to give more emphasis in the years to come.

In Part III, law enforcement practitioners and academic experts— reflecting upon the research results and their own experiences—discuss where law enforcement has been with community policing and where it may be going. These commentators provide practical direction for law enforcement professionals, particularly agency executives, on how the promise of community policing can be fulfilled in the challenging years ahead. Bonnie Bucqueroux (Chapter 6) draws on the survey data to demonstrate how departments have been deficient in their partnership work and she provides guidance on how to fully realize this critical element of community policing. Paul Grogan and Lisa Belsky (Chapter 7) describe the results of successful community development corporations-police partnerships across the nation, citing activities that reduce disorder, strengthen neighborhood social controls, increase the political power of residents, and promote economic development. Dennis Rosenbaum (Chapter 8) also addresses the importance of the relationship between police and the community—highlighting how new technologies can be harnessed to move community policing into the future. Barbara McDonald and Ron Huberman (Chapter 9) then describe one such technology: a very comprehensive information system the Chicago Police Department uses to advance citizen interactions with police, facilitate problem solving and crime investigation, and promote effective performance measurement— particularly measures of community satisfaction.

Nancy McPherson (Chapter 10) emphasizes the importance of structures and processes internal to police agencies that support community policing as they move into the future. She highlights the importance of leadership at the line level; the need for research, education and technology to support problem solving; internal organizational mechanisms that reinforce community policing; ethical competence among personnel; and management-union collaboration. Jerry Flynn draws on his experience as a police officer and union leader to demonstrate how community policing can be advanced through the efforts of dedicated, creative street officers. Ellen Hanson (Chapter 12) raises the critical issue of resources for continued support of community policing. She emphasizes the need for partnerships among government agencies and private social service agencies to ensure limited resources are used efficiently and effectively to meet common community goals. Wesley Skogan (Chapter 13) reviews the key principles of community policing and cautions agencies against partial, "on the cheap" implementation. He delineates reasons why some community policing efforts fail, including resistance from officers, police unions, and police managers; competing demands and expectations; lack of interagency cooperation; and an unresponsive public. Richard Myers (Chapter 14) also examines the impediments to community policing, but from the perspective of one who has fully considered the *possible* and *preferable* futures of community policing. Based on his experience and feedback from several working groups of police futurists, he discusses the potential impact trends and emerging technologies could have on community policing.

Ellen Scrivner (Chapter 15) next addresses the issues related to community policing associated with the terrorist attack of September 11, 2001 and the ongoing threat to domestic security. She describes how community policing, including problem solving, can serve the goals of homeland security. Chief Darrel Stephens (Chapter 16) also outlines the significant challenges to the full implementation and continued existence of community policing, such as the potential impacts of September 11, 2001 and rising crime rates. He calls upon practitioners to implement community policing department-wide, to expand community involvement, and to use COMPSTAT in a way that facilitates community policing.

In the final chapter (Part IV, Chapter 17), Mary Ann Wycoff discusses what is required to ensure that community policing is sustained in agencies around the country. She describes the perils of incomplete implementation and provides guidance to ensure both internal and external institutionalization of community policing.

Though most law enforcement agencies across the nation believe themselves to be engaged in some aspect of community policing, this book provides concrete assessments of what implementing this form of policing really means, and explores the progress and promise of community policing. It provides an opportunity to compare current practices against aspirations for true community policing. We hope it will make an important contribution to the efforts of those agents of change who want to take community policing to the next level by strengthening the bond between police and the people they serve.

Bart Lubow   Chuck Wexler
The Annie E. Casey Foundation   PERF

Part I

The Community Policing Model

1

The Defining Characteristics of Community Policing

by Lorie Fridell, Director of Research,
Police Executive Research Forum

The Community Policing Consortium defines community policing as "a collaborative effort between the police and the community that identifies problems of crime and disorder and involves all elements of the community in the search for solutions to these problems."[1] Community policing is based on the premise that police alone cannot control crime and disorder and promote residents' quality of life (Community Policing Consortium 1994). In community policing—in contrast to traditional policing—the public's involvement is viewed as a "co-producer" of community safety and wellness (Whitaker 1980; Parks et al. 1981; Parks et al. 1982). Community policing also expands the role of police beyond crime fighting

---

1. The Bureau of Justice Assistance created the Community Policing Consortium, which is currently housed within the Office of Community Oriented Policing Services (COPS Office). The Consortium is composed of the International Association of Chiefs of Police (IACP), the National Sheriffs' Association (NSA), the National Organization of Black Law Enforcement Executives (NOBLE), the Police Executive Research Forum (PERF), and the Police Foundation. These five organizations play a principal role in developing community policing research, training, and technical assistance. Each is committed to advancing the community policing philosophy.

to maintaining order and promoting improved living conditions for residents. While traditional policing has been characterized by reactive responses to crime, community policing emphasizes proactive problem solving to prevent and otherwise control crime (Sparrow, Moore, and Kennedy 1990; Sparrow 1988). The goals of community policing are to reduce crime and disorder, promote citizens' quality of life in communities, reduce fear of crime, and improve police–citizen relations (Community Policing Consortium 1994). These goals are achieved through three essential efforts: community engagement, problem solving, and organizational transformation. The following discussion focuses on how each of these elements is understood in the community policing context and raises key questions about their effective implementation.

Community Engagement

Sir Robert Peel said "the police are the public and the public are the police" (Braiden 1992). This statement reflects a key tenet of community policing: the police should not be separate from, but rather joined in partnership with, the community. A major impetus for the move away from traditional policing was the recognition that the police cannot control crime and disorder alone. With community policing, the police and community are expected to co-produce safe and healthy communities (Parks et al. 1981, 1982). The partnerships can and should serve to empower residents to take responsibility for their neighborhoods. As stated by Kelling (1988, 2–3), "police are to stimulate and buttress a community's ability to produce attractive neighborhoods and protect them against predators."

Important to this relationship are agency activities that promote interaction and familiarity with jurisdiction residents.[2] Agencies generally achieve stronger links with citizens using myriad approaches including long-term assignments of officers to specific geographic areas; foot and bike patrols; mini-stations in communities; community meetings; citizen police academies; and other forms of outreach such as Police Athletic Leagues, educational programs in schools, and citizen volunteer programs. But, however important these outreach programs are for promoting a

---

2. In *Citizen Involvement: How Community Factors Affect Progressive Policing*, Correia (2000) affirms the need for police to pay more attention to how communities mobilize and develop bonds of trust to involve them in community policing. His book is based on an analysis of six sites and other survey data, interviews, and reports.

strong police-community relationship, other activities are required to cement a true partnership with the community. One key activity is collaborative problem solving. As discussed in detail below, police and citizens engaged in collaborative problem solving join together to identify the problems facing a community, prioritize them, and develop and implement viable responses. In a true partnership, the police and citizens make important decisions together about agency policies, practices and direction.[3] This level of citizen involvement in the workings of the department might take several forms (for instance, residents' participation on advisory councils to the chief or their involvement in hiring, evaluating, and/or promoting personnel; developing agency policies; or reviewing complaints).

Agencies should form partnerships not only with residents but also with organized groups and private and public agencies. These organized entities are stakeholders in a healthy community, as well as potential resources for addressing community problems. They include public and private service agencies (for example, housing agencies, other public assistance agencies and nonprofit groups serving high-need groups), interest groups (for example, the Urban League, Mothers against Drunk Driving, neighborhood organizations), and public works agencies.

Any agency that wants to gauge the effectiveness and potential of its police-community partnerships should be prepared to answer a number of key questions that have been raised about these partnerships across the United States:

- In what ways are agencies reaching out to communities to facilitate familiarity and trust?
- Are agencies moving beyond these outreach efforts to truly engage the community as partners?
- Do residents have sufficient trust in the police and understanding of community policing to become and stay involved?
- Is the role of involving the community relegated to a unit or team of officers, or is community involvement a core principle of the department, underlying all that it does?

---

3. "Community may be defined by the following three factors: geography (people who live or work in a given place), shared character or identity (people share common characteristics, such as ethnicity, age, economics, and religion), and common concerns or problems (people tend to join together when they share common concerns or problems). Groups of people who more or less exhibit each of these three factors can be considered a community, at least for the purposes of community policing" (Flynn 1998, 9).

- Are agencies successfully engaging in partnerships with organized groups and private and public agencies to cooperatively address issues of crime, disorder, and quality of life?

The survey results presented in Chapter 4 as well as the commentaries throughout this book address these questions and consider the challenges for the future.

Problem Solving

The second element of community policing, and an objective of police partnerships with communities, is collaborative problem solving. In problem-oriented policing, police work with residents, organizations, and agencies to identify and solve community problems related to crime, disorder, and the quality of life. But problem solving is not just a mechanism for linking with the community and developing trust; it is good policing, as Herman Goldstein, the father of problem-oriented policing, explains. "Smarter policing in this country requires a sustained effort within policing to research substantive problems, to make use of the mass of information and data on specific problems accumulated by individual police agencies, to experiment with different alternative responses, to evaluate these efforts and to share the results of these evaluations with police across the nation" (Goldstein 1993, 5). Problem solving is essential to effective prevention. With this tool, police are not merely responding to the same locations and individuals over and over to address crime; they are addressing underlying problems that can eliminate, or at least reduce, future occurrences.

While police could conceivably conduct their problem solving in isolation, their effectiveness is greatly enhanced when the police partner with residents, organized groups, and agencies. The community's first critical task is to work with the police to identify the crime, disorder, and quality-of-life issues residents want to be addressed. Police all over the country have found that citizens' priorities may be very different from those that police might identify; both sets of priorities can be addressed and ordered in a partnership. The community can be helpful in gathering critical information to determine the nature and scope of the problems being analyzed for priority action (Eck and Spelman 1987; U.S. Department of Justice 2001, 2002). The community is then involved in working with the police to identify and implement viable responses to the problems.

Often police and individual residents lack the necessary resources and expertise or authority to implement long-term change. Therefore, public and private organizations and entities can be important partners in these endeavors. As reported by Sadd and Grime (1995), the problems identified by residents can go beyond the purview of police agencies. Alternatively, the problems themselves may be well within the traditional reach of law enforcement agencies, but effective responses may require external resources. The regular involvement of outside entities can stimulate such innovative responses as using building code enforcement and other regulatory codes to address drug dealing; training apartment-complex managers on crime control efforts; and supporting crime prevention pacts with specific neighborhoods. These partnerships can promote the use of non-criminal-justice responses for even traditional crime and disorder problems.

Within some police agencies, the executives assign the task of problem solving only to designated officers, problem-solving units, or patrol officers. Other police agencies consider problem solving to be an effective tool for all personnel. A recent PERF project examined the involvement of investigators in problem solving (Wycoff 2001). In many departments, detectives now have geographic or neighborhood assignments, thus facilitating information sharing with officers assigned to the same areas. In some departments, detectives and patrol officers are partners in problem-solving teams. For example, detectives in the Spokane County, Washington, Sheriff's department have had the primary responsibility for working with citizens to identify and resolve problems. Detectives in Mesa, Arizona, have developed a number of programs that involve citizens in crime prevention. Other agencies find that even the chief and other command staff need to become involved in implementing problem-solving responses. Partnerships with other public agencies, including other components of the criminal justice system, or local or state legislative changes may be required to solve the problem.

As discussed more fully below, agencies can support or promote problem solving internally through training, policies and procedures, and individual and agency-level performance measures. Those interested in assessing police agencies' problem-solving acumen should ask these basic questions:

- Are the law enforcement agencies engaging in problem solving?
- Are they implementing problem solving collaboratively with residents, organized interest groups, and public and private agencies?

- Is problem solving relegated to a special unit or just to patrol, or are other components of the agency involved?
- Are agencies implementing innovative responses?
- Do agencies support problem solving internally through training, performance measurement, and other means?

Light can be shed on progress in the field by reviewing the survey results in Chapter 4 and the commentators' observations. Consideration of these questions is also useful for any agencies interested in self-assessment and for the citizens integral to their efforts.

Organizational Transformation

In 1988 George Kelling asked, "How will community policing fit into police departments, given how they are now organized?" He conjectured that "radical alterations will be required if police are to respond more effectively to community problems." Similarly, Goldstein (1993, 9) reported that "the initiatives associated with community policing cannot survive in a police agency managed in traditional ways. If changes are not made, the agency sets itself up for failure" (see also Zhao 1996). Organizational transformation facilitates community engagement and problem solving and sustains community policing implementation over time.

A major theme in discussions of successful agency transformation for community policing is the need for pushing power downward in the agency. As described in "Understanding Community Policing: A Framework for Action,"

> Community policing requires the shifting of initiative, decision making, and responsibility downward within the police organization. Under community policing, patrol officers are given broader freedom to decide what should be done and how it should be done in their communities—they assume managerial responsibility for the delivery of police services to their assigned areas. Patrol officers are the most familiar with the needs and strengths of their communities and are thus in the best position to forge the close ties with the community that lead to effective solutions to local problems (Community Policing Consortium 1994, 22).

Physical decentralization—in addition to the decentralization of power and command—are important for supporting the new role of officers. This physical decentralization corresponds to personnel assignments. Long-term assignments to specific geographic areas are needed so that police are accessible to the residents they serve and acquire a sense of 24–7 responsibility for their neighborhoods. They can be physically stationed within those assigned communities in, for instance, precinct stations, beat offices, or storefronts. Some agencies, as mentioned above, decentralize not just patrol, but other agency components such as investigations and crime analysis. When managers are made responsible for geographic areas rather than police functions, all types of police services in an area can be coordinated to meet objectives for that neighborhood or zone.

Other types of organizational transformation also support critical field-level work. The role of management is not to *direct* the activities of the field personnel so much as *guide* them and ensure that they have the resources that they require to do their jobs (Community Policing Consortium 1994). Some advocates of community policing recommend flattening the organization, or reducing the number of management levels, to facilitate communication and decrease the amount of time and bureaucratic effort needed for decision making. Agencies also can free up time for field personnel to engage in their community policing responsibilities by developing alternative mechanisms for handling calls for service. This can take the form of call classification and prioritization, which reduces the number of calls to which field personnel are immediately dispatched. Specifically, nonemergency calls may be handled in another manner or delayed if immediate assistance is not required.[4]

Other agency changes to support community policing relate to hiring, training, personnel evaluation, and agency performance measurement. In terms of hiring, agencies need to hire officers with characteristics well suited to community policing. These officers have been described by Hough (2002) as conscientious, emotionally mature and stable, influential, amicable, service-oriented, and having practical intelligence. Police executives need to work with their training directors, academy personnel, and perhaps even budget and legislative leaders to ensure the resources and

---

4. Some jurisdictions handle requests for assistance differently than emergency calls for service. These jurisdictions provide a nonemergency call number to citizens, such as the 311 system in Baltimore, Maryland. In addition, some agencies have provided automated burglary reports or permit nonsworn personnel to take reports, primarily for insurance purposes, for certain routine matters. For example, nonsworn personnel may take car accident reports in which there is no injury.

mechanisms are in place to offer academy recruits quality training in community policing and problem solving—preferably with community policing concepts infused throughout the entire academy curriculum. In-service officers, too, need training in community policing and problem solving, including training in advanced topics, such as organizing groups and communities, community interactions, human resources management, and crime analysis or mapping, to name a few.

Agencies should develop job descriptions that recognize community policing and problem-solving responsibilities. Personnel evaluations should review and assess skills and behaviors related to these roles. The evaluation system, as well as the disciplinary system, should recognize that mistakes will be made. Community policing is a model of policing that promotes well-intentioned risk-taking. In the same way that personnel evaluations are an important management tool for promoting desired behavior on the part of individuals, agency-level performance measurement should examine community policing inputs, outputs, and outcomes to promote and sustain its implementation.[5]

To find out about the nature and extent of organizational transformation in community policing agencies, one might ask the following questions:

- Are field personnel given authority to make decisions regarding which activities are necessary to promote the health of their assigned neighborhoods?
- Has command or decision making been tied to defined geographic areas?
- Have patrol, crime analysis, and/or investigations been physically decentralized?
- Have agencies implemented alternative response methods for calls for service?
- Have recruiting/selection criteria been modified to reflect the skills and characteristics needed by community policing officers?
- Are recruit and in-service officers trained in community policing and problem solving?

---

5. Moore et al. (2002) advocate comprehensive agency-level performance measurement systems that provide for both internal and external accountability. Examples of outcome measures for agencies include the extent to which they control crime, hold offenders to account, reduce fear, and regulate public spaces.

- Do role definitions and personnel evaluations reflect community policing and problem solving?
- Do agencies incorporate community policing and problem solving into measures of their own performance?

This chapter has defined community policing in terms of three key features: community engagement, problem solving, and organizational transformation. The next chapter elaborates on community policing practices and suggests that the best practices, surprisingly, may be invisible.

References

Braiden, Chris. 1992. "Enriching Traditional Police Roles." *Police Management: Issues and Perspectives.* Washington, D.C.: Police Executive Research Forum, p. 108.

Community Policing Consortium. 1994. *Understanding Community Policing: A Framework for Action.* Washington, D.C.: Bureau of Justice Assistance. Reprinted in Willard M. Oliver, ed. 2000. *Community Policing: Classical Readings.* Upper Saddle River, N.J.: Prentice Hall.

Correia, Mark. 2000. *Citizen Involvement: How Community Factors Affect Progressive Policing.* Washington, D.C.: Police Executive Research Forum.

Eck, John, and William Spelman. 1987. *Problem Solving: Problem-Oriented Policing in Newport News.* Washington, D.C.: Police Executive Research Forum.

Flynn, Daniel. 1998. *Defining the "Community" in Community Policing.* Washington, D.C.: Community Policing Consortium

Goldstein, Herman. 1993. *The New Policing: Confronting Complexity.* National Institute of Justice, Research in Brief. Washington, D.C.: U.S. Department of Justice. Reprinted in Oliver, Willard M., ed. 2000. *Community Policing: Classical Readings,* 71–80. Upper Saddle River, N.J.: Prentice Hall.

Hough, Laeatta M. 2002. *Hiring in the Spirit of Service: Definitions, Possibilities, Evidence and Recommendations.* St. Paul: Community Policing Consortium.

Kelling, George L. 1988. "Police and Communities: The Quiet Revolution." In Perspective on Policing, no. 1 Washington, D.C.: National Institute of Justice, U.S. Department of Justice, and the Program in Criminal Justice Policy and Management, John F. Kennedy School of Government, Harvard University. Reprinted in Willard M. Oliver, ed. 2000. *Community Policing: Classical Readings,* 60–70. Upper Saddle River, N.J.: Prentice Hall.

Moore, Mark, with David Thacher, Andrea Dodge, and Tobias Moore. 2002. *Recognizing Value in Policing: The Challenge of Measuring Police Performance.* Washington, D.C.: Police Executive Research Forum.

Parks, Roger B., Paula C. Baker, Larry Kiser, Ronald Oakerson, Elinor Ostrom, Vincent Ostrom, Stephen L. Percy, Martha B. Vandivort, Gordon P. Whitaker, and Rick Wilson. 1981. "Consumers as Coproducers of Public Services." *Policy Studies Journal* 9 (Summer): 1001–1011.

————. 1982. "Coproduction of Public Services." In Richard C. Rich, ed., Analyzing Urban-Service Distributions, 185–199. Lexington, Mass.: Lexington Books.

Sadd, Susan, and Randolph Grime. 1995. *Issues in Community Policing: Lessons Learned in the Implementation of Eight Innovative Neighborhood-Oriented Policing Programs,* vol. 2 of a report submitted to the National Institute of Justice. Http://www.ncjrs.org/txtfiles/inopvol2.txt

Sparrow, Malcolm K. 1988. "Implementing Community Policing." In *Perspective on Policing,* no. 9. Washington, D.C.: National Institute of Justice, U.S. Department of Justice, and the Program in Criminal Justice Policy and Management, John F. Kennedy School of Government, Harvard University. Reprinted in Oliver, Willard M., ed. 2000. *Community Policing: Classical Readings.* Upper Saddle River, N.J.: Prentice Hall.

Sparrow, Malcolm, Mark H. Moore, and David M. Kennedy. 1990. *Beyond 911: A New Era for Policing.* New York: Basic Books.

U.S. Department of Justice, Office of Community Oriented Policing Services. 2001. *Problem-Oriented Guides for Police.* Washington, D.C.

————. 2002. *Problem-Oriented Guides for Police.* Washington, D.C.

Whitaker, Gordon P. 1980. "Coproduction: Citizen Participation in Service Delivery." *Public Administration Review* 40(3) (May–June): 240–246.

Wycoff, Mary Ann. 2001. *Investigations in the Community Policing Context.* Unpublished report submitted to the National Institute of Justice by the Police Executive Research Forum. Grant No. 96-IJ-CX-0081.

Zhao, Jihong. 1996. *Why Police Organizations Change: A Study of Community-Oriented Policing.* Washington, D.C.: Police Executive Research Forum.

2

The Best Community Policing Practice May Be Invisible

by Mary Ann Wycoff, Independent Researcher/Consultant

Community policing, either as proclamation or practice, tends to be highly visible, a fact that yields both substantive and political payoff. The announcement that a department is adopting community policing is made so that the public, press, and politicians will take appropriate note. The new storefront office, district station, or police-community center is opened with fanfare designed to generate press coverage and applause. The officer who teaches a class or meets with community groups or walks through a neighborhood is intentionally visible—and should be. An invisible approach to community policing would make it difficult for the public to know when and where to make better contact with the police. Such an approach also would make it difficult to know that the police are attempting to do something different.

In addition to these publicized aspects of community policing, there is a less visible, "undercover" side. While largely unknown to press or public, this feature is essential to identifying and successfully implementing the best community policing practices for any given community. Philosophy and programs are visible (or audible) and tend to be well publicized, but every department that aspires to community policing should have an undergirding all-but-invisible corporate strategy that is essential for the implementation of the best and the most enduring practice of the philosophy.

The Visible Philosophy

The philosophy of community policing has received broad public acclaim. It is likely that every major newspaper and news magazine has, by now, carried multiple stories about the concept and about some of the more glamorous operational approaches to its implementation. The philosophy is publicly well received. There can be nothing but applause for the notion that police and citizens should know one another and should work together to produce safer communities. Who (other than criminals perhaps) would not celebrate such an idea? It has so much democratic "face" appeal that almost all police leaders in the country embrace it publicly. Indeed, it is such a commonsensical and appealing notion that many chiefs claim to have been implementing it for years, if not decades. While this might be true in some places, many chiefs supporting the philosophy reported in a 1992 survey that they were unsure how to operationalize the community policing philosophy. [1]

This uncertainty has diminished with time as community policing practices have been showcased. The 1992 survey was an unintentional part of the publicity process. For the first time in the long career of this researcher, there were calls to the research organization from police leaders who wished to express gratitude for the survey. Because the survey instrument asked questions about a number of different community policing practices in which responding agencies might be engaged, it helped some agencies with operational specification of the concept. The philosophy had attracted them and they were eager to know how it might look in reality.

Since 1992 there has been a cascade of such information about the implementation of community policing. The National Institute for Justice, the Bureau of Justice Assistance, the Office of Community Oriented Policing Services (COPS), the Police Executive Research Forum, the Police Foundation, the National Organization of Black Law Enforcement Officers, the International Association of Chiefs of Police, the National Sheriff's Association, the International City/County Management Association, the Ford Foundation, Harvard University, and a host of other public and private agencies—along with the media ever eager for a new police story—have hosted conferences, funded or conducted research, produced publications, and otherwise promoted and publicized community policing and its companion philosophy, "problem-oriented policing." The philosophy

---

1. This 1992 survey conducted by the Police Foundation is described in Chapter 4.

has not lacked publicity and with it has come a substantial body of information about programs and practices.

Visible Programs

With the exception of notable efforts by COPS and the seminar series conducted by Harvard University and the National Institute of Justice, the primary focus of the publicity about community policing has been on programs. For example, articles have been written about storefronts in Detroit, Michigan, or Houston or Dallas, Texas, or Madison, Wisconsin; foot patrols in Flint, Michigan, or Newark, New Jersey; and problem-solving units in Baltimore, Maryland. Nationwide there have been mentoring/tutoring programs for struggling students; citizen police academies; community meetings involving police and residents; citizen surveys; specific problem-solving efforts; and department websites. City after city has had its highly acclaimed community policing officer or group of officers made locally famous by the media for using the idea to provide better police service in a troubled neighborhood.

Stories about programs and individual officers were easy to tell and often could be accompanied by appealing photographs of the officers at work, perhaps in the company of young children or an adult in need of assistance. Fifteen years ago these stories made good copy. In one community, a newspaper article told the dramatic tale of a neighborhood officer who was able to lead terrified but trusting children from an apartment building where an assailant was believed to be hiding. In another, an officer was profiled who created a storefront office in a post-Vietnam Asian neighborhood and found volunteers to assist him, each of whom could speak one of the three languages spoken in the community. This officer, a Vietnam veteran, provided a wide variety of policing and other social services to a previously neglected community. In a midwestern city, the television news covered a group of officers and citizens who, together, waved down speeders on a heavily traveled neighborhood street to appeal to their sense of neighborliness and good citizenship in an effort to convince them to drive more slowly. In a Florida community, there were newspaper and television stories about a police department that used drug forfeiture monies to build a recreational and learning center in a neighborhood where families had been devastated by predations of drug dealers and by police activity that jailed them. In a Texas city, storefront officers were reported hosting a Halloween party for children that resulted in a child revealing to an officer the location of a large quantity of stolen property. Other officers were written about because they walked door to door in their neighborhoods, becoming acquainted with residents and asking them whether there were any problems in the neighborhood police should know about.

These are all compelling stories, and in 2004 community policing stories still make good copy. We read that Arlington, Texas, has neighborhood teams that provide a wide range of police services. We read that in Lakewood, Colorado, and Fremont, California, there are parenting classes for parents who feel they do not know how to control their children. The "Kids' Corner" program in Reno, Nevada, helps prevent child abuse and neglect. The Appleton, Wisconsin, police department partners with the local Boys and Girls Club to help prevent children from running away from home. Officers in Mesa, Arizona, work with community groups to prevent a variety of crimes by hardening targets. Police in Portland, Oregon, work with apartment managers who want to learn how to reduce crime and to handle problems before they escalate. We read about community policing efforts in Arlington, Virginia; Charlotte-Mecklenburg, North Carolina; Portland, Oregon; and San Diego, California. Stories still abound. And we can hope that they always will.

Best Practices: A Cautionary Note

The tales—whether told in the popular press, at conferences, or in government or professional publications—help the public and police practitioners alike gain an understanding of what community policing is and what it can do. The result, not infrequently, is that these stories elevate specific activities to the status of "best practices." Police practitioners, political leaders, and/or community members in some other city will decide that the activity or program described is something that should be adopted by their own department. After all, if Community A is a "community policing department" using this program, then adoption of the program elsewhere should spread community policing to other communities.

Perhaps. There always is a solid argument to be made for borrowing a good idea rather than investing resources in an attempt to develop something unique. At the same time, risks are associated with ready replication. Six of those risks are explained in this section.

First, simple replication can result in a shallow and overly simple examination of the philosophy. When the concept of community policing was first gaining popularity, many people confused the tactic of foot patrol with the philosophy, and some community leaders and police managers considered foot patrol to be the *sine qua non* of community policing. Do this one thing, and your department would be a community policing department. Indeed, when foot patrol was discontinued in the 1980s in Flint, Michigan, the city where this ancient practice had been modernized and popularized, there was national crepe hanging about the imminent death of community policing. With hindsight, we now know that community policing was just beginning to live, but the confusion between specific programs (such as the once popular foot patrol) and the community policing philosophy also lives.

A second risk of adopting a seeming "best practice" is that the effectiveness of an attractive idea is seldom evaluated in advance of program publicity. There is no guarantee that it accomplishes its goal at the implementation site, let alone in a different setting. Despite having theoretical or political appeal, the program might have no measurable impact, or it might even have an impact that is the opposite of the one desired. When the Houston Police Department was testing several fear reduction strategies in the early 1980s (Pate et al. 1986), it experimented with calling crime victims to see whether they had received the information they needed about their case and whether they were having any problems with which the department might help them. An evaluation determined that, while the telephone contacts were well received by a majority of the experiment's subjects, they had a negative impact on Hispanic victims who apparently feared any contact with the police. Because the strategy was well researched, this outcome was known. But had the contact strategy simply been described by the media or the police department, the reader might never have suspected the Hispanic reaction.

A third risk has to do with program transferability. Project descriptions— particularly, but not peculiarly, journalistic reports—seldom identified relevant conditions under which the original project was implemented. What was the neighborhood like? How large was it in square miles? Was there a commercial area? What were the population demographics? Did residents occupy houses or apartments? Were residents well organized? How many were homeowners? And what were their problems? A program that is effective in one site might be worthless in another, not because the idea isn't good but because it doesn't fit the needs or conditions of the population for which it is being adopted.

Before the crisis in Flint, a consultant to one major city police department strongly advocated the adoption of foot patrol by that agency until he drove through the city and realized it had very few sidewalks outside the central business district. The misfit of idea and local conditions was blatant and readily identifiable. Other mismatches might not be so glaringly apparent, but they might be just as great a roadblock to successful replication. The "right" practice (even the "best" practice") adopted in the wrong setting will do nothing to advance community safety or community policing. The "best practice" for any given community is the one that fits the needs and conditions of a specific community and is compatible with the resources of the city, its citizens, its police, and its other institutions.

A fourth risk of replication arises from the fact that programs often come attractively packaged but without instructions for assembly. Even a program that is "best" in terms of its local appropriateness will do no good if it is not properly implemented. If summary program descriptions tend to lack detailed discussion of the context in which the program has been implemented, they even more commonly lack discussion of the organizational and community resources required for successful implementation. What was required politically and organizationally to make the work of a lauded community policing officer possible in the first place? And what was required to keep him or her effective over the long run? (The story almost never is about the long run.)

Sometimes little is required. One officer assigned to a neighborhood and given considerable latitude to work with residents to solve problems does not require much organizational adjustment or support. Even a dozen such officers assigned to work out of storefronts or engage in problem solving in neighborhoods can accomplish their tasks without significant realignment of the organization. They can simply be added to (or subtracted from) the routine business of the department. But even in simple applications of the community policing concept, there is more work required than typically is documented. These special officers have to be recruited and selected for an assignment that someone has articulated for them and has articulated for the communities in which they will work. These officers have to be trained and, in the case of storefront officers, supplied with a workspace outfitted for their needs. They have to be supervised by someone who understands and supports the nature of their assignment and has been trained (or selected) for the capacity to supervise in a manner less rigid than the style of supervision that historically may have been used in the department. The officer and supervisor must then be managed by someone who can integrate the functions of the specialized officers and traditional patrol officers so they do not work at crosspurposes.

All of that sounds easy only if you never have attempted it. At first glance, a police manager might assume this new effort is manageable in the same way any number of other specialized units or details in the department have been managed. A manager may have directed community relations units that were charged with developing positive contacts with the community and assume that a unit engaged in community policing can be managed similarly. But, until recently, few police managers had ever set officers free to take charge of a neighborhood in order to know its people, know its problems, and attempt to solve them. Few chiefs and, more importantly, very few supervisors and managers had ever relinquished to first-line officers the kind of operational and political power necessary to do the job they were expected to do—or which they would come to understand as being necessary to do. New management philosophies and practices are required. If they are not developed, individual officers and special units (even those providing material for glowing newspaper accounts) become isolated and frustrated in their efforts to deal effectively with their communities.

A fifth potential drawback of program replication is the subsequent lack of a sense of program ownership on the part of its participants, both police and citizens. A proprietary feeling is important for the generation of initial support and the maintenance of dedication to the effort. Idea adoption does not necessarily preclude ownership, but a deliberate and structured effort needs to be made to involve potential participants in a survey of various ideas and the selection of the one to be used locally. If resources allow, a highly effective way to accomplish this is for a team (or teams) of officers and citizens to visit other communities engaged in community policing, most preferably cities that share characteristics and problems with the city that is seeking new ideas. If the team has first researched efforts in other communities (and there now exists a substantial body of information that can serve this purpose), and has chosen the sites to visit, these visits can serve multiple purposes. They can inform decision making about program ideas and promote a sense of ownership about the ultimate choice. Just as important, they can foster strong bonds between police and citizens. Absent actual travel, the team research effort can strengthen working relationships and foster ownership of the adopted idea.

Perhaps the biggest hazard of adopting a "best" community policing practice from another community is not that it will fail for any of the reasons suggested above. The biggest hazard is that it may succeed, thus causing the department and community to conclude that the department now is engaged in community policing. Community policing is not a program. It is not a strategy. No number of imported programs can be substituted for the adoption of a department-wide management philosophy and organizational structure that truly orient the department toward the community rather than toward itself.

Clearly, a philosophy without representative programs can yield no change in the kind of policing a community receives. But tactics, practices, or programs—even the "right" ones—that are not undergirded by a corporate strategy to guide and sustain them (the less visible but essential component of community policing described in this chapter) will be short lived. When the practice or program ends, because interest or resources wane or the problem has been solved, there will be nothing to replace it but "business-as-usual" policing and the next new idea to make headlines. Community policing, when fully implemented, ensures that "best practices" for a given community come, not in fits and starts and not in misfits and failures, but in a fitting and ongoing way from the nature of the police-community relationship.

Invisible Insurance of Best Practices

The practices or programs that are "best" for a particular community will have certain common characteristics. They will be

- responsive to community needs,
- capable of implementation with available (or accessible) resources, and
- supported by citizens and police and other partnering agencies.

The organizational structure and strategy of a police agency that foster responsiveness to the community it serves are the most essential and the most enduring aspects of a serious (as opposed to cosmetic) approach to community policing. And they may be all but invisible to the media and the public. They may be invisible to police managers if they have the opportunity to read only about the performance of some acclaimed community policing department. And this is often the case because, as researchers and publicists, we are more likely to write about a performance than about what goes on behind the curtain to make the performance possible.

The behind-the-scenes elements critical to the performance might include

- first-line personnel who are capable of conducting community policing (because appropriate recruitment and training strategies were implemented),

- supervisors who are selected, trained, and authorized to coordinate, monitor, and support community policing and problem-solving activities of officers,
- police managers who have responsibility for geographic areas of the community,
- managers with authority to make decisions at the operational level that are appropriate for the area for which they are responsible,
- long-term assignment of personnel (first-line, supervisory, and managerial) to a geographic area so that they have the opportunity to know the residents of the area,
- accountability of personnel at all levels for safety within the geographic area to which they are assigned,[2]
- easy access to police (officers, supervisors, managers) by residents and businesspeople in the area policed,[3]
- regular structured contact between citizens and police (for example, door-to-door visits, community meetings, surveys) to determine community needs,
- involvement of citizens in decision making about appropriate responses to area problems,
- involvement of citizens in the implementation of responses to the problems,
- training for citizens to facilitate their involvement in decision making and problem solving,
- collaboration with other city and county agencies and private organizations for the purpose of problem solving,
- organizational policies and procedures that mandate and facilitate the above, and
- individual and organizational performance assessment to determine whether the practices and objectives listed above are accomplished.

The list of organizational practices, procedures, or policies that undergird and ensure community policing is akin to a list of best programs: some or all of the elements may be needed in some agencies, while other subsets

---

2. This almost certainly will require new methods of performance measurement.

3. If a community is large, and the police department is centralized, this may require physical decentralization of police facilities and technology that facilitates such decentralization.

of these elements may be required in other agencies. There is no one formula for all communities, and no simple formula for any community. In
the past, when funding agencies stipulated the elements that should exist in
a police agency in order for it to be considered a community policing
department, some police managers responded appropriately that their
departments didn't *need* to be structured that way in order to know their
community and be responsive to it. And they may have been right. It is a
judgment call that is difficult to make from the outside. The appropriate
mix of the elements listed above will depend on community size, population heterogeneity, and resources. Local decision makers will have to determine the appropriate organizational characteristics for local needs and
capacities.

Whatever the mix, it must provide for close contact between police and
citizens and guarantee that police decision makers are fully aware of the
needs of the community today and are positioned to be fully aware of
needs as they change. And this last is important. There have been numerous community policing efforts or "beginnings" in which the police have
made special efforts to contact the community, often through meetings
that are arranged to discuss area problems. And that's all that happens. If
and when those particular problems are addressed, the relationship
between citizens and police reverts to whatever it was before that meeting
or series of meetings. There is no plan or structure to ensure ongoing contacts that will keep police and citizens informed about changing community conditions and working together to address them. Without structures,
procedures, and policies in place that make routine police-citizen interaction inevitable, the department will always be in the position of "starting
over" with community policing. The department (or community leaders)
will always be tempted to import some other community's "best practice"
to solve a need that seems suddenly to have sprung up. (Needs only "spring
up," of course, when there is too little regular contact with the community
to see them developing over time.)

Conclusion

When a police agency and its community are aligned and working together,
there will not even be a need for "community policing." As some observers
have noted, the very use of a label for a style of policing suggests that something is amiss with traditional police practice that needs to be remedied
by adopting the new approach. When alignment and partnership exist,

community policing will become traditional policing, and adjustment to changing conditions and needs in the community will occur automatically. Constant improvement and reform will be the norm.

The essential, undergirding elements of community policing have been described here as being invisible. They are not always invisible, of course. A new neighborhood police station is going to be highly visible. Community meetings will be visible. But many of the other procedures are internal and are not easily seen. Certainly, they are given short shrift in the policing literature. As a result, many police administrators continue to voice the opinion that community policing does not require significant organizational change. As has been explained, the fact that they know little about the behind-the-scenes work of well-known community policing departments is not their fault. For the most part, they are not the authors of the literature and the "model" departments. Writers and researchers and the funders of such research have that responsibility. They are the ones who must make their audience as familiar with the back-stage preparations as they are with the on-stage performance. It is a responsibility that is not easily met.

The kinds of organizational changes outlined in this chapter take a long time to accomplish. A researcher or journalist must be familiar with an organization and stay affiliated with it over an extended time in order to see the changes that are made. There is little available support or institutional structure for that kind of long-term attachment. Alternatively, the researcher must be a skillful interviewer—and be motivated to ask the boring questions. Police organizations seldom keep records that identify practices that once existed as compared to practices that now exist, and they seldom keep records about when the change was made. As organizations, police departments probably are no worse than any other agencies when it comes to being keepers of their own organizational history. For a raft of reasons, this information is seldom written down. If the researcher is fortunate, the organization will have made a deliberate effort to embark on community policing (as opposed to gradually slipping into it), and there will exist a strategic plan that identifies the organizational changes to be made. There will be follow-up records that document the progress made at regular intervals. I would not want to guess how many such documents exist in American policing today. The fact is that it is difficult to identify the internal changes and even more difficult to write about how they were made—the problems that were encountered and how they were overcome. It is hard work, and it doesn't make for especially interesting reading. Some will even argue that if we focus on the difficulties of implementing community policing, we will discourage departments from taking even the first step. "Let them begin and discover for themselves what they need to do," these people argue.

The result is that, for the most part, we do not write about the quiet (if sometimes bloody) dramas of organizational change that are vital to the institutionalization and survival of community policing. We write about performers. We write about performances. We write about outcomes. We write about "best practices." The spectacle behind the curtain remains invisible. Unless we bring those unexposed efforts to light, we perpetuate the mistaken idea of many police leaders that major organizational change is not required to produce effective and enduring community policing. Unless we accept this responsibility, we may one day have to accept the responsibility for the failure of community policing.

References

Pate, Anthony M., Mary Ann Wycoff, Wesley G. Skogan, and Lawrence W. Sherman. 1986. *Reducing Fear of Crime in Houston and Newark: A Summary Report.* Washington, D.C.: Police Foundation.

3

Community Policing Is Good Policing, Both Today and Tomorrow

by Edward A. Flynn, Secretary of Public Safety of the Commonwealth of Massachusetts

ommunity policing reduces crime, helps minimize fear of crime, and enhances the quality of life in communities nationwide. The success of community policing lies in the development of trust-based partnerships between law enforcement agencies, local government officials, and citizens. It is a collaborative effort in which law enforcement and community members identify, prioritize, and address crime and disorder problems. The result is strong and confident communities.

Community policing recognizes that the police cannot effectively deal with crime and disorder by only reacting to individual incidents. It broadens the police mandate beyond narrow goals of *law enforcement* as an end in itself. It recognizes the importance of the police in developing and maintaining the idea of "community." To explain why community policing is so important to police leaders of my generation, I begin by telling my story.

A Rookie Cop's First Experiences

In 1971 I began my police career with high ideals. I firmly believed that every U.S. resident was either a part of the problem or a part of the solution.

American cities were in a state of crisis, and I wanted to make a difference. My police work provided me with a strong sense of satisfaction, even though I experienced varying degrees of frustration. I quickly understood why police officers become cynical. They deal with human degradation and learn that people are capable of true evil. This experience can erode the idealism of even the most naïve rookie cop.

Despite my best intentions, I was frequently reviled by the same people I was trying to protect. As I worked what was then called a "ghetto" precinct, I was not only exposed to great human need, I also felt for the first time in my life that I was hated for being a police officer. It was unnerving. The community demanded we do something about crime, but when we responded with conventional police tactics, that very same community accused us of harassment. No matter how many arrests we made, crime continued to escalate. No matter how many "sweeps" or "crack downs" we undertook, neighborhoods continued to deteriorate. No matter how fast we got to calls, no matter how many calls we answered, no matter how many fights or disorderly groups we broke up or tickets we wrote, things just seemed to get worse. Meanwhile, my fellow officers and I increasingly felt frustrated, isolated, and more than a little resentful. Our morale was further undermined by our growing awareness of the effect partisan politics could have on the police. As city after city fell into poverty and despair, politicians fought over patronage. As the police department struggled with declining resources and increasing demands for service, politicians expected campaign contributions in return for coveted police assignments.

Yet there was some reason to hope. Federal funds were being allocated to assist law enforcement agencies in educating officials. One example was the Law Enforcement Education Program (LEEP). Federal funds helped to create a generation of leaders in law enforcement who would prove more resistant to political pressure and more committed to progressive policing. As I stated to my friends at the time, "As long as you aren't afraid to wear a uniform and work nights, you can own your soul." Further, it seemed that many cities were gradually escaping their machine-dominated pasts. Scandals, indictments, and trials were replaced by politicians' "reform" administrations. Although reform administrations were often followed by a return of the old order, the reforms nonetheless seemed to accumulate, impeding a complete return to the past. Mayors and their reforms came and went, but the police made little progress. A political reformer might leave a legacy of newly constructed office buildings and malls, yet some neighborhoods continued their steady decline.

Broken Windows Theory Makes Sense

Back in 1982, while a member of a street-crime unit (a plainclothes unit specializing in stakeouts and decoy operations), I was greatly influenced by an *Atlantic Monthly* article written by James Q. Wilson and George Kelling (1982). It was entitled "Broken Windows: The Police and Neighborhood Safety." Wilson and Kelling made the argument that what police did to control disorderly behavior in the long term has more to do with neighborhood safety than what the police have tried to do to control crime. They described citizens who were fearful of using their own streets and contributing to their neighborhood's vitality because of what they witnessed and experienced. Most people never experienced crime, but they saw graffiti and garbage in their neighborhoods. They viewed menacing youths hanging out on the corner; they were accosted by drunken and disturbed panhandlers; and they were propositioned by prostitutes. These behaviors led them to abandon their streets. Next, predators moved into the neighborhoods and, inevitably, serious crime rose as criminals were emboldened by the disorder they saw. Another neighborhood had deteriorated and was gone.

The observations in the article absolutely matched my own experience. We in the police profession were always husbanding our limited resources to deal with serious crimes: robberies, burglaries, rapes, and assaults. We did not have the time for the "minor stuff," even though it was the minor stuff we always heard about from residents. As my precinct captain once said, "When I go to community meetings I never hear any complaints about bank robberies. I do hear complaints about noisy kids, loud music, and disorderly groups."

Was it possible the police could do something to save our neighborhoods? Despite years of efforts to heighten police efficiency to "fight crime," years that had seen the police perfect the tactics of random mobile patrols, rapid response to calls, and follow-up investigations, cities were in continued decline. Furthermore, research was demonstrating that random patrol produced random results; rapid response to crimes did not significantly affect arrest rates; and most criminal investigations were fruitless. Even though the jails were full, it was clear that there was no police solution to the crime problem and no way that the police alone could save the neighborhoods from themselves.

A Quiet Revolution in Policing

During the 1980s, what was described as the "Quiet Revolution" in American policing began to emerge. Police agencies soon came to realize that although traditional policing tactics would continue to generate seemingly impressive statistics, they would not, in fact, improve the quality of life in neighborhoods. Strategies designed to resolve this problem were evolving, such as "problem-oriented policing," "neighborhood policing," and "community policing." These terms may be phrased and defined somewhat differently, but they all share common elements that would advance the delivery of police services to all members of our communities.

"Community policing" was not a new idea by any means, but one that had been emerging for years. The community policing philosophy includes two important assumptions. First, the most effective barrier against crime and disorder is a healthy and self-confident neighborhood. Second, police officers are an untapped creative resource in most police departments who are ready and willing to develop practical solutions to neighborhood problems by forming trust-based partnerships within the community. Community policing recognizes the preeminence of the police role in apprehending criminals and providing emergency services. It also recognizes that the police cannot effectively deal with crime and disorder by only reacting to individual incidents. Along with enlisting community support, the police learn to recognize problems that lead to criminal conditions, and they develop solutions to those particular problems.

I attended my first conference on community policing in Arlington, Virginia, while I was the police chief in Chelsea, Massachusetts. Back then, Chelsea was in state-imposed receivership as the result of a corruption scandal and the city's bankruptcy. This conference interested me because the topic of how community policing could improve the quality of life in distressed cities was being discussed. I was in the process of implementing a community-oriented strategy, and I was emphasizing to my officers its potential to "Bring down the crime, the disorder, and the 'for sale' signs." In a city where politics had been a problem, I was giving them this message: "Before, the politicians inserted themselves between the police and the community. Now the community will be between the police and the politicians."

Herman Goldstein gave the keynote address at the conference. The title of his remarks was *The New Policing: Confronting Complexity* (Goldstein

1993). Goldstein expressed concern that the term "community policing" was being used widely, without regard for its meaning or substance. In his words, "oversimplification can be a deadly enemy of progress." Because community policing expands the police function, police need to be aware that "the avalanche of business that this expansion brings can invite a self-inflicted wound." Goldstein commented further that it could be important for the police to reduce public expectations. Just because the police and public identified new problems did not mean that there would be easy solutions to them. Realistic expectations are a key to success and an inoculation against despair. He observed that through the implementation of community policing strategies, the police were redefining their relationships with the rest of the criminal justice system. Finally, he warned that "the initiatives associated with community policing cannot survive in a police agency managed in traditional ways. . . . [O]fficers will not be creative . . . if a high value continues to be placed on conformity. They will not be thoughtful if they are required to adhere to regulations that are thoughtless. And they will not aspire to act as mature, responsible adults if their superiors treat them as children" (Goldstein 1993, 9). Though much progress has been made in the past decade on community policing, Goldstein's remarks still stand as warnings for the future.

An Agenda for the Future

What about the future of community policing? Many challenges must be faced before we can remove the prefix *community* from *community* policing and be assured that this philosophy has become ascendant. Among the challenges are the following:

- training reforms at all levels,
- research that is current and practical,
- measurement and data systems tailored to the elements of community-oriented policing,
- technology that supports community policing, and
- leadership advances.

Training

With a few exceptions among large police departments, very few departments have control over their basic training. Most agencies participate in regional police training academies. State training councils usually set the curricula for these academies. The course of study at most police academies is overwhelmingly dominated by concerns about liability, criminal law, and tactical procedures. While officer and public safety are paramount, at most of the academies 90 percent of the curriculum is approximately 20 percent of the job. The values and strategies that reflect true community policing must be integrated into all recruit training. Engaging citizens in ways that will build mutual trust, learning to work collaboratively to identify and solve problems, and employing other key community policing approaches will better prepare officers for what is truly expected of them when they take their first assignments.

Another problem we face is the content of our management training courses. By common acceptance, the FBI National Academy is our elite training ground for the future leaders of community policing. Yet the American local police establishment does not have any control over the course content. One hopes that a Department of Justice commitment to community policing results in a reexamination of the National Academy's curriculum in support of community policing initiatives.

Research

Much of the research on community policing needs to be reevaluated. Practical research is still lacking that would advance community policing. The valuable research done to date must be continually updated. The early works of Jerome H. Skolnick (1966), William A. Westley (1970), Arthur Neiderhoffer (1967), and James Q. Wilson (1968) were crucial to the development of modern policing. Their research, however, was often based on interviews and surveys of officers who had been retired for decades. We should not be relying on research that is older than our officers. It is time to conduct research that retests previous assumptions and findings in light of the new generations of police leaders and officers who are working in a new and very different social environment.

Performance Measurement

A challenge related to research but with political ramifications is the notion of measuring the effects of community policing. Although the Office of Community Oriented Policing Services (COPS) and the National Institute of Justice (NIJ) have facilitated useful discussions in this area, additional research needs to be conducted. The National Incident-Based Reporting

System (NIBRS),[1] although tremendously valuable, is inadequate; it does not answer the need for police to have statistical standards of accountability beyond the 20 percent of their work that directly relates to crime reports. We desperately need a Uniform Crime Reporting (UCR) index to be used for making comparisons in and among jurisdictions regarding disorderly conditions. We also need accurate standardized survey instruments that can measure citizens' fear of crime and satisfaction with the police, measurements that can be compared over time against other jurisdictions. Many measures can be employed to assess how police are doing their jobs, and we need to understand and apply those measures that reflect community policing values.

Technology

The law enforcement profession must carefully scrutinize the effects of computer-aided dispatch and E-911 on community policing strategies. Goldstein's caution against self-inflicted wounds is most applicable here. Every police agency that has attempted to expand community policing beyond special units and into the mainstream of the patrol function has been stressed to breaking points by the unremitting pressure of calls for service. The COPS Office has acknowledged this tough issue and has solicited grant applications that would address the related problems. Technological and policy-oriented research is needed to produce communications and dispatch systems that allow the police to prioritize their call load in a way that is properly responsive yet does not undermine their ability to engage in problem solving. The truth of the matter is that police chiefs are more likely to lose their jobs if a 911 call is mishandled than if there is a failure to implement community policing.

Scrutiny also must be extended to the many other advances in technology that are finding their way into police agencies. How do we best employ

---

1. The Federal Bureau of Investigation in collaboration with the U.S. Department of Justice's Bureau of Justice Statistics recognized the limitations of the Uniform Crime Reporting system. As a summary or "snapshot" of the most serious crimes known to the police, the UCR provides limited information (although it does give an easily understood glimpse of crime). During the 1980s, a new system was developed to address the new information needs that both police and policy makers had for a more comprehensive information system. This system, the National Incident Based Reporting System, collects incident-specific crime data on a wide range of offenses.

and integrate crime mapping, mobile data, records management, resource allocation, and other systems to support community policing? The challenge is formidable, but there is now an opportunity to meet this challenge that we must not lose. It is a good time to evaluate how technology can support community policing while we are working to create standards for interjurisdictional information sharing and joint systems integration that will address the new terrorism threat.

Leadership

Though we examine leadership from the perspective of policing agencies themselves, we must be willing to confront the limitations of the "great man" or "great woman" theory of police leadership. The entire burden for the success of community policing should not rest solely on the Executive Office of the Chief of Police. Community policing will work only when police managers and officers recognize that it has value for them.

Community policing is the best antidote to police cynicism that the profession can provide. It is the sole strategy that we possess that places our officers in nonconfrontational contact with members from every stratum of society. It should not come as a surprise when officers see the worst in people and people at their worst that some may become cynical. By creating positive working opportunities for officers and communities, we can prevent police from becoming demoralized and unable to inspire others to join in their problem-solving efforts.

The impediments to implementing new strategic visions, particularly in states dominated by strong collective bargaining laws, must be acknowledged. The power of such associations should never be underestimated. The factory union mentality, as George Kelling characterized it, undermines notions of professionalism and public service by concentrating on organizational issues. This cannot be changed by enlightened police leadership alone. If anything, the enlightened police chief too often becomes the lightening rod for these associations. Given this, police officers must accept the leadership challenge of helping create organizations more useful to their communities. It is very easy to defy the police chief. Officers with the moral courage to defy their peers in pursuit of elevated notions of public service are what we need. Ironically, as the public demands more and more accountability from police agencies, many of our labor associations find themselves fighting to protect the marginal and even sometimes the dangerous police employee. As a result, public confidence is undermined, and it may appear to citizens that police organizations put their members' interests ahead of public interests. This long-term cultural issue cannot be swept under the rug if we want to advance our profession in meaningful and profound ways. Goldstein was correct: The greatest challenge in institutionalizing community policing lies inside police agencies. Ultimately, that challenge will be won by officers, managers, and chief executives who are brave enough to work in unison for the public interest as represented by community policing.

Our greatest resources for meeting future challenges are the skills and ideals of police officers themselves. The leadership of officers, managers, and chief executives is based upon teamwork, flexibility, innovation, adaptability, and notions of loyalty to one another. It is a privilege to lead the officers of today in a way that capitalizes upon their energy and idealism. This can be done best by supporting the strategy and philosophy of community policing. If properly implemented, the community policing philosophy will provide an environment in which the promise of our officers can be best realized, and communities can be best protected. This must remain our challenge and our mission.

Community Policing after September 11

Community policing is more important now than ever. After September 11, 2001, homeland security issues (preventing and responding to terrorist acts as well as community stabilization) became law enforcement's primary focus. These issues are issues of local and national importance. Although terrorists may "think globally," they "act locally." I was the chief in Arlington County, Virginia, and was among the first responders to the Pentagon, which is located in that county, after it was hit by a hijacked plane. I have been immersed in homeland security issues for some time. Through the many briefings on resource allocations, new technologies, interoperability, and other plans to counter the new terrorist threats, I remain convinced that one of the greatest weapons against terrorists is community policing.

A vital component of community policing requires law enforcement and communities to work together, to connect with one another, and establish trust. Across the country there are many *communities of interest* with respect to the fight against terrorism. While some are clearly defined geographically as districts or neighborhoods, others are defined by race or ethnicity. For example, Arlington County has the most diverse zip code in the D.C.-metropolitan area. After Spanish, the second most frequently spoken foreign language is Amharic (spoken by Ethiopians). I know that Arlington County is not alone in its struggle to overcome the challenges that will result in better services to diverse communities.

Law enforcement officials appreciate that residents provide information only when they trust the police. There have been instances when members of the community who have provided law enforcement with information about crime have put themselves at great personal risk, particularly in regard to drug dealing cases and homicides. It is not difficult to imagine that some communities are privy to information they could share regarding terrorist activities or cells. If they trusted law enforcement, they would be more inclined to cooperate with officials and provide them with critical information regarding terrorists and other threats. If community members believe that the police are *their* police and not just *the* police, they will become partners in the war on terrorism as well as the war on crime.

Conclusion

The research data presented in Chapter 4 makes it possible to compare 1992 and 2002 studies. On a personal level this means a great deal. It was about 1992, as the police chief of Chelsea, Massachusetts, that I saw the promise of community policing. It was there in Chelsea, with the assistance of Weed and Seed and COPS grants, that I first implemented a strategy based on partnerships with the community as well as problem solving, crime prevention, geographic accountability, and officer empowerment. As a result of community policing efforts, the crime rate in Chelsea decreased, officers' job satisfaction increased, citizens' approval ratings of the police improved, and the city evolved from state-imposed receivership to designation as an All-American City by the National Civic League.

In 1997 I was appointed the police chief in Arlington County. In many ways Arlington was the antithesis of the Chelsea I knew. Arlington County's political environment was stable, its local government practice was very professional, and its police force was the longest and continually CALEA-accredited agency in the country. The community policing strategy had great power and promise in Arlington—a community experiencing rapid demographical diversification. Fours year after community policing became the dominant strategy there, a decentralized, community policing model was in place that emphasized partnerships, problem solving, crime prevention, officer empowerment, and geographical accountability. As a result of employing the community policing model, the

Arlington County Police Department had a very high approval rating, and twenty-year lows in crime when I left in January 2003.

As a police chief making my first attempt to implement community policing, I can recall the rolling of the eyes and the crossed arms over chests of doubting and unconvinced officers. I attended many conferences on the subject of what the true definition of community policing was, and whether or not it qualified as something new and innovative. A decade later, the bulk of my patrol force in Arlington County had known no other strategy than community policing. Yes, they still like to respond rapidly to emergency calls. Yes, they still enjoy the thrill of a good "pinch." But police officers, managers, and chief executives all understand their responsibilities. The development of trust-based partnerships in neighborhoods, the critical importance of problem solving, and collaborative problem identification remain central components of crime control efforts. Ten years from now, when data from 1994 to 2014 are assessed, what will be measured will not be "community" policing but rather "good" policing because it will finally be evident that policing *is* about communities.

References

Goldstein, Herman. 1993. *The New Policing: Confronting Complexity*. National Institute of Justice, Research in Brief. Washington, D.C.: U.S. Department of Justice.

Neiderhoffer, Arthur. 1967. *Behind the Shield: The Police in Urban Society*. Garden City, N.Y.: Doubleday.

Skolnick, Jerome H. 1966. *Justice without Trial: Law Enforcement in a Democratic Society*. New York: John Wiley and Sons.

Westley, William A. 1970. *Violence and the Police: A Sociological Study of Law, Custom and Morality*. Cambridge, Mass.: MIT Press.

Wilson, James Q. 1968. *Varieties of Police Behavior: The Management of Law and Order in Eight Communities*. Cambridge, Mass.: Harvard University Press.

Wilson, James Q., and George Kelling. 1982. "Broken Windows: The Police and Neighborhood Safety." *Atlantic Monthly* 249, 29–38.

Part II

The Implementation of Community Policing

4

The Results of Three National Surveys on Community Policing

by Lorie Fridell, Director of Research,
Police Executive Research Forum

I s community policing being implemented fully by law enforcement agencies that say they have adopted this model of policing? This is a question that has been raised by a number of scholars and practitioners. To determine the extent to which community policing is being implemented, we must examine whether agency executives fully understand what community policing is, and what is entailed for the department that adopts it.

As Herman Goldstein (1993, 1–2) has noted, the term

> "community policing" is widely used without any regard for its substance. Political leaders latch onto the label for the popular image it evokes but do not invest in the concept itself. . . . Indeed, the popularity of the term has resulted in its being used to encompass practically all innovations in policing, from the most ambitious to the most mundane, from the most carefully thought through to the most casual.

National Surveys in 1992 and 1997

The data from national surveys in 1992 and 1997 help us understand how agency executives have *interpreted* and *implemented* the community policing model within agencies that report adopting community policing. From these data we can see what agencies have done in the past decade to engage the community, in terms of problem-solving efforts, and with regard to organizational transformation.

In both surveys, agency executives were asked to agree or disagree with this statement: "It is not clear what community policing means in practical terms." In 1992 and 1997, 47 percent and 31 percent of the executives, respectively, agreed or strongly agreed with this statement.

Another issue pertains to the distinction between a department's adoption of various "tactics" or "programs" that might reflect one or more principles of community policing versus the wholesale adoption by an agency of the community policing strategy or philosophy to guide all that it does (Kelling and Moore 1988).

The 1992 survey was conducted by the Police Foundation with funding from the U.S. Department of Justice's National Institute of Justice (NIJ). The Police Foundation sent a comprehensive survey about community policing to 2,337 U.S. agencies. Responding agencies indicated whether or not they had adopted community policing. They also reported on community policing-related programs and practices, organizational arrangements, the nature of citizen participation, and other matters. Many of the items in the survey, including the item assessing whether community policing had been implemented, were included verbatim in the 1997 follow-up survey, which also received funding from NIJ.

The 1997 survey was conducted by ORC MACRO International and the Police Executive Research Forum (PERF). ORC MACRO and PERF sent their survey to the same 2,314 agencies selected by the Police Foundation for the 1992 survey. They received responses from 1,637 agencies (a response rate of approximately 71 percent); of these 1,637 agencies, 1,264 had responded to the Police Foundation survey (Rosenthal et al. 2000). (That is, the ORC Macro/PERF team produced a panel of 1,264 agencies that had responded to both surveys.[1]) The combined results of these two surveys provide information on the extent of *self-reported* implementation of community policing, as well as comprehensive information about the nature of that implementation.[2]

---

1. Some agencies responded to the ORC Macro/PERF survey that had failed to return results to the Police Foundation five years earlier.

2. It is important to highlight the fact that the responses reflect *self-reported* community policing implementation. Experts and practitioners over the years have

TABLE 4-1. Implementation of Community Policing, 1992 and 1997

Question: Which of the following statements best describes your agency's current situation with respect to the adoption of a community policing approach?

Response Options	1992	1997
We have not considered adopting a community policing approach.	28%	5%
We considered adopting a community policing approach but rejected the idea because it was not the appropriate approach for this agency.	3%	2%
We considered adopting a community policing approach and liked the idea but it is not practical here at this time.	18%	8%
We are now in the process of planning or implementing a community policing approach.	31%	27%
We have implemented community policing.	20%	58%

As Table 4-1 shows, both the 1992 and 1997 surveys asked agency executives, "Which of the following statements best describes your agency's current situation with respect to the adoption of a community policing approach?" Response options were

- We have not considered adopting a community policing approach;
- We considered adopting a community policing approach but rejected the idea because it was not the appropriate approach for this agency;
- We considered adopting a community policing approach and liked the idea, but it is not practical here at this time;
- We are now in the process of planning or implementing a community policing approach; and
- We have implemented community policing.

Figure 4-1 presents the results for this item from the 1,264 agencies that responded to both the 1992 and 1997 surveys. These results reflect significant changes over time in the implementation of community policing. By 1997, 58 percent ($p < .05$) of the responding agencies reported that they had implemented community policing; an additional 27 percent ($p < .05$) reported that they were in the process of doing so. These results contrast significantly with the 1992 results. Then only 20 percent of the agencies

---

expressed concern about whether agencies that self-identify as community policing agencies are, in fact, implementing it, to what extent, or, indeed, whether they even know what implementation would entail.

FIGURE 4-1. Implementation of Community Policing, 1992 and 1997

Question: Which of the following statements best describes your agency's current situation with respect to the adoption of a community policing approach?

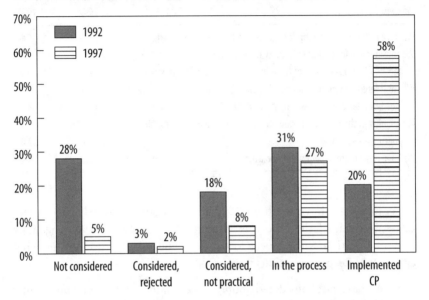

reported that they had implemented community policing, and another 31 percent of the responding agencies claimed that they were in the process of doing so. In 1992, 28 percent of the agencies reported that they had not considered community policing, compared with only 5 percent in 1997.

In both 1992 and 1997, municipal agencies were significantly more likely than sheriffs' departments to report having implemented community policing. In 1997, 61 percent of the municipal agencies, compared with 44 percent of the sheriffs' departments, reported implementing community policing. Large agencies were also much more likely to have implemented community policing than smaller ones.

National Survey in 2002

According to the agency responses to the surveys in 1992 and 1997, community policing has been implemented widely in the United States. It was unclear, however, to what extent and to what effect. In 2002 PERF conducted a modified third survey of a subset of the agencies that had responded to the 1992 and 1997 surveys. The goal was to collect additional information on how self-identified community policing agencies have changed over time. PERF sent a survey composed of the key items contained in the first two surveys to the 282 agencies that (1) had responded to both previous surveys and (2) had reported in both of those surveys that they had implemented community policing.[3] A 90 percent response rate produced a three-wave panel of 240 self-identified community policing agencies with information regarding their community policing implementation from 1992 through 2002.

The next section draws upon the data in all three surveys to detail the perceived impact of community policing on police-citizen relationships, fear of crime, crime, and other factors, and to explain how agencies have implemented it. These data help to identify the strengths and challenges of community policing implementation across the nation.

The Reported Effects of Community Policing

An item in all three surveys asked respondents: "To what extent has your agency's approach to community policing had the following effects?" Figure 4-2 shows the percentage of agencies reporting each possible effect in 1992, 1997, and 2002. Several of the items that were included in the 1997 and 2002 surveys were not contained in the 1992 survey. For these items, there are two bars, instead of three, in the figure. The bars on the left side of Figure 4-2 denote the community policing effects that did not manifest statistically significant changes over time.[4] The bars on the right reflect the effects that changed significantly between 1992 and 2002.[5] All five of the effects for which responses did not increase significantly over time could

---

3. Readers are cautioned that the population of 282 agencies is too small to allow for broad generalizations to police agencies nationwide.

4. In this and all subsequent figures, the response items in this group (solid bars) are ordered from left to right in terms of their proportionate change over time—from least amount of change between 1992 and 1997 (at left) to the most amount of change. To determine proportionate change over time, we divided the difference between the percentages of agencies reporting the effect in 1992 and in 1997 by the percentage of agencies reporting the effect in 1992. For instance, "reduced crime against persons" has the largest proportionate change between 1992 and 2002—45.2 percent. We calculated 45.2 percent as the difference between the 1992 percentage of 59.1 and the 2002 percentage of 85.8, divided by 59.1.

5. The items within this group (striped bars) are also ordered from left to right in terms of the level of proportionate change over time. If the item was not included in the 1992 survey, the changes over time were calculated by comparing 1997 and 2002.

FIGURE 4-2. Reported Effects of Community Policing, 1992, 1997, 2002

(Percent of responding agencies reporting each effect.)

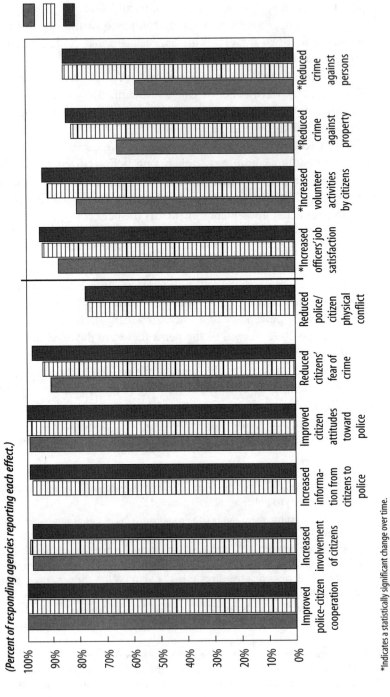

*Indicates a statistically significant change over time.

not have produced changes because they were reported in very large percentages by respondents in the earliest surveys. In 1992, 1997, and 2002 more than 90 percent of the responding agencies reported that community policing

- improved cooperation between citizens and police,
- increased involvement of citizens,
- increased information from citizens to police,[6]
- improved citizens' attitudes toward police, and
- reduced citizens' fear of crime.

For other effects, there were significant reported increases between 1992 and 2002. These include the following (in order of smallest proportionate change to the largest proportionate change):

- reduced physical conflict between police and citizens,[7]
- increased job satisfaction of officers,
- increased volunteer activities by citizens,
- reduced crime against property, and
- reduced crime against persons.

In the 2002 survey, we expanded the response options to the question regarding community policing effects. Instead of reporting merely whether or not there was an effect on "increased involvement of citizens," for example, respondents indicated whether the effect was manifested "not at all," "to some extent," or "to a great extent." These results from the 2002 survey indicate that the respondents perceived the greatest effects in improved cooperation between citizens and police, and increased involvement of citizens (see Figure 4-3). Close to 65 percent of the agencies responding to the 2002 survey reported improved cooperation between citizens and police "to a great extent," and close to 55 percent reported increased involvement of citizens "to a great extent." Relatively large proportions of agencies also reported that community policing "to a great extent" improved citizen attitudes toward police (48 percent), increased volunteer activities by citizens (37 percent), and increased information from citizens to the police (31 percent). More than 80 percent of the agencies (82.2 percent) reported that community policing increased officers' job satisfaction "to some extent."

---

6. This item was not included in the 1992 survey.

7. This item was not included in the 1992 survey.

FIGURE 4-3. Reported Effects of Community Policing, 2002

(Percent of responding agencies reporting each effect.)

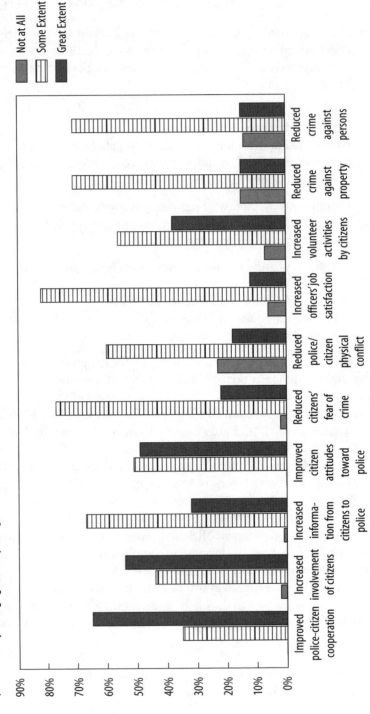

Agencies also reported whether they experienced increased or decreased calls for service from citizens and whether response times increased or decreased between 1992 and 2002. In 2002, one-fourth of the agencies reported decreases in citizens' call for service either "to some extent" or "to a great extent." Three-fourths reported increases in citizens' calls for service. Half of the 2002 respondents reported reductions in their response times; one-third reported increases in their response times.

The Nature of Community Policing Implementation

In this section we focus on the policies, programs, and practices of law enforcement agencies that have self-identified as community policing agencies. As indicated in Chapter 1, key elements of community policing implementation include

- community engagement,
- collaborative problem solving, and
- organizational transformation.

The information obtained from the 240 agencies that reported implementing community policing in the 1992, 1997, and 2002 surveys provide a glimpse into how these three core elements are finding their way into some U.S. police agencies.[8]

Community Engagement

Figure 4-4 provides information from the three surveys on how the 240 agencies have involved citizens in their work. Over the 1992–2002 period, more than 90 percent of the agencies reported citizen participation in the form of attending police-community meetings, participating in Neighborhood Watch, and helping police identify and resolve problems.[9] At least 40 percent of the agencies over all three time periods reported citizens serving as volunteers within the police agency, serving on jurisdiction-level advisory councils, serving on neighborhood-level advisory councils, and/or

---

8. With this small number of agencies, however, the reader cannot presume that these results are generalizeable to all self-reported community policing agencies.

9. Items included in the 1997 and 2002 surveys but not included in the 1992 survey are indicated in Figure 4-4 by two bars instead of three.

FIGURE 4-4. Methods of Citizen Participation, 1992, 1997, 2002

(Percent of responding agencies reporting each method.)

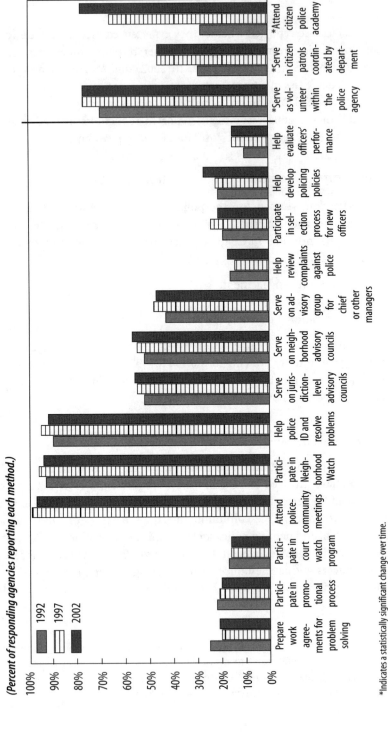

*Indicates a statistically significant change over time.

serving on advisory groups for the chief or other managers. The bars on the left represent items for which no statistically significant changes occurred between 1992 and 1997. The bars on the right indicate that, for three items (attending citizen police academies, serving in citizen patrols, and acting as volunteers within police agencies) statistically significant increases occurred over time.

Small percentages of agencies involved citizens in decisions regarding the internal workings of the department. Even as of 2002, less than 30 percent of the agencies reported that citizens participated in promotional processes, helped review complaints against police, participated in the selection of new officers, helped to develop policies, or helped evaluate officers' performance. This issue is discussed further in the commentaries and in the concluding chapter of the book.

Other survey items queried the existence of particular policies, practices, and/or programs that reflected partnerships or outreach. As seen in Figure 4-5, more than three-fourths of responding agencies reported regularly scheduled meetings with community groups, interagency involvement in problem identification/resolution, police-youth programs, and victim assistance programs in 2002. Additionally, in 2002 at least half had written policies on interactions with citizens and groups, had written policies regarding interactions with government agencies, provided regular radio or television programs or spots, or engaged in interagency code enforcement.

Although relatively few agencies reported integration with community corrections or involvement in alternative dispute resolution, these two activities manifested the greatest increases between 1992 and 2002.

Collaborative Problem Solving

As described above, problem-oriented policing involves police working with citizens, organizations, and agencies to identify and solve community problems related to crime, disorder, and the quality of life. Figure 4-6 provides the survey results for questions pertaining to problem-solving policies and procedures. By 2002 more than 80 percent of the responding agencies reported that they work with citizens to identify and resolve problems, work with other agencies in identifying and resolving problems, and use building code enforcement and other regulatory code enforcement to solve problems. By 2002 at least 50 percent of the agencies reported that they had adopted organizational performance measures reflecting problem

FIGURE 4-5. Partnership/Outreach Activities/Policies, 1992, 1997, 2002

(Percent of responding agencies reporting each activity/policy.)

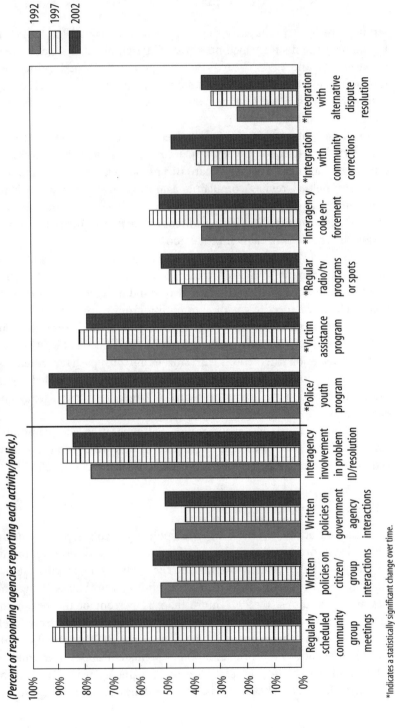

*Indicates a statistically significant change over time.

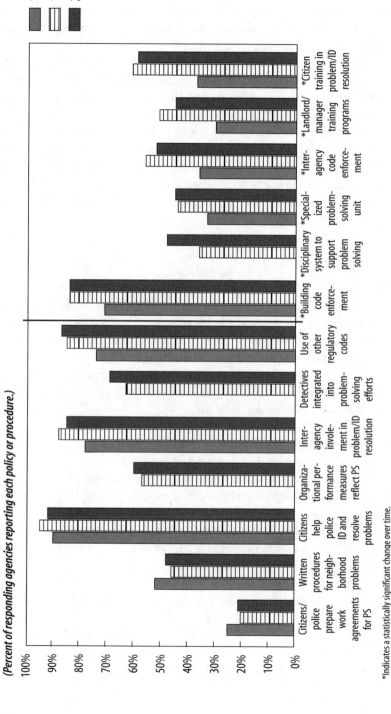

FIGURE 4-6. Problem-Solving Policies and Procedures, 1992, 1997, 2002

(Percent of responding agencies reporting each policy or procedure.)

Legend:
- 1992
- 1997
- 2002

Categories (left to right):
Citizens/police prepare work agreements for PS · Written procedures for neighborhood problems · Citizens help police ID and resolve problems · Organizational performance measures reflect PS · Inter-agency involvement in problem/ID resolution · Detectives integrated into problem-solving efforts · Use of other regulatory codes · *Building code enforcement · *Disciplinary system to support problem solving · *Specialized problem-solving unit · *Inter-agency code enforcement · *Landlord/manager training programs · *Citizen training in problem/ID resolution

*Indicates a statistically significant change over time.

solving, had integrated detectives into problem-solving efforts, worked with other agencies to enforce various codes, and had trained residents in problem identification and resolution.

The bars on the right in Figure 4-6 convey the extent to which problem-solving activities and practices significantly increased between 1992 and 2002 (or in some cases between 1997 and 2002). Of the thirteen items in the survey reflecting problem-solving activities, six showed statistically significant increases over time. The largest increases were seen in citizen training in problem identification and resolution, landlord/manager training programs, and interagency code enforcement. Also showing an increase over time was the use of specialized problem-solving units. In 1992 only 33 percent of the agencies reported this specialized unit compared with 45 percent in 2002.

Organizational Transformation

Organizational changes that support community policing include pushing power downward in the agency, physical decentralization, geographic responsibility, and reducing levels of management. Transformation of a police department involves changes in hiring, training, personnel evaluation, and agency performance measurement.

Figure 4-7 shows the responses to the three surveys pertaining to organizational transformation. By 2002 more than 70 percent of the responding agencies reported that they had

- a management approach to support well-intentioned risk taking,
- fixed assignments to specific beats or areas,
- beat/patrol boundaries that coincide with neighborhoods,
- special recognition of good community policing and/or problem-solving officers,
- foot patrol as a periodic expectation,
- alternative response methods for calls,
- methods for classifying/prioritizing calls,
- geographically-based crime analysis,
- role definitions and/or job descriptions that reflect community policing,
- a citizen survey to help the agency identify needs and priorities,
- permanent neighborhood-based offices/stations, and
- a citizen survey to evaluate police services.

FIGURE 4-7. Organizational Transformation, 1992, 1997, 2002
(Percent of responding agencies reporting each item.)

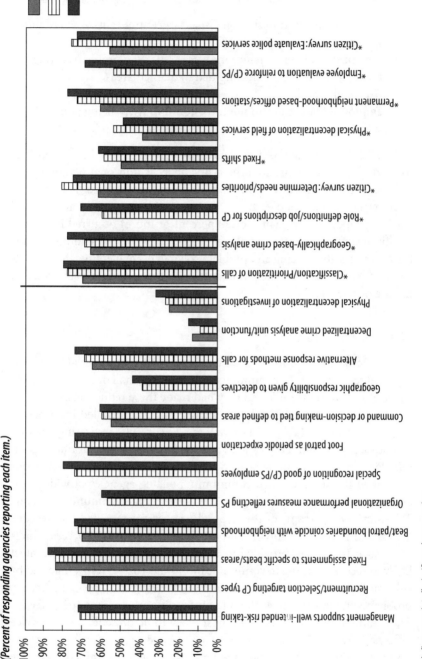

*Indicates a statistically significant change over time.

Additionally, by 2002 more than 50 percent of the agencies had adopted

- recruitment/selection strategies that target applicants who are suited to community policing work,
- organizational performance measures reflecting problem solving,
- command or decision making tied to defined areas,
- fixed shifts, and
- employee evaluations to reinforce community policing and problem solving.

By 2002 less than half of the agencies had given geographic responsibility to detectives, decentralized the crime analysis unit or function, physically decentralized investigations, or physically decentralized field services.

In terms of changes over time, the largest increases between 1992 and 2002 (a proportionate change of 20 percent or more) occurred in the use of citizen surveys to evaluate police services, employee evaluations to reinforce community policing and problem solving, permanent neighborhood-based offices or stations, the physical decentralization of field services, and the use of fixed shifts.

Management and Training

The agencies surveyed in 2002 were asked whether managerial levels had been reduced to support community policing. Less than one-quarter of the agencies (22 percent) indicated they had made these reductions.

Also of note, the 1997 and 2002 surveys solicited detailed information related to training. Table 4-2 portrays the 2002 results indicating whether or not various training topics were included as part of recruit training, in-service training, or training of field training officers (FTOs). Seventy-four percent of the self-identified community policing agencies provide academy and/or in-service training on the concepts of community policing. Two-thirds (65 percent) of the responding agencies reported that recruits are trained in problem solving and nearly three-fourths (74 percent) indicated such training is provided to in-service officers. Recruits were most likely to receive training in communication skills (82 percent), followed by cultural diversity (77 percent), community policing concepts (76 percent), problem solving (65 percent), and community interactions (62 percent). These same topics were the ones most likely to be presented to in-service officers; between 70 and 85 percent of the agencies reported in-service training in these topics. About one-half of the agencies trained in-service

TABLE 4-2. Training Topics by Training Type, 2002
Question: For each of the following types of officer training, please indicate whether initial (recruit), in-service, and/or FTO specialized training is provided by your agency.

Topic	Recruit	In-Service	FTO
Organize groups and communities	23%	53%	18%
Community interactions	62%	70%	51%
Cultural diversity	77%	85%	35%
Problem solving	65%	74%	52%
Concepts of community policing	76%	74%	51%
Communication skills	82%	73%	58%
Human resources management	17%	59%	20%
Crime analysis or mapping	14%	48%	14%

officers in organizing groups and communities. In general, field training was least likely to address the various topics.

Not presented in the table are the changes in training between 1997 and 2002. During this five-year period, there were statistically significant increases in the proportion of community policing agencies that provided training to recruits on community policing concepts, communication skills, problem solving, and organizing groups and communities. The only other significant increase was the inclusion of problem solving in field training.

The Impact of September 11, 2001

In the 2002 survey, PERF asked agencies "To what extent do you think the events of September 11, 2001, will impact your agency's community policing efforts?" The possible responses were "to a great extent," "to some extent," "not at all," and "don't know." As indicated in Figure 4-8, the majority of agencies (58 percent) reported that the attacks in the United States by terrorists on September 11 would affect their community policing efforts "to some extent." Eleven percent conjectured that the impact would be to "a great extent," and nearly one-third said the events would not affect their community policing efforts at all.

The extent of the perceived impact on community policing of the attacks corresponded with agency size; that is, the smaller the agency, the less likely it was to report an impact of September 11 on its community

FIGURE 4-8.   Extent of the Impact of 9-11 on Community Policing Efforts, 2002

Question: To what extent do you think the events of September 11, 2001,
will impact your agency's community policing efforts?

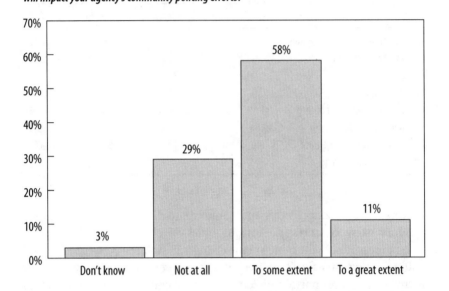

policing efforts. Approximately, 61 percent of small agencies reported an impact "to some extent" or "to a great extent," compared to 72 percent of medium-size agencies, and 80 percent of large agencies.[10]

Agencies indicating an impact of September 11 events on their community policing efforts were asked to explain. Two themes predominated in these open-ended responses. First, many agencies reported that community policing activities had been negatively impacted because personnel had other priorities and because of military call-ups of their department's staff. Representative comments include the following:

- "Line officers moved from patrol to security assignments (i.e., airport security)."

---

10. Small agencies serve jurisdictions up to 49,999 residents; medium agencies have populations of 50,000 to 149,000, and large jurisdictions have 150,000 or more residents. Again the reader should be cautioned about the small sample size and thus limited ability to generalize these results.

- The need to "focus on domestic terrorism in terms of training, protection, etc. may pull time and resources away from community policing initiatives."
- "Activation of members to military service created many holes in the schedule."
- "For the time being, our personnel are reassigned to a much higher level of routine patrol—such as patrolling the villages' infrastructures such as government buildings, schools, water supply, etc. This takes away from some of the time-heavy community policing activities."

The second theme was much more positive. Many agencies reported greater support from residents. They attributed this to the heroic actions of law enforcement personnel in response to the terrorist attacks of September 11, 2001, and a renewed appreciation for the dangers associated with the job. A few of the respondents linked the increased support and appreciation to new opportunities for partnerships and trust building. Representative comments include the following:

- "Overall, I feel the community has a greater respect for the officers that serve them. I believe the impact will increase the cooperation that we receive from the community."
- "The events of September 11th have increased the public's awareness of our department and concern for our officers. This has created an atmosphere that fosters cooperation. Community-based program involvement has increased."
- September 11 "brought the community and different agencies together . . . to work towards new goals and better preparedness."
- "The rekindled respect for public safety professionals will allow us to overcome some of the pre-existing barriers to communication in our community."
- "9-11 further solidified a strong community bond already in place."

Some comments referenced activities after September 11 that reflected community policing:

- "The terrorist attacks of September 11, 2001, have made it increasingly vital to increase community policing efforts in order to remain aware of potential terrorist threats which may exist within the community."
- "[We] must get in touch with new immigrant populations and establish trust and collaboration in order to fight terror and reduce crime."

- "September 11th has made our department realize that problem solving is not just about drugs, gangs, robbery, etc. It is now about a much greater problem—terrorism. We are working with businesses and other government agencies more closely to help prevent terrorism."

Conclusion

There are myriad interpretations that one can draw from the 1992, 1997, and 2002 survey data. PERF asked practitioners with diverse perspectives and academic experts in law enforcement and community development to reflect on the implementation and future of community policing in the United States. In this book they have aptly drawn on the survey data and their own experiences to put forward interpretations that can help guide law enforcement into the future.

References

Goldstein, Herman. 1993. *The New Policing: Confronting Complexity*. National Institute of Justice, Research in Brief. Washington, D.C.: U.S. Department of Justice. Reprinted in Willard M. Oliver, ed. 2000. *Community Policing: Classical Readings*, 71-80. Upper Saddle River, N.J.: Prentice Hall.

Kelling, George, and Mark Moore. 1988. "The Evolving Strategy of Policing." In *Perspectives on Policing*. Washington, D.C.: National Institute of Justice.

Rosenthal, Arlen M., Lorie A. Fridell, Mark L. Dantzker, Gayle Fisher-Stewart, Pedro J. Saavedra, Tigran Markaryan, and Sadie Bennett. 2000. *Community Policing: 1997 National Survey Update of Police and Sheriffs' Departments*. Final report submitted to the National Institute of Justice. Grant No. 96-IJ-CX-0045.

5

The Survey Data:
What They Say and Don't Say
about Community Policing

*by Gary Cordner, Dean of the College of Justice and Safety
at Eastern Kentucky University and Director of the
Regional Community Policing Institute*

The data presented in this chapter are based on three national surveys of police agencies and can be used to describe the current state of community-oriented policing (COP). The data also track changes in COP during the past decade. Of course, surveys of police departments, typically completed by one individual per agency, have their shortcomings. It is difficult to discover complex organization-level phenomena, not to mention the reality of programs implemented on the street and in neighborhoods (see Maguire and Mastrofski 2000 for a discussion of these issues as they relate to community policing; see also Maguire and Katz 2002). Although the surveys described in this chapter have those shortcomings, they also have a particular advantage: they were administered to a panel of agencies three times between 1992 and 2002, and this permits at least an estimation of change over time.

Limitations of Survey Data

It should be emphasized that these data do not cover the whole history of community policing. In particular, it would be inappropriate to regard the 1992 survey as a real *baseline* measurement of community-oriented policing in the United States, since community policing began its ascendancy in the early 1980s (Wilson and Kelling 1982) and was being widely promoted and debated by the late 1980s (Greene and Mastrofski 1988; Kelling 1988; Kelling and Moore 1988).

A further limitation of these data should be acknowledged at the outset. Most of the survey items asked police executives whether their agencies had or had not implemented specific aspects of community-oriented policing. There are at least two consequences of this methodology. One is that it takes a reductionist approach to defining and measuring community policing. It assumes that the sum of the parts accurately reflects the whole. It assumes that an agency that has implemented more of the parts of COP has more fully adopted community policing than an agency that has implemented fewer of the parts. Similarly, it assumes that if an agency (or the sum of all agencies) has implemented more of the parts of COP over time, then community policing has been more fully adopted over time. To use a well-worn cliché, community policing is a philosophy, not just a program. Therefore, this reductionist approach has some obvious weaknesses in measuring the real quality and quantity of community policing implementation.

The second specific limitation of these survey data derives from the yes/no nature of most of the items. These items measure whether agencies do or do not employ certain COP activities, but not the *extent* to which they are employed. For example, more than 90 percent of agencies had citizens participating in Neighborhood Watch in 1992, 1997, and 2002 (see Chapter 4, Figure 4-4). The proportion of agencies using this program increased somewhat in 1997 and then decreased somewhat in 2002, but those changes were not statistically significant. The reader should conclude from the data presented that there were no changes over time, due to the lack of statistical significance, although the reader might also be concerned about the small decrease from 1997 to 2002. Missing from the figure, however, is any measurement of the number of organized neighborhoods, the number of citizens participating, or the intensity of participation. Thus, a police department might have responded "yes" to this item on all three surveys (as most did), suggesting no change, when in fact the number of organized neighborhoods or the number of participating citizens might have increased (or decreased) dramatically.

These comments are not meant as criticisms of the surveys. They merely acknowledge the surveys' limitations. All research methods have strengths and weaknesses. It is important to be aware of the limitations of the data being used to describe the state of community policing in America today and to assess what progress has been made over the past decade.

A Snapshot of Community Policing in 2002

One way to use these survey data is to identify those COP activities that, in 2002, were most and least commonly adopted. This can provide a recent snapshot of the state of community policing.

Out of a total of fifty-six community policing activities that were analyzed, the sixteen *most common* listed below were claimed by at least 75 percent of responding agencies on the 2002 survey (see Figures 4-4, 4-5, 4-6, and 4-7):

- Citizens attend police-community meetings,
- Citizens participate in neighborhood watch,
- Citizens help police identify and resolve problems,
- Citizens serve as volunteers within the police agency,
- Citizens attend citizen police-academies,
- Police hold regularly scheduled meetings with community groups,
- Police have interagency involvement in problem solving,
- Police have youth programs,
- Police have victim assistance programs,
- Police use regulatory codes in problem solving,
- Police work with building code enforcement,
- Agencies use fixed assignments to specific beats or areas,
- Agencies give special recognition for good community policing work by employees,
- Agencies classify and prioritize calls,
- Agencies do geographically based crime analysis, and
- Agencies use permanent neighborhood-based offices or stations.

These most common activities characteristic of community policing paint a fairly positive picture of citizen participation, partnerships, outreach, problem solving, and organizational change in place in American policing in 2002. More than half of these activities had registered below the

75 percent implementation threshold on the first survey in 1992, indicating that real progress has been made over the past decade in the implementation of community policing.

The seven *least common* community policing activities listed below were claimed by less than 25 percent of the responding agencies on the 2002 survey:

- Citizens help prepare work agreements for problem solving,
- Citizens participate in the police promotional process,
- Citizens participate in a court watch program,
- Citizens help review complaints against the police,
- Citizens participate in the selection process for new officers,
- Citizens help evaluate officers' performance, and
- Agencies have decentralized crime analysis.

These COP activities that were the least common illustrate the limited role that the community has thus far taken in police administration and policy making. It has become common for citizens to participate in neighborhood watch and neighborhood problem solving, attend meetings with the police, attend citizen police academies, and do volunteer work within the police agency. It has not become common for citizens to play a role in evaluating their neighborhood police officers, selecting and promoting police officers, or reviewing complaints against the police.

Changes in Community Policing over Time

The survey data not only give us a snapshot of community policing in 2002; they also allow us to assess changes in the implementation of community policing activities during two time periods: 1992 to 1997 and 1997 to 2002. While increases in the implementation of COP are indicated during both time periods, it appears that increases were more common during the earlier period (see Table 5-1).

TABLE 5-1. Community Policing Activities Showing Increases in Implementation by Time Period

Time Period	Percent of Activities Showing Increases
1992–1997	82%
1997–2002	62%

This picture of when COP implementation changes occurred is not surprising. The 1992–1997 time period seems to correspond with increased awareness about community policing throughout the police profession and the wider community (Oliver 2000). Certainly, it coincides with the first three to four years of federal funding for community policing through the Office of Community Oriented Policing Services (COPS) in the U.S. Department of Justice.

The lower numbers for the period from 1997 to 2002 should not necessarily give rise to a gloomy interpretation, however. First, more than half of COP activities showed increased implementation during this period, so the general direction was still forward. Second, because of the yes/no measurement method, there was no way for agencies that had reported "yes" about implementing a particular COP activity in 1997 to register any increase in 2002. Thus, a suggestion of a plateau over time is inevitable even if there is no backtracking.

The Nature of Changes in Community Policing

Survey items were broken down for both time periods into four categories of COP activities: citizen participation, partnership outreach, problem solving, and organizational change (Table 5-2). In both periods, COP activities in the organizational change category were most likely to show increased implementation, as indicated in Chapter 4 (Table 4-7), while those in the citizen participation category showed the least increase in adoption (Table 4-4). Within each category of COP activity, increased adoption was greater in the 1992–1997 time period than in the 1997–2002 time period.

A positive interpretation of these patterns in changes would be that police agencies are becoming more serious about implementing and institutionalizing community policing, as reflected by the increased emphasis

TABLE 5-2. Categories of COP Activities Showing Increases in Implementation by Time Period

Activities	1992–1997	1997–2002
Citizen participation	73%	38%
Partnership outreach	80%	60%
Problem solving	80%	62%
Organizational change	93%	81%

on organizational change. A more critical interpretation would focus on the decreasing emphasis on citizen participation as evidence that there was less community involvement in community policing in 2002 than in the earlier period.

None of the fifty-six COP activities analyzed for this report showed a 10 percent or greater decrease in adoption between 1992 and 2002. The community policing activities listed below showed a 10 percent or greater *increase* in implementation between 1992 and 2002 (or between 1997 and 2002, if the item was not included on the 1992 survey):

- Citizens participate in citizen patrols,
- Citizens attend citizen police academies,
- Police engage in interagency code enforcement,
- Police work with community corrections,
- Police work with alternative dispute resolution,
- Police use regulatory codes in problem solving,
- Police work with building code enforcement,
- Agencies have a disciplinary system to support problem solving,
- Agencies have a specialized problem-solving unit,
- Agencies have landlord training programs,
- Agencies provide citizen training in problem solving,
- Agencies classify and prioritize calls,
- Agencies do geographically-based crime analysis,
- Agencies have job descriptions that include community policing,
- Agencies do citizen surveys to determine needs and priorities,
- Agencies do citizen surveys to evaluate police services,
- Agencies use fixed shifts,
- Agencies have physical decentralization of field services,
- Agencies use permanent neighborhood-based offices or stations, and
- Agencies use employee evaluations to reinforce community policing.

The nature of the preceding activities that became more widely adopted over the past decade lends solid support to the positive interpretation of COP progress since 1992.

Overall Assessment

According to these surveys, circa 1997, the vast majority of U.S. police agencies (85 percent) were at least in the process of implementing community policing, and most (58 percent) had implemented it. As of 2002, police executives whose agencies had adopted community policing expressed very positive views about the effects of this model of policing on community relations, fear of crime, police officer job satisfaction, and even crime. It might seem to be time to declare victory in the campaign to promote the diffusion and adoption of community policing throughout America.

The other side of this coin is that police agencies have tended to adopt a relatively modest version of community policing, according to the surveys. Increases in the implementation of internal organizational aspects of COP have outpaced the adoption of most forms of citizen participation. Police agencies have been more willing to engage citizens in problem solving and citizen patrols than in police performance evaluation, complaint review, and personnel decision making.

Information from other sources tends to corroborate the sometimes limited or modest nature of community policing as implemented. For example, community police officers seem to spend relatively little time actually engaging citizens (Parks et al. 1999). There is little evidence that community policing affects community processes in ways that would be expected to subsequently affect fear, disorder, and crime (Kerley and Benson 2000). The adoption of community policing *strategies* at the managerial level does not always lead to the utilization of community-based *tactics* in the field (Bennett 1998). Everyday problem solving by police officers typically does not conform very closely to the analytical and collaborative problem-solving model promoted by the advocates of problem-oriented policing (Cordner 2002). These sources support the picture of modest implementation presented in the surveys.

The Next Level of Community Policing

For the past several years, community policing enthusiasts have often discussed "taking COP to the next level." There has not been much consensus, however, about what the next level is or how to get there. The survey data do not help directly in that respect, but they provide a useful description of what community policing is today, and how it has changed over the past ten years.

One aspect of "the next level" might be continuing efforts to push toward the adoption of community policing by 100 percent of police agencies. As of 1997, 15 percent of agencies reported that they had either not considered implementing COP or had rejected it for some reason. Since the

2002 survey only included agencies that had implemented community policing, we do not have an updated measure of the number of non-COP agencies. Although the Office of Community Oriented Policing Services in the U.S. Justice Department may have made inroads with these recalcitrant agencies since 1997, it is also likely that some agencies have moved away from community policing following the change in administrations in Washington, the continued uncertainty of COPS Office funding, and the new demands on police agencies after September 11, 2001.

Another aspect of taking community policing "to the next level" might entail further elaboration of basic community policing (Cordner 2000). The tendency of the COPS Office and others at the national level to limit the officially endorsed version of COP to community engagement, problem solving, and organizational change has had the positive effect of retaining flexibility in community policing and not scaring agencies away with a rigid national model of COP. However, this loosely defined model has had the negative effect of not providing much guidance to those agencies looking for direction in their community policing efforts. Perhaps the list of sixteen COP activities implemented by 75 percent or more of the surveyed agencies in 2002 would be a good starting point for describing basic community policing in more detail. Such elaboration would provide police agencies with specific ideas for enhancing their approaches to community policing.

"The next level" also could entail efforts to promote adoption of those aspects of community policing that the 2002 survey showed were least common. In particular, few police agencies seem to have been willing to engage in real power sharing with the community (Brown 1985), such as by inviting the community to help select, promote, and evaluate officers. Police agencies have taken great strides over the past decade in welcoming citizen participation in community meetings, neighborhood problem solving, and even citizen patrols. The next frontier of community policing might be characterized by greater input and participation by citizens in police department policy making and decision making.

Another avenue for COP enhancement could include improvements in the quality of police officers' implementation of community policing. Officers could allocate more of their time to interaction with citizens and community engagement instead of falling into the easy habit of motorized patrol. They also could devote more time and energy to identifying and analyzing problems and demonstrate more creativity when trying to solve those problems. Field studies of community policing and problem solving consistently reveal shortcomings in how these strategies are implemented at the street level.

To improve the quality of community policing at the street level will require improvements in police selection, academy training, field training, supervision, and performance evaluation. A few police agencies have systematically changed these aspects of their infrastructure in support of community policing (Oettmeier and Wycoff 1998), but most have not. Revising the academy training component is particularly problematic for those many agencies that send their recruits to a regional or state academy. Agencies often have little input into the academy's curriculum and modes of instruction. Some of these academies have been slow to change, despite the availability of model curricula that integrate community policing throughout all classes and documented examples of the use of problem-based adult learning techniques in police training (Himelfarb 1997; Barbian 2002).

New approaches to training might provide an important means of taking community policing "to the next level," although we should be careful not to harbor unrealistic expectations about the extent to which training can accomplish changes in policing philosophy (Buerger 1998). Exhortation aside, police academies today have an opportunity to introduce an entirely new body of knowledge into police training. They can use COP case studies and the elaborate series of problem-solving guides currently being published by the COPS Office that are focused on specific crime and disorder problems. Officers whose education and training about their new jobs is totally oriented around community engagement and methods for solving specific types of community problems might be able to implement better quality COP than officers whose indoctrination into policing took a more traditional form.

Finally, in the years ahead community policing must find a way to be more relevant to the experiences of teenagers and young adults, especially young males of color (Williams 1999). For reasons that are not entirely clear, the increased implementation of community policing over the past decade has coincided with heightened concerns about racial profiling and excessive use of force by police. Some regard this situation as a sad coincidence; others see it as the result of two worlds of policing (COP vs. SWAT, or COP vs. zero tolerance). Still others see a sinister motivation within community policing itself. Regardless of the explanation, it seems clear that community policing, although popular with many residents, has not worked for everyone. As police agencies strive to implement COP more fully in order to more effectively control crime, disorder, and fear, they need to figure out how to improve their relationship with all segments of the community, not just young kids, soccer moms, and old folks.

References

Barbian, Jeff. 2002. "A New Line of Defense." *Training* 39,9 (September): 39–47.

Bennett, Trevor. 1998. "Police and Public Involvement in the Delivery of Community Policing." In Jean-Paul Brodeur, ed., *How to Recognize Good Policing: Problems and Issues,* 107–122. Thousand Oaks, Calif.: Sage Publications.

Brown, Lee. 1985. "Police-Community Power Sharing." In William Geller, ed., *Police Leadership in America: Crisis and Opportunity,* 70–83. New York: Praeger.

Buerger, Michael. 1998. "Police Training as Pentecost: Using Tools Singularly Ill-Suited to the Purpose of Reform." *Police Quarterly* 1,1: 27–63.

Cordner, Gary. 2000. "Community Policing: Elements and Effects." In Geoffrey Alpert and Alex Piquero, eds., *Community Policing: Contemporary Readings,* 2nd ed., 45–62. Prospect Heights, Ill.: Waveland.

———. 2002. *Problem-Oriented Policing in San Diego: A Study of POP in Practice in a Big-City Police Department.* Report submitted to the National Institute of Justice, Washington, D.C.

Greene, Jack, and Stephen Mastrofski, eds. 1988. *Community Policing: Rhetoric or Reality?* New York: Praeger.

Himelfarb, Frum. 1997. "RCMP Learning and Renewal: Building on Strengths." In Quint Thurman and Edmund McGarrell, eds., *Community Policing in a Rural Setting,* 33–39. Cincinnati, Ohio: Anderson.

Kelling, George. 1988. "Police and Communities: The Quiet Revolution." *Perspectives on Policing.* Washington, D.C.: National Institute of Justice.

Kelling, George, and Mark Moore. 1988. "The Evolving Strategy of Policing." *Perspectives on Policing.* Washington, D.C.: National Institute of Justice.

Kerley, Kent, and Michael Benson. 2000. "Does Community-Oriented Policing Help Build Stronger Communities?" *Police Quarterly* 3(1), 46–69.

Maguire, Edward, and Charles Katz. 2002. "Community Policing, Loose Coupling, and Sensemaking in American Police Agencies." *Justice Quarterly* 19(3), 503–536.

Maguire, Edward, and Stephen Mastrofski. 2000. "Patterns of Community Policing in the United States." *Police Quarterly* 3(1), 4–45.

Oettmeier, Timothy, and Mary Ann Wycoff. 1998. "Personnel Performance Evaluations in the Community Policing Context." In Tara O'Connor Shelley and Anne Grant, eds., *Problem-Oriented Policing: Crime-Specific Problems, Critical Issues and Making POP Work,* 351–398. Washington, D.C.: Police Executive Research Forum.

Oliver, Willard. 2000. "The Third Generation of Community Policing: Moving through Innovation, Diffusion, and Institutionalization." *Police Quarterly* 3(4), 367–388.

Parks, Roger, Stephen Mastrofski, Christina DeJong, and Kevin Gray. 1999. "How Officers Spend Their Time with the Community." *Justice Quarterly* 16(3), 483–518.

Williams, Brian. 1999. "Perceptions of Children and Teenagers on Community Policing: Implications for Law Enforcement Leadership, Training, and Citizen Evaluations." *Police Quarterly* 2(2), 150–173.

Wilson, James Q., and George Kelling. 1982. "Broken Windows: The Police and Neighborhood Safety." *Atlantic Monthly* 249, 29–38.

Part III

The Future of Community Policing

6

Community Policing in the Years Ahead: And Now for the Really Hard Part

by Bonnie Bucqueroux, former associate director of the National Center for Community Policing at Michigan State University

For the tens of thousands of police officers who are working hard to make the most of community policing, the title of this chapter must be disconcerting. What do you mean the hard part has yet to be done?

The reality is that the hard part of making the community a full partner with the police has not happened. The results of the 1992, 1997, and 2002 surveys presented in Chapter 4 confirm that departments are doing a good job of reaching out to the community for help and support. They also indicate that there is still an obvious reluctance to share power and decision making with citizens. These features of community policing are ultimately necessary if community residents are to shoulder their fair share of the work of and responsibility for making their communities safer.

The good news is that, of the departments that say they embrace community policing, the vast majority have implemented basic outreach strategies. More than 90 percent participate in Neighborhood Watch and nine out of ten also have their officers regularly attend community meetings. Four out of five community policing agencies conduct citizen academies and encourage people to volunteer.

But when it comes to true power sharing, the numbers are consistently far lower. Fewer than one in five self-described community policing agencies allow citizens to help evaluate officers or review complaints. The number of community policing departments where citizens participate in producing the work agreements for problem solving has actually dropped, from roughly 25 percent in 1992 to 21 percent in 2002. The number of agencies that allow citizens a role in the promotional process has also declined slightly to below 20 percent.

Departments clearly find it easier to engage the community as volunteers who help, rather than as partners who share in decision making. Only through building equal partnerships with the community, however, can the full power of community policing be unleashed. The hard part is to make this most democratic form of policing as open and inclusive (and thereby as powerful) as it can be.

The Importance of Informal Social Control

The ultimate goal of community policing is to strengthen communities so that they have the power to police themselves. Studies uniformly confirm that a small percentage of people commit the vast majority of crimes. Moreover, this small group typically gravitates to high-crime hotspots that are not strong enough to repel or control them. Unfortunately, when the lawbreakers achieve the upper hand, the downward spiral gains momentum. A brief exploration of how this happens and what role the police can play in reversing such trends helps to highlight the importance of informal social control.

Face-to-Face Interactions

Sir Robert Peel, the renowned British policing theorist, said it best when he argued that the people are the police and the police the people. Not only is it cost prohibitive to have a cop on every corner; most of us do not want to live in that kind of society. The ideal is when the community enjoys the leadership, structure, and resources necessary to deal with most of its problems; occasionally, the community's efforts to resolve its problems will be supplemented as needed by the police, whose unique authority spans the broadest possible range of options, including arrest and deadly force.

Yet during the past 50 years in the United States, as the policing profession modernized and professionalized, two profoundly dangerous but unanticipated results occurred. First, proliferation of the telephone, the police radio, and the patrol car inadvertently severed the relationship between people and their police. In the past police officers who walked the beat knew they had to form personal relationships with the people in their communities. The officers needed to have citizens who were willing to share information—and to watch the officer's back if trouble erupted.

Second, as the police applied scientific management to policing, the perception grew that it was the police department's job to keep the community safe. In the past the community understood that it was ultimately up to its citizens to establish and reaffirm certain norms of behavior that promote public safety.

At the same time the police role was changing, many of those same forces created a culture of alienation and atomization within many communities. Geographic aggregations of isolated strangers often replaced cohesive neighborhoods where people felt they shared a common destiny.

Particularly in high-crime neighborhoods, the face-to-face interactions that support and strengthen informal social control declined as the crime rate skyrocketed during the 1960s and 1970s. While the rates of violence nationwide have recently declined, the gains have still not taken us back to the demonstrably safer era of the 1950s, a time fondly remembered by many who are still alive today.

Examples of Social Restraints and Mechanisms

Many of us are old enough to remember firsthand the power of informal social control. In earlier times, if Mrs. Smith looked out her window and saw young Bobby abusing younger kids, she might well march Bobby home to his mother, even if Mrs. Smith did not have a child in the fray. Through such informal interactions, communities wielded enormous power to set standards and to raise the next generation within them.

In rich neighborhoods as well as poor ones today, however, Mrs. Smith is far less likely to have a personal relationship with Bobby's parents, for a variety of reasons. Where we once had stay-at-home moms, we now have two wage-earner and single-parent families. This means fewer people have the time for frequent face-to-face interactions with their neighbors. Adding to that dynamic is the reality that people today spend hours in front of the TV, hours that were previously spent out in the community or visiting friends who lived within walking distance.

The rising crime rate has also driven Mrs. Smith indoors, where she lives behind dead-bolted doors and barred windows. She may have good reason to fear that Bobby's parents will not welcome her intervention. Indeed, she may have evidence to support the fear that young Bobby himself will draw a gun on her if she challenges him alone.

When people like Mrs. Smith, who previously reinforced good behavior, retreat from community life, the downward spiral accelerates. Neighborhoods can spin out of control, emboldening the handful of lawbreakers to the point where they overwhelm the law-abiding majority.

Indulging in a nostalgic yearning for a safer past is not the answer. But we need to remember that informal social control is the most effective and affordable way to keep communities safe. Community policing asks police departments to explore ways to harness the power of social control by borrowing from the best of the past, filtered through today's reality.

Ways to Promote Positive Social Norms

Police agencies have yet to fully embrace the community. One reason may be a continuing undercurrent of thought within some police agencies that "there are communities that want crime." During the early 1990s, when violence was reaching its peak, I spent more than 18 months working with some of the most crime-riddled housing developments. I can say unequivocally that in those 18 months I never met a mother who thought it was OK for children to die by gunfire. What has happened in high-crime communities is that the law-abiding majority has effectively been silenced. Dr. Carl S. Taylor of Michigan State University calls this the dangerous and increasing normalization of ignorance and violence.

As Robert Axelrod's *The Complexity of Cooperation* (1997) reminds us, coercion, force, and punishment are not the only (or the best) ways to promote positive societal norms. Others are as follows:

Law: The law serves as a framework for defining and codifying proper behavior. It enshrines the rules in a formal system that has the power to employ punishment to enforce compliance.

Dominance: Dominance means that a group with superior power and status can enforce compliance from groups with less of both. This is the underlying relationship between parents and children, as well as between groups in the dominant culture and the so-called underclass.

Deterrence: This approach promotes compliance by using individuals as examples of the bad things that happen to people who do not follow the rules. Holding up those who pay the penalty—whether that means doing time, losing a job, or being shunned by neighbors—is designed to keep others in line.

Membership: Rules can be enforced through contracts, covenants, and alliances.

Internalization: This occurs when the rules are so well inculcated in the individual that they become a part of him or her. Instead of outside coercion, a person's conscience dictates to the person what he or she should do.

Reputation: People follow norms for fear of harming their reputations if they stray.

Metanorms: When a norm becomes so widely embraced that it reaches metanorm status, community members enforce compliance by challenging and even punishing anyone who disagrees.

Social proof: When an individual sees people in the community exhibiting behavior that supports the norm, this reinforces the idea that these are rules everyone should follow.

The police and the rest of the criminal justice system traditionally have relied almost exclusively on strategies involving the law, dominance, and deterrence to promote public order. Community policing instead encourages police to become the catalyst to empower the Mrs. Smiths, so that the law-abiding but often silent and intimidated majority can use tactics like membership and reputation to promote the norms that support community safety. Community policing needs to encourage and protect the Mrs. Smiths who intervene with youngsters, so that they grow up to internalize law-abiding behavior. The police have a valuable role to play in ensuring that the Mrs. Smiths and Mr. Smiths achieve critical mass on the streets so that they provide the social proof that the community will not tolerate being victimized.

The Need for Nonarrest Strategies

The late Dr. Robert Trojanowicz, a renowned community policing pioneer, recognized the importance of informal social control. "Arrest must always be an integral part of police work—it's what makes the police what they are," he said. "But we have ignored the power of the police to support community-based non-arrest strategies to solve problems" (Trojanowicz n.d.).

Trojanowicz viewed arrest and incarceration as precious but expensive tools best used sparingly.

If he were alive today, Trojanowicz would no doubt be heartened to see that the vast majority of police agencies have embraced some form of community policing. But he would be horrified to find that we now have more than 2 million people behind bars, arguably the highest incarceration rate in the world, in large part because of mandatory drug sentences. The brand of community policing that he and other progressive police leaders promoted was one that urged police to do more to help struggling communities harness informal social control in the service of public safety.

The Challenge Ahead

The community policing philosophy adds two new strategies to traditional police work—collaborative, community-based problem solving and community building. The Police Executive Research Forum (PERF) has been instrumental in training police in the SARA (Scanning, Analysis, Response, and Assessment) method of collaborative problem solving advanced by Dr. Herman Goldstein. The U.S. Department of Justice's Office of Community Oriented Policing Services (COPS) reinforces those skills and also helps police departments connect to communities, offering much-needed information and advice on how to help crime-ravaged communities build the infrastructure they need to be partners in the problem-solving process.

Police professionals have done a good job of partnering with other government, private, and nonprofit professionals. Many have also done a good job of connecting with the community. But what has been lacking is that last crucial link where the community becomes a participating partner in the problem-solving process, so that residents can contribute the power of informal social control to long-term strategies.

If we think about low-level drug dealing, for example, there are limits to the strategies that professionals alone can implement. The most successful long-term interventions may include police sweeps and code enforcement to close dope houses, but those that survive the test of time typically involve community efforts to change the prevailing norms. When the community takes a stand that it will not tolerate open drug dealing and drug use, the tide turns. Tactics can range from developing citizen patrols to having former addicts talk to kids in school, but the bottom line is the community's commitment to doing whatever it can to make a positive difference.

Those of us fortunate enough to live in safe, well-tended, middle-class communities know that there may well be drug dealing and drug use within our midst. But it is a not a visible and dangerous presence that corrodes community life and teaches youngsters the wrong lessons. If an armed drug dealer decides to open shop on a corner of my street, the community would rise up as one to do whatever it takes to solve the problem.

We would demand that the police spend whatever times it takes to work with us on a variety of strategies. If we did not receive satisfaction from the police, we would pressure every politician within reach—and communities like mine have the clout to be taken seriously. It wouldn't take long to organize citizen patrols and telephone trees, and we have the money to buy our own jackets, two-way radios, cell phones, and laptops.

The challenge for police in dealing with communities that lack structure, cohesion, clout, and resources is to help them build from within so that they can function as true partners. What has not been made clear is that even seemingly unrelated community-building activities, such as starting a Police Athletic League or a faith-based mentoring program for kids, are not worthwhile only for their own sakes. They also serve as the first steps toward building the foundations for future community-based problem solving.

Educating and Nurturing New Community-Based Leaders

For community members to function as full partners at the problem-solving table requires nurturing a new generation of leaders. In the mid-1990s, the U.S. Department of Justice's Bureau of Justice Assistance and the U.S. Department of Housing and Urban Development's Office of Resident Initiatives funded the community policing training for public housing developments. The training was delivered by a consortium composed of the Police Executive Research Forum, the International City/County Management Association, the National Center for Community Policing at Michigan State University, and the Institute for Law and Justice (1994). The training was unique. At least two community residents were required to be part of the ten-person training team that attended the three-day training sessions. More than sixty public housing developments around the country were involved in the training.

The training proved that the collaborative problem-solving process benefits tremendously from participation by community residents. Residents often identified why plans considered brilliant by professionals would founder on the rocks of reality in their neighborhoods. They also contributed innovative strategies that involved having the residents deal with the problems on their own, often asking only for modest resources and support.

But what the training also made clear was that nurturing this next generation of leaders requires special effort and understanding. For example, a common challenge for facilitators was often to carve out a space for the residents to speak. While a few community participants were eager to hold forth, many were hesitant to speak up. Some appeared to be intimidated by the highly educated professionals at the table for whom such sessions were second nature. Another challenge was to ensure that the residents' ideas and needs were acknowledged by the rest of the group.

The training provided some skill-building sessions for residents on organizing and hosting community-based meetings. However, it was clear that these sessions would not be enough. For full and sustained participation by residents, additional opportunities over time to build their leadership skills are needed.

Professionals, too, need training in working with the community. Action-oriented police are often quick to skip over some of the steps required to implement their plans. Police may not recognize that some community residents do not understand their inner workings or their lingo. While many professionals at the training sessions quickly realized the importance of the residents' input, others needed to learn the importance of patience in building consensus and to accept people whose grammar, idioms, experiences, and lifestyles differed from theirs.

Perhaps the biggest obstacle to full community participation is the danger that community voices will be marginalized. Reserving seats at the table for community participants can end up being little more than a token action if decisions are reached by quick votes. As anyone who has been on the losing side knows, a 51–49 vote may be fair, but it is hard to get members of the forty-nine-person group enthusiastic about helping to implement the plan. The challenge is to stay at the table and work together until a plan that everyone can endorse and sell to others is reached.

Professionals and community members alike would also benefit from sessions that explore the power of informal social control. Many of the community policing strategies employed around the country still place too much of the burden on the police and the other professionals. The result is over-reliance on expensive and time-consuming arrest and incarceration strategies to solve problems.

Educating the Community about Community Policing

As attention shifts to new concerns about homeland security and the threat of terrorism, some fear many police agencies that have done an excellent job of taking community policing as far as they have will not be eager to do even more. It may be time to train the community about its power to implement the community policing philosophy. In addition to attending skill-building and leadership sessions, community residents need to be provided with the tools to make the most of informal social control, to augment, supplement, and even supplant the efforts of professionals.

As Internet visionaries Greg Kearsley and Ben Shneiderman (1999) explain, a sense of community is developed by providing opportunities for people to create, relate, and donate. Given the chance, people are inspired by the chance to create something new, to relate with one another, and to donate to something bigger than themselves, something that offers the next generation a better chance at the American dream. We can do a better job of tapping into those universal human impulses by giving people the tools they need to engage in problem-solving efforts that can make their neighborhoods better and safer places in which to live, work, and raise families.

Perhaps the most appropriate goal for the next decade is to give communities the training they need to take the lead in problem solving. Maybe it's time to educate and empower community residents so that they are the ones who approach the police to join them.

References

Axelrod, Robert. 1997. *The Complexity of Cooperation: Agent-Based Models of Competition and Collaboration.* Princeton, New Jersey: Princeton University Press, Princeton Studies in Complexity.

Bucqueroux, Bonnie, Drew Diamond, and Carl S. Taylor. Forthcoming. *Community Policing: Taking It to the Next Level.* Cincinnati: Anderson Publishing.

Kearsley, Greg, and Ben Shneiderman. 1999. *Engagement Theory: A Framework for Technology-Based Teaching and Learning.* Available at http://home.sprynet.com/~gkearsley/engage.htm

Police Executive Research Forum, the International City/County Management Association, the National Center for Community Policing at Michigan State University, and the Institute for Law & Justice. 1994. *Community Policing in Public Housing Training Manual.* Washington, D.C.: U.S. Department of Justice's Bureau of Justice Assistance and the U.S. Department of Housing and Urban Development's Office of Resident Initiatives.

Trojanowicz, Robert (n.d.). Personal communication.

7

The Promise of Community Development Corporations

By Paul Grogan, President of the Boston Foundation,
and Lisa Belsky, Senior Program Director at
Local Initiatives Support Corporation in New York

Afirst reading of the survey results presented in Chapter 4 reveals an important milestone in the evolution of law enforcement: According to the comparative findings, community policing, as policy, finds itself increasingly in the mainstream, perhaps even part of the new "conventional wisdom." This is welcome news for all those working on the broader revitalization of urban America.

As paper policy, the pragmatism and promise of community policing precepts are difficult to argue. Indeed, as Commissioner Paul Evans of the Boston Police Department recently noted (Geller 2002b), "it's common sense that economic vitality and safety go hand-in-hand. So it's just more common sense to align police and community." Unfortunately, in too many places, concepts of community policing remain just that—well-intentioned (at best) yet superficial notions of amorphous connections between street-level officers and community residents. Community policing may be defined more by meetings held than by collaborative problem solving and concrete action.

The good news, however, is that for those departments that do seek meaningful and productive alliances with their communities, highly capable neighborhood partners—in our lexicon "community development cor-porations" (or CDCs)—stand at the ready to help transform philosophy into action.

This basic notion arises from our experience working at the Local Ini-tiatives Support Corporation (LISC), based in New York. It was founded more than twenty years ago by the Ford Foundation. LISC's mission is to deliver private-sector financial support and technical help to inner-city revitalization efforts nationwide. These efforts are carried out by CDCs—neighborhood-based, citizen-formed organizations that have a broad mis-sion of rebuilding communities. The first of these groups appeared in the late 1960s, and their numbers have grown exponentially since then. Today more than 4,000 community development corporations operate through-out the country. They have become a major positive force for the recovery of very damaged and distressed inner-city neighborhoods.

The founders of LISC believed there was enormous potential for ordi-nary people—the residents of these largely poor, minority communities—to take the lead and accomplish things that neither the public nor the private sector had the will or capacity to do. But they also believed that without access to expertise and capital, even the most courageous and tena-cious of these efforts would be limited. The Local Initiatives Support Cor-poration is a cross between a foundation and an investment bank. It was created to provide just such access. Since its inception, the organization has been able to deliver more than $4 billion of private capital in the form of grants, loans, and equity investments to several thousand of these commu-nity development corporations around the country. This money has been used to build or renovate more than 100,000 homes and apartments and more than 20 million square feet of commercial facilities.

CDCs and Community Policing

Our views on community policing come largely from the perspective of our long-term engagement in LISC and in the community development field more generally. They derive, as well, from what that experience tells us about the prospects for safety in these communities and for partnerships with police. On that topic we offer three basic arguments.

1. Ordinary people in poor communities intuitively ascribe to the "bro-ken windows" theory (Wilson and Kelling 1982). If you look at how CDCs have evolved and behaved over time, at their strategy, and at

what they do on the ground in low-income neighborhoods, what you find is an overwhelming implicit confirmation of what has come to be known in the criminal justice world as the "broken windows" theory. This is the idea that disorder, often in the form of blighted and abandoned property, produces fear, spawns crime, and speeds the decline and deterioration of troubled communities. This is by no means the only negative force at work in these neighborhoods, but it is an extraordinarily powerful one. CDCs believe very strongly that this is the case and addressing it is at the core of their strategy.

2. CDCs help control crime. The rise of the CDC phenomenon—the development of a robust community revitalization movement in this country—is enormously good news for the prospect of safety, tranquility, and order in inner-city communities that have historically seen chaos, even virtual anarchy. By themselves, even leaving aside any particular relationship they have to the police or to any other part of the criminal justice system, community development corporations are making enormous progress in changing whole environments in communities.[1] We ought to understand what this movement is all about and learn from it.

3. Enduring, stable partnerships between police and CDCs should be central to community policing. A particularly promising frontier in community policing is the creation of formal, systematic, comprehensive alliances between police departments committed to community policing and these kinds of community organizations. We have already seen tremendous results from such partnerships in Seattle, New York, Boston, Toledo, Kansas City, Missouri, and elsewhere.

Halting Physical Signs of Disorder

Residents who form CDCs absolutely embrace the broken windows theory, although few if any have ever read the 1982 *Atlantic Monthly* article by James Q. Wilson and George Kelling. They've never read *Disorder and Decline* by Wes Skogan (1992), nor, for the most part, are they familiar with

---

1. We maintain that networks of CDCs are largely responsible for the spectacular recovery of formerly ravaged neighborhoods like the South Bronx and Harlem in New York City, and significant rejuvenations of neighborhoods in cities as diverse as Boston, Kansas City, Houston, and Seattle.

the host of other literature on problem-oriented policing. But instinctively, given what life in these communities is like, the residents who form CDCs understand that disorder is not only a symptom but also a cause of neighborhood decline and rapid increases in crime. Wes Skogan captures their viewpoint well when he says that disorder has a social and a physical connection evident in the widespread appearance of junk and trash in vacant lots, in decaying homes, boarded up buildings, and the vandalism of public and private property, and in graffiti and the stripped and abandoned cars that litter streets and alleys. Disorder is signaled by bands of teenagers congregating on street corners, by the presence of prostitutes and panhandlers, by public drinking, by verbal harassment of women, and by open gambling and drug use. All of these conditions indicate a breakdown in social order.

Such evidence of decline prompted the formation of many of the community development corporations in existence today—by churches, neighborhood coalitions, block clubs, and civic associations, or merely by groups of neighbors sitting on a stoop and saying, "We can't let this go on. We've got to do something. We can't wait to be rescued by some outside force. We've got to take action now." Initially focused on something concrete and perhaps quite small, like cleaning one vacant lot of garbage, these groups often grow to be large forces in their communities by piling one small accomplishment on another. For these groups, generating positive physical change in communities—usually begun by rehabilitating and building housing—is a bedrock element of their strategy. They regard boarded-up buildings and vacant, weed-filled lots as blights in their neighborhood. If you think of a neighborhood as a living organism, these are the wounds in which social infection gathers, becomes more virulent, and spreads, taking the entire community down. CDCs believe that they can start to replace these very negative "signal senders" with positive ones. This will begin to affect the whole perception of the neighborhood, influencing behavior in the process.

Rebuilding Social Norms

The downward spiral of community disintegration is propelled not just by the physical condition of an environment but also by the behavior residents display—behavior often licensed by the physical disarray (Skogan 1992). This is the breakdown of social norms. The community development corporations seek to rebuild and recreate the civic norms and sanctions that are at the root of secure community life. They often try to establish what political scientist Richard Nathan in 2000 called "the mutual obligation society." In other words, CDCs recreate the web of reciprocal relationships that marks healthy communities.

These CDCs are effective for many reasons. They bring tangible benefits into communities—quality housing, jobs, and revitalization. They produce visible victories that can begin to replace the psychology of decline that has taken hold in communities with a contagion of success, progress, and possibility, infecting people with a new spirit that is critical to true revitalization and order. CDCs repair damage to private markets. The private economy, as most Americans know it, is severely impaired in most inner-city communities. But by bringing housing, new investments, and hope, CDCs capture the attention of merchants, entrepreneurs, and bankers. Retail businesses in inner-city communities—supermarkets, pharmacies, apparel stores, and other shops—begin to reappear.

Recapturing Political Power

Community development corporations also help communities recapture lost political power. It is axiomatic that declining communities lose public services. They don't get good schools, the police don't respond as quickly, and garbage doesn't get picked up as often. Why does that happen? Is it because local government is somehow perversely invested in a given neighborhood's decline? No, it is not that conscious. People get good services because they insist on getting them and have the power to enforce that demand at the ballot box and in all the informal ways that our political system allows.

In declining communities, that ability has been lost or eroded. But CDCs begin to restore that ability. Part of the multiplier effect of community development is seeing public services and investment reappear. This is happening across America. One example is Linwood-Prospect in Kansas City, Missouri, the heart of the African-American community, the site of the TV movie of twenty years ago entitled *The Day After*. The producers looked for the site in America that most resembled the aftermath of a nuclear holocaust, and they found it at the intersection of Linwood and Prospect Boulevards. Go there today, and you'll find two thriving shopping centers, hundreds of new homes and apartments, community centers, and more—all produced by CDCs.

One of the largely uncredited aspects of the great crime-success story in New York City is the huge rebuilding process that went on in neighborhoods across the city. There are tens of thousands of homes and apartments, developed by community development corporations and now backed heavily by private capital and public investment. The steepest drops in crime in New York neighborhoods occurred precisely where the redevelopment activity was most concentrated.[2]

The Potential for Future Alliances

So what is the potential of formal cooperation and alliance between such groups and the police? Police all too often look out at a community and see merely a host of conflicting interests. They hear a chorus of confusing and disparate voices—most of which are raised in complaint. We want to argue that within that cacophonous mass, CDCs—builders and owners with the power, capital, credibility, and capacity to get things done—are a special class of community institution that ought to be of great interest to police. CDCs have existed in a kind of parallel universe, often getting street-level cooperation from police as part of their community-building programs but not penetrating the command structure or strategy of police departments in any significant way.

Historically, a key factor inhibiting progress on crime has been the deep and long-held mistrust between some community residents and police. As we have described, CDCs generally seek to create stable, healthy, economically vibrant, and safe communities. Police share this goal and know the characteristics of a healthy community are vital to their own core mission. However, despite the natural confluence of goals, police and CDCs are, in the context of this country's cultural, racial, and economic history, seemingly unnatural allies. Community groups often organize against institutions. Perceptions of racism, other prejudice, or misconduct can make them wary (at best) of police. Police operate within a rigid bureaucracy. Too often they experience the streets they patrol as war zones, and they see some community organizations as one of many voices demanding change. Real cooperation can be elusive with these types of organizations.[3] The

---

2. While many factors were no doubt at work (including an improving economy), the dramatic abatement of blight in the neighborhoods, along with the creation of significant new housing, played a larger role than acknowledged.

3. Many police agencies, however, have successfully partnered and involved citizens eager to support their law enforcement officers. Neighborhood watches, Police Athletic Leagues, and citizen volunteer programs are just a few of the positive partnerships that are routinely formed with police agencies.

challenge has been to overcome historic mistrust and help each see the other as a valuable and trustworthy partner.

Beginning in the mid-1990s, the Local Initiatives Support Corporation engaged in a national effort to help communities rise to that challenge. Since then LISC has demonstrated that once cooperation is achieved, much can be accomplished. The menu of positive outcomes is long: new and productive partnerships and programs, physical improvements (less graffiti, better street lighting, fewer crack houses), housing and economic development opportunities, real reductions in crime, and attitudinal changes (less fear and better rapport between police and CDC members).

The national program is called the Community Safety Initiative (CSI). Launched with crucial assistance from PERF, the CSI has a straightforward mission: put CDCs and police together to create and sustain the kind of concrete outcomes described above. The methodology for achieving this mission is also deceptively simple: create robust working partnerships between CDCs and police officers and managers.

Police-CDC Partnerships

With its collaborators, LISC identifies like-minded or potentially like-minded partners among police departments and CDCs; provides resources to staff the partnership and fund the myriad creative ideas and projects that emerge from it; offers technical assistance on an on-site and off-site basis; and documents the progress. A body of learning is created that can be shared not just within the CSI network, but more broadly throughout the community-development industry, the policing world, and beyond.

What is unique is not the strategy *per se* but what the partners bring to the table. An astonishing positive spiral of benefits flows from the partners' work together—benefits no individual could have achieved alone. This collaboration has had lasting effects.

At the outset of the Community Safety Initiative, there was more emphasis on building relationships than on getting results on the street. But the program's core methodology—grow the partnership, nurture it, support it for the long term, and, most of all, exercise patience as it stumbles—has fostered its most notable successes. As the older CSI sites have demonstrated—and as we expect the newer sites will confirm—staying the course pays off.

"Police–CDC partnerships are not simply another version of the police–resident partnerships that have become popular in community policing," writes David Thacher (2002) in a paper published by the John F.

Kennedy School of Government at Harvard University. "They are a specific type of relationship that commands the distinct resources of an important institution. They also are not simply a separate 'security' program of the sort that a few CDCs have added to their portfolio. They are a tool that helps CDCs to pursue sustainable revitalization and influence a range of conditions relevant to neighborhood quality of life. Looking to future projects like those in Seattle and New York, it seems especially important to recognize the breadth of strategies that police and CDCs can pursue together. In sum, these projects offer ample evidence for the value of police–CDC partnerships."

Progress in policing comes at various paces in various places. Something as ambitious as the partnerships described in this chapter is probably not for every police department—at least not until its leadership or its service population sees the need for a deeper and more meaningful engagement with community change agents. But many police agencies are ready, willing, and able—and have local CDCs comparably positioned, even if the two have not yet met—to forge potential strategic alliances for safer, more livable communities. Enlightened police leadership bolsters our confidence. The former chief of the Charlotte-Mecklenburg Police Department, Dennis Nowicki, describes CDCs and police as "key allies" (Geller 2002a). "If a police agency is doing real community policing and problem-solving—spending its resources and reputation to support officers who work effectively with the community," he writes, then it "should jump on opportunities to significantly improve the neighborhood, which is just what a talented CDC is good at. . . . [W]orking with CDCs is just common sense" (Geller 2002a).

In considering the fears engendered by the current domestic and international landscape, some wonder whether meaningful community–police partnerships can survive, or, more pointedly, are even appropriate. Our view is well expressed in the words of Boston's Commissioner Evans: "Our best defense against terrorism is healthy communities in which residents know each other, and key stakeholders work with the police. The terrorists thrive in an atmosphere of anonymity. Nothing could be more to our advantage than strong working relationships. . . . [T]he investment is not trivial, but it can pay huge dividends" (Geller 2002b).

The good news is that most major cities now have thriving networks of CDCs. To launch a productive partnership in your city,

- identify a high-potential partner CDC (feel free to contact LISC for assistance),

- craft together an ambitious statement of your shared mission,
- hire a project coordinator to do the leg work of the partnership,
- procure support from technical assistance providers who can help guide the strategies and day-to-day operations of your partnership, and
- document your progress.

A successful CDC–police partnership will

- bring together community groups and police departments in a non-confrontational atmosphere,
- bridge communication gaps within and between the organizations,
- bolster organizational infrastructures with specially tailored assistance and training,
- pinpoint systemic and persistent neighborhood crime problems,
- integrate the participating CDCs' development agenda with broader public safety goals,
- develop and maintain a strong advisory committee and community participation,
- identify and utilize technical assistance (from CSI, for example, or other experts in this brand of partnership),
- craft dynamic plans to resolve identified problems,
- achieve real accomplishments on both the safety and community revitalization fronts,
- facilitate long-term cooperation, strategic planning, and bold thinking by participants,
- assess progress periodically with participants,
- provide opportunities for learning, documenting, and disseminating "best practices,"
- engage in public relations to broadcast results, and
- leverage resources from within the community and beyond.

As noted at the beginning of this chapter, today community policing characterizes the mainstream of the policing profession. It is our hope that in the not too distant future collaborations between police and community development corporations also will become firmly embedded in the mainstream.

References

Geller, William 2002a. "An Interview with Dennis Nowicki: CDCs and Cops—Key Allies." *CSI in Action* (Winter 2001–2002): 2. New York City: Local Initiatives Support Corporation–Community Safety Initiative.

————. 2002b. "An Interview with Boston Police Commissioner Paul Evans." *CSI in Action* (Summer 2002): 2. New York City: Local Initiatives Support Corporation–Community Safety Initiative.

Grogan, Paul S., and Tony Proscio. 2000. *Comeback Cities: A Blueprint for Urban Neighborhood Revival.* Boulder: Westview Press.

Nathan, Richard P. 2000. *Social Science in Government: The Role of Policy Researchers.* Rockefeller Institute Press: Albany, New York.

Skogan, Wesley G. 1992. *Disorder and Decline: Crime and the Spiral of Decay in American Neighborhoods.* Berkeley: University of California Press.

Thacher, David. 2002. "The Community Security Initiative: Lessons Learned." Working Paper No. 00-05-15, 29–30. Program in Criminal Justice Police and Management of the Malcolm Weiner Center for Social Policy, John F. Kennedy School of Government, Harvard University, Cambridge, Mass.

Wilson, James Q., and George Kelling. 1982. "Broken Windows: The Police and Neighborhood Safety." *Atlantic Monthly* 249, 29–38.

8

Community Policing and Web-Based Communication: Addressing the New Information Imperative

by Dennis P. Rosenbaum, Professor and Director, Center for Research in Law and Justice, Department of Criminal Justice, University of Illinois at Chicago

American policing in the twenty-first century has embraced community policing and experimented with myriad other approaches, including data-driven policing, problem-oriented policing, "broken windows" policing, zero-tolerance and paramilitary policing, and even traditional policing—obviously not all at the same time or by the same agency. To support these orientations, American policing has also adopted new systems of accountability and state-of-the-art information technology. At times, these major trends have clashed, masqueraded as one another, or provided mutual support; but regardless, they represent the diverse faces of organizational change (and stability) in municipal policing today.

The future of community policing cannot develop independently from these other trends, and its ability to survive and flourish will depend on its ability to successfully accommodate, assimilate, or, if necessary, challenge these coinciding forces. The history of policing suggests that technological innovation, such as the introduction of automobiles and radios, is among the few forces able to alter the nature and style of policing in Western democracies. Today the world is witnessing how information technology can alter the way we engage in everyday social and commercial transactions. Seeing the power of this technology, reformers and change agents have high expectations about the capacity of technology to improve municipal policing (Brown 2000; Dunworth 2000).

Beginning with the premise that information will be a driving force in future police organizations, I address in this chapter a key question about the future of community policing: What types of information and data systems are needed to facilitate the goals of community policing and improve public safety? Technology has the capacity to either undermine or strengthen community policing. Neither outcome is inevitable. One way for police organizations to harness the power of technology is to address one of the most persistent problems in urban neighborhoods—namely, the problem of poor police–community relations. More generally, I will discuss how information is important to building genuine anticrime partnerships.

The Future of Community Policing: Strong or Weak?

The prospects for community policing are strong or weak, depending on how one reads the current evidence.

Reasons for Optimism

On the strong side, there is little question that, over the past decade, the language or discourse of community policing has become fundamentally ingrained in the psyche of American police executives, politicians, and the public. Mother, apple pie, and community policing are good for America. Police executives also report that their organizations have changed substantially in structure and function since the early 1990s in response to the community policing agenda. The national surveys presented in Chapter 4 show that self-reported implementation of police–community partnerships, collaborative problem solving, and organizational change more than doubled between 1992 and 1997. Other studies (for example, Roth et al. 2000) confirm sizable self-reported changes in police organizations during the 1990s in a direction favorable to community policing.

In addition, there is growing evidence that community policing, if implemented with high integrity and intensity, can make a difference in public safety outcomes (Rosenbaum 1994; Skogan and Hartnett 1997).

Arguably, the success of problem solving is also linked to community polic-ing and the ability to identify problems that are a priority to the public, and not just the police. Finally, support for this model of policing comes from outside the public safety arena. Internationally, there appears to be growing support for community roles in local governance and for interagency part-nerships (Crawford 1997; Rosenbaum 2002). Citizens are becoming increasingly dissatisfied with traditional bureaucracies and their inability to be responsive to the needs of the public. The general public likes the idea of *community* policing and wants municipal police to continue on the road to full-scale implementation.

The Critics' Perspective

Critics would argue that the findings from national studies are little more than self-promotional smoke and mirrors from police executives who know what people want to hear. There is little doubt among police schol-ars that these self-reports overestimate the amount of real change in Amer-ican policing, and anyone who spends time riding along with police officers knows that the basic style of policing and how police bureaucracies respond to problems have not changed fundamentally for decades.

If anything, we have witnessed the split of many urban police forces into several functional groups. Traditional patrol and detectives have been sup-plemented by specialized units, including problem solvers/community policing officers and aggressive tactical units. Despite all the rhetoric about compatibility or similarity, where zero-tolerance policing is practiced, it rarely reflects a community-sensitive or prevention-oriented approach to solving crime problems. It more often resembles a unilateral quasi-military assault on specific target populations and hot spots. Nevertheless, these actions can be proactive, problem-oriented, and information-driven, rely-ing on state-of-the-art information technology, modern data systems, and good undercover work.

Finally, the real challenge to community policing is evident on the faces of community residents in every major city. If community policing has been so successful, why are inner-city neighborhoods across America so often disappointed in the police? Why are many African-American and Hispanic communities so angry today? Why does the Justice Department feel compelled to order consent decrees in so many cities? Is community policing only for middle-class neighborhoods, while many low-income neighborhoods are required to have zero-tolerance policing? The success of community policing in the future will be linked to the capacity of municipal police organizations to seriously address the festering problem of police–community relations.

The IT Factor

Granted, the problem is complex, but improved communication and greater public accountability are essential ingredients for strengthening police–community partnerships and improving the institutional legitimacy of the police. Given the availability of Internet-based information technology, a more transparent police organization, with fast two-way flow of information, has never been easier to achieve. Thus, the future of community policing will depend, in part, on how effectively police agencies can integrate and exploit new IT in the service of community policing goals.

Defining Community Policing and Its Objectives

To see how information technology might help or hurt the future of community policing, we must first decide how to define this style of policing. Notwithstanding a range of definitions, I argue that future conceptions of community policing must give more attention to the most distinctive aspect of the model—namely, the police's relationship with the "community." Therefore, a working definition should include but not be limited to (1) *organizational changes* that encourage a closer relationship between police officers and the neighborhoods they service, such as decentralization of authority, attendance at community meetings, and, yes, foot and bike patrols; (2) serious *problem solving* that is based on the real concerns and problems expressed by neighborhood residents rather than police priorities; and (3) *community engagement* designed to stimulate and empower community residents in the prevention of crime and disorder.

In theory, the community policing model gives special attention to a variety of related objectives: empowering the community; expanding the police function to emphasize crime prevention; building partnerships between law enforcement, community residents, and public and private agencies; personalizing services based on community needs; engaging in data-driven problem solving; and being accountable to police "customers" for the services rendered (Cordner 1997; Rosenbaum, Lurigio, and Davis 1998; Skogan and Hartnett 1997; Greene 2000).

Why have progressive police leaders faced such resistance when seeking to adopt these functions? An organizational analysis of the many factors that restrict change in bureaucracies cannot be attempted here. One thing, however, is clear: change is much more difficult when management does not have the information it needs to shape and reinforce the desired behaviors. At present, municipal police organizations are not driven by information that will enhance and support the community policing model.

The Information Imperative

Community policing engenders a new information imperative. If policing organizations are serious about decentralization of authority, then beat officers must be empowered with up-to-date information about neighborhood characteristics, and they should be accountable for their relationships with neighborhood residents. If data-driven problem solving is a priority, then police officers and supervisors need timely geo-based information relevant to all phases of the SARA process—scanning, analysis, response, and assessment. Especially important (and often neglected) are data about the concerns and priorities of local residents and community organizations, as well as factors in the local environment that are either preventative or criminogenic. If community engagement is a priority, then police officers need reliable information about the crime prevention behaviors of neighborhood residents, as well as data on local resources that can be leveraged to help prevent crime and disorder.

The information imperative of community policing is larger and more demanding than I have suggested here. The Information Systems Technology Enhancement Project, funded by the Office of Community Oriented Policing Services in the U.S. Justice Department, is examining how information technology can be applied to community policing and has grouped these information needs into seven major categories: community interface, interorganizational linkages, workgroup facilitation, environmental scanning, problem orientation, area accountability, and strategic management (Dunworth et al. 2000). Here I will give primary attention to the "community interface" category because of its importance and relative neglect.

The community interface is critical for achieving two missing elements in community policing: (1) strong and positive relations between police and the community and (2) serious community-based crime prevention. Both are needed to create the partnerships that theorists tell us should be at the heart of community policing (Cordner 1997; Rosenbaum 2002).

Police–community relations are the first priority. From Rodney King in 1992, to Amadou Diallo in 1999, to the sixteen year-old in Inglewood,

California in 2002, media coverage of excessive force incidents has tainted the image of police professionalism. Research has shown that these rare incidents are followed by dramatic increases in unfavorable attitudes about the police (Weitzer 2002) and thus contribute to a crisis of confidence in the institution of policing. Looking beyond these cases, however, I am suggesting that the day-to-day interactions between police and average citizens also play a critical role in solidifying lasting impressions of local law enforcement agencies. Too often, some municipal police organizations have not responded appropriately and professionally to citizens as victims, witnesses, suspects, complainants, and concerned human beings.

If the philosophy and values of community policing were communicated and reinforced at all ranks of the organization, citizens who have contact with the police would be less disgruntled than they are today.[1] The history of tension with minority communities is long and repetitive. Some of the hostility in both directions is unavoidable given the ugly job that we ask police officers to do in high-crime communities. But the severity, persistence, and pervasiveness of the problem demand that we give it greater attention than we have in the past. One of the biggest "neighborhood problems" that needs to be addressed in urban America is the troubled relationship that exists between the police and local residents, especially persons of color who live in high-crime neighborhoods. Again, without data systems that collect relevant community-based information about police performance and local community issues, and without new channels of communication, behavior on both sides is unlikely to change.

The second priority is the creation of self-regulating neighborhoods where citizens play the primary role in maintaining a safe environment. Despite the many community-oriented activities engaged in by police organizations today, a serious gap remains in their knowledge of the communities they serve and their knowledge of "best practices" with respect to creating true partnerships in the fight against crime and disorder. Community input, for example, is critical for empowering local residents and transforming them from passive recipients of service to co-producers of public safety. Again, police organizations need new types of information to build both organizational and community capacity for preventing crime. Thus, understanding and measuring citizens' perceptions, beliefs, attitudes,

---

1. I am not suggesting that all citizens are unhappy with the police. In fact, most are quite satisfied. However, minority race, lower class status, and any type of contact with the police are factors that are associated with dissatisfaction.

and behaviors with respect to neighborhood conditions become an important police function.

Various methods have been employed for collecting new information from citizens, ranging from surveys to beat meetings (Skogan and Hartnett 1997). According to the national data presented in Chapter 4, one of the largest changes in police organizations between 1992 and 1997 was the use of citizen surveys to gauge public reactions. By 1997 roughly three out of four departments used citizen surveys to help them identify needs and priorities, and nearly as many used them to evaluate police services. The challenge, as laid out here, is to institutionalize this process using Web-based technology.

Technology and Accountability

A convergence of forces in the public and private sectors has resulted in two big trends in policing today: (1) the desire to use advanced information technology more effectively, and (2) a push for greater accountability and hard evidence of success in achieving goals.[2] While these organizational changes could be used to support community policing, they also have the capacity to derail it. At present, technology and accountability are combining forces in a way that seems inconsistent with the primary goals of community policing. As Janet Chan and her colleagues note (Chan et al. 2001), police are investing in information technology for three main reasons: to improve effectiveness and efficiency (see first trend noted above), to meet the requirements of new forms of management and accountability (second trend noted above), and to satisfy external demands for information. The first two reasons are dominant and deserve elaboration.

Improving Effectiveness and Efficiency

Police organizations are building bigger and faster data systems. The basic idea is that better analysis of crime patterns and a more integrated data warehouse will increase the efficiency of resource deployment and improve investigations, which will, in turn, lead to the arrest of more criminals and reduce crime at certain hot spot locations. While I applaud the efforts of

---

2. These forces include public pressure for greater openness and accountability in government, private sector advances in information technology, and police success stories using technology like COMPSTAT.

administrators to develop information-driven organizations, I am concerned about this trend. These new systems tend to reinforce the long-held misconception that police can win the war on crime alone, without any additional information or support from the community. Information systems that are built around offender databases may encourage in-house, reactive searches with a focus on solving known crimes. These systems restore the traditional authority of the investigative function (although not necessarily the detective role per se) and unintentionally divert the organization's attention away from more important questions about how neighborhood crime can be prevented. Either way, feeling empowered to catch the "bad guy" faster, and witnessing quick results from their investment, police organizations will be less inclined to see the value of long-term prevention or community involvement. Unfortunately, as most seasoned law enforcement executives will admit, we cannot "arrest our way out" of the urban crime problem. Increasing the number of arrests, given the virtually *unlimited* supply and demand for drugs and guns, is only a partial answer to the problem of neighborhood crime and disorder.

At the foundation of community policing theory (as well as community crime prevention theory) is the recognition that violent crimes and property crimes are preventable, in large part, by modifying the informal social actions of local citizens, changing the physical environment, and leveraging social services to address human needs (Rosenbaum, Lurigio, and Davis 1998). Citizens are not only the best informants for the police; their territorial surveillance and intervention can limit criminal opportunities. Hence, when we think about "measuring what matters" and creating new IT-driven performance measures for policing, we should think about strategies that are likely to achieve important police goals such as preventing crime, increasing the public's sense of safety, and improving police–community relations. Information and accountability systems should reflect a police department's commitment to strengthen community through the monitoring, evaluation, and revision of police (and citizen!) activities that promote community engagement and that strengthen residents' feelings of "collective efficacy" in fighting crime (Sampson 1998).

Management and Accountability

When police organizations believe they can solve neighborhood problems with police resources alone, they are more likely to get themselves in trouble with the community. Policing without the consent or knowledge of the community can result in inequitable policing (for example, racial profiling), aggressive and insensitive policing (for example, verbal abuse, excessive force), and corrupt policing (for example, theft, false testimony, tainted evidence, coerced confessions). The price paid by the police organization is high: loss of the community's trust and confidence, damage to the agency's legitimacy, weakened capacity to prevent civil unrest, costly civil and criminal litigation, and greater political scrutiny from external agencies. The price paid by individual officers also must be considered: alienation from the community, compromised safety, increased risk of punishment, and lower morale.

Traditionally, police accountability has been an internal and legal process, focusing on the control of officers through punitive enforcement of rules, regulations, and laws. Today police organizations are under pressure to be responsive to the public both for crime control and police conduct. As Chan et al. (2001, 4) note, this new public accountability "has transformed the traditional police force into organizations with mission statements, business plans, marketing strategies and a new emphasis on crime management, customer service and performance measurement." While police administrators have expressed a growing interest in customer satisfaction, they unfortunately have yet to *systematically measure and monitor* the important dimensions of customer satisfaction. In contrast, we have seen widespread interest in computer-supported measurement of police performance in changing traditional crime indicators, following the lead of New York City.

The apparent success of New York's technology-driven COMPSTAT model has made "accountability" the new buzzword in policing. Accountability, an undeniable good, is arguably something that has been lacking in law enforcement agencies for some time. But two important questions must be posed. To whom are the police accountable? For what are they accountable? Unfortunately, the COMPSTAT model requires the beat officers and their supervisors to be accountable primarily to central management in the traditional police hierarchy. Hence, information systems are being used to reinforce the quasi-military bureaucracy rather than to help decentralize decision-making authority or open the organization to public scrutiny, as called for by community policing.

For what are officers accountable? By far, the biggest problem for community policing involves the type of performance standards used for accountability. Despite new technology systems, police organizations continue to rely on the traditional "big four" to measure their performance:

reported crime rates, overall arrests, clearance rates, and response times (Alpert and Moore 1993).[3] Police departments also reward individual officers for activity associated with drug and gun seizures and for income-producing activity such as traffic and parking tickets. In general, too many law enforcement agencies have blindly followed the narrow application of COMPSTAT technology to hold police managers and officers accountable for jurisdictional crime rates. The use of information technology is a good thing, but for what purpose is it being used? What end does it serve?

Traditional measures of police performance are grossly inadequate for satisfying the new information imperative of community policing and for taking urban police organizations to the next level of performance (Dunworth 2000; Rosenbaum 2002). Simply put, these indicators of performance do not address the key factors that contribute to public safety or attempt to gauge in a meaningful way the satisfaction of customers with the quality of police service. Because law enforcement agencies are assumed to be the experts on crime and public safety, and because they receive the lion's share of the funding for these issues, they carry the biggest responsibility for educating the community and involving the community in both enforcement and prevention activities (Rosenbaum, Lurigio, and Davis 1998). Some cities, like Chicago, have taken this responsibility seriously by institutionalizing community beat meetings and other activities (Skogan and Hartnett 1997; Skogan et al. 2000). Unfortunately, when the community becomes involved in problem solving, traditional police data systems are not capable of incorporating the new data that are generated. As Skogan (2002) notes, the community's assessment of disorder problems often does not fit neatly into existing police data fields, and consequently the assessment does not get recorded in any systematic and representative way. This suggests, again, that new data systems are needed to capture what is important to community residents and what should be important to the police.

Once the overall "bean counting" system changes, the behavior of the typical front-line police officer will change, but not before.[4] While police chiefs regularly talk about the importance of community policing at public meetings, their police officers are in the streets being rewarded for

---

3. See Moore et al. (2002) for an extensive discussion of who holds police accountable and what measures are appropriate for assessing police performance.

4. Many officers engage in the "right" behaviors without a new evaluation system, either because of their personal orientation or because they are situated in a special unit that rewards such behavior.

a completely different set of behaviors. Only when the performance evaluation system changes can we expect police–community interactions to change. The implication is clear: we need to collect and monitor new types of information about police and community performance in achieving goals.

This system of accountability must expand to incorporate new performance standards based on the goals of partnership building, community engagement, and problem solving—outcomes being demanded by the public in the twenty-first century. Today there is considerable public pressure on government to be open and responsive to community priorities. Indeed, the legitimacy of the police as a public institution depends heavily on its ability to strengthen public confidence and trust in them at a time when police practices are being heavily criticized.

Public confidence in the institution of policing will be strengthened only when police organizations engage in an open, honest, understandable, and mutually beneficial dialogue with the public. There are many avenues for creating this dialogue. One of them is sharing information through the use of new technologies. This can dramatically increase the transparency of the police organization (Fulla and Welch 2002) and strengthen its partnership with the community.

New Web-Based Reporting System

In order to satisfy the information needs of community policing and problem-solving models, police organizations need to exploit the Internet more fully. Although information technology has been promoted as the vehicle to help catch the bad guy, little has been said about its capacity to expand communication with the public, build stronger partnerships, and prevent crime.

A growing number of police departments nationwide now offer online information about their services, programs, and crime statistics. Some departments even offer crime mapping for the public.[5] To date, however, few police departments nationwide have moved beyond simply posting information to embracing the Internet as a proactive tool for obtaining new information about neighborhood conditions, solving problems, building partnerships, evaluating programs, and assessing unit performance.

---

5. Two examples are the Chicago Police Department, http://www.ci.chi.il.us/ CommunityPolicing/Statistics/Statistics.html, and the San Diego Police Department, http://www.sannet.gov/police/stats/index.shtml.

For departments that are ambitious, I suggest adding the following five components to your Web-based initiative: Incident-Reporting Program, Citizen Monitoring Program, Neighborhood Profile Report, Enhanced Police–Community Program, and the Public Service Links. Each component will be discussed in turn.

Incident Reporting

Reporting incidents through the Internet is now a reality. In some locations, citizens are given the opportunity to use online reporting for traffic accidents, property crimes, and a broad range of quality-of-life problems.[6] My impression is that these services are offered more frequently in smaller cities and towns where the volume of activity is more manageable, although there is little, if any, research on this topic.[7]

Using the Internet for taking minor crime reports will allow officers to devote less time to filling out reports, thus freeing them to address more pressing issues. A faster method for filing reports, it will also allow police departments to build a more representative database quickly and move toward the goal of a "paperless" agency. Providing citizens with the option of reporting criminal activity confidentially opens an avenue that previously has been denied to those residents who fear retaliation. Online reporting and anonymous tips may lead indirectly to improved clearance rates for violent crime, notably in neighborhoods where visible cooperation with the police is problematic. If new crimes and new leads come to the attention of the police, this information may help detectives solve more cases. Entirely new patterns of crime may be observed and strategically addressed through targeted crime prevention initiatives.

Citizen Monitoring

The public should be the primary source of data for any community-oriented police organization, and Web-based surveys represent the preferred methodology of the future. Hundreds of police departments

---

6. For online reporting of traffic accidents, see, for example, Colorado State Police, http//crash.state.co.us/splash.jsp. On property crime reporting, see, for example, San Jose Police Department, www.sjpd.org/. The Philadelphia Police Department encourages online reporting of quality-of-life problems. See www.ppdonline.org/.

7. My colleagues and I are conducting a national study of law enforcement Web pages to answer this question.

nationwide conduct telephone and mail surveys (see survey data reported in Chapter 4), but Internet surveys are much less common. Some departments choose to evaluate specific police functions, such as the performance of the communications division,[8] while others seek a wide range of data on diverse topics.[9] Instead of merely offering the public information, these agencies are actively seeking community input and two-way communication to improve the delivery of police services.

Despite these promising developments, the state of the art in police Web-based surveys remains very primitive. Efforts are needed to establish (a) representative samples of community residents, (b) regular reporting periods, (c) comprehensive survey content to measure the important dimensions of policing and public safety, (d) data analysis or feedback mechanisms, and (e) plans for the systematic use of these data for strategic or tactical planning.

I recommend a model for Web surveys in urban or suburban communities: Web survey data should be collected from a randomly selected panel sample of households that can serve as "beat monitors." The sample should be clustered or stratified so that households are randomly selected from each block or from each police beat. (The time has come to move beyond the biased samples of civic-minded residents who regularly attend community meetings, belong to church organizations, etc.) Such a sample can be achieved through a random-digit-dialing telephone survey of all listed and unlisted phone numbers; households willing to serve as survey respondents are sought. For families that do not have a personal computer or Internet access, the necessary equipment and services should be provided, along with some minimal compensation, in exchange for their participation in monthly surveys over a twenty-four-month period. These individuals will serve as the primary source of data for the new information system proposed here. By providing equipment and Internet access, at least for randomly selected households, the government can begin to close the large "digital divide" that separates Americans by race and class (U. S. Department of Commerce 2000, 2002)—a divide that will prohibit the creation of representative samples of urban households.

This system of citizen monitoring will allow police departments to institutionalize previously sporadic efforts to "measure what matters" in the twenty-first century (Masterson and Stevens 2002; Mirzer 1996). These

8. See Metropolitan Nashville Police Department, www.police.nashville.org.

9. See South Pasadena Police Department, www.sppd.org.

new data elements, if collected systematically and shown to be reliable and valid over time, should gradually achieve legitimacy as "official police data." A citizen monitoring program could do the following:

- **Monitor neighborhood conditions.** Citizen performance measures should capture levels of community involvement, collective efficacy, perceptions and fears about safety and crime, problem-solving skills, and preventive behaviors. Knowing the level of community efficacy and involvement will allow police to determine the scope of community development needed before satisfactory community–police collaboration can occur. Reductions or increases in citizens' perceptions of crime problems and fears will help direct and evaluate policing efforts for particular communities. The early identification of crime and disorder patterns is possible with this reporting program, thus enhancing proactive policing. Tracking changes in levels of physical disorder (abandoned cars, graffiti, and broken windows, for example) and social disorder (for example, prostitution, youth loitering, loud music) can alert police to developing problem areas and may indicate communities in a "cycle of decline" (Skogan 1990).

- **Monitor police performance.** These measures gauge citizens' perceptions of police performance. They essentially capture three aspects of police performance important to the community: effectiveness, equity, and efficiency (Eck and Rosenbaum 1994). Assessing police responsiveness, demeanor, fairness, and effectiveness, these items measure citizens' overall satisfaction with police. A wide range of attitudinal (trust and confidence) measures can be employed, capturing the public's sentiments about the organization, the local precinct, and beat-level performance.

- **Evaluate anticrime interventions.** By conducting surveys on a monthly or bimonthly basis in every neighborhood, police will continually receive data suggesting whether problems are increasing, decreasing, or staying the same. Also, with data collection in comparable neighborhoods that did not receive localized police interventions, a built-in evaluation design can be employed to increase confidence in any conclusion that observed changes in problem levels were caused by the intervention.

- **Offer recommendations.** Web-based surveys present a great opportunity for police agencies to receive new ideas and suggestions from citizens. Multiple perspectives on problems, programs, and policies should be welcomed.

In sum, a citizen monitoring survey program serves many functions. It can monitor neighborhood conditions, identify emerging problems, evaluate the performance of both police and citizens, evaluate anticrime interventions, and solicit new ideas.

Neighborhood Profile Report

Police departments are ready to receive information from the public, but many are not skilled at giving information back to members of the community. A two-way flow of information is critical. If citizens take the time to participate in a Web reporting system, the police should provide some analysis and feedback on the information supplied. A neighborhood profile report might include crime information, such as aggregate information about incidents, arrests, and locations (mapping is an excellent example), and citizen monitoring results, such as summary reports of the data collected from citizens' Web surveys. This feedback might include neighborhood or beat profiles and performance summaries for both police and citizens. Sharing information via neighborhood profile reports should increase "organizational transparency," thus fostering greater trust among local residents and increasing their desire to collaborate.

Enhanced Police–Community Program

Departments that have institutionalized community policing programs (for example, community beat meetings, neighborhood watches, police citizen academies, school programs), can use the Internet to extend the reach of these programs and to improve the efficiency of communications with participants. The Chicago Police Department, for example, is exploring the idea of using the Internet to enhance its well-known CAPS beat meetings.[10]

---

10. CAPS stands for the Chicago Alternative Policing Strategy. The Chicago Police Department (CPD), famous for its success with community policing (Skogan and Hartnett 1997; Skogan et al. 2000), is now developing a state-of-the-art advanced information technology system called CLEAR (Citizen and Law Enforcement Analysis and Reporting program). This initiative should dramatically strengthen the department's ability to deliver services that are efficient, effective, and equitable. To date, the focus has been on internal performance—using information for police management and operations. In the final analysis, the most difficult test will be whether the Chicago Police Department can address the information needs of local residents and beat officers in the context of community policing. Given that CLEAR is largely a Web-based information system, the CPD is ready to explore new Web-based avenues of communication for building information-driven, crime-fighting partnerships with the community.

Beyond maintaining pertinent information about CAPS meetings (meeting times, locations, agendas, guest speakers), "Virtual CAPS" might serve as a communication center for beat officers and residents. A virtual community might complement the physical community fostered through beat meetings. For reasons ranging from work schedules to disabilities, many citizens cannot attend beat meetings. This inability to participate physically should not preclude these residents from participating in police–community decision making.

Efficient and inexpensive, chat rooms allow for synchronous communication, or conversation between two or more individuals, and would enable police officials to hold "virtual meetings" at the neighborhood or citywide levels. "Live chats" can be arranged with featured speakers, such as the chief of police. Listservs and message boards, both asynchronous forms of communication, are also possible. In addition to reminding residents of community meetings and relaying current information, a listserv can alert them to immediate threats to their community. An initial means of notification in emergency situations, a listserv merits special consideration since the terrorist attacks of September 11, 2001. Message boards allow participants to post questions and suggestions to which others may respond. These postings remain visible to eliminate duplication and provide a forum for citizens to engage in proactive problem solving.

Public Service Links

If police departments are seriously committed to *preventing* crime (as opposed to *reacting* to reported incidents of crime), they should be willing to address the root causes of crime (child abuse and neglect, poor nutrition, poor education, unemployment, and lack of treatment services, to name a few). Criminologists have clearly documented that public safety is not achieved by defensive or offensive anticrime measures alone. Rather it is the product of a larger constellation of personal, social, environmental, economic, and political forces that impinge on neighborhoods (Rosenbaum, Lurigio and Davis 1998; Sampson 1998). Given this reality, police agencies should use the Internet to link residents with a wide array of resources that might assist them in solving personal problems and thereby reduce their risk of offending or being victimized.

The public services component of the Web page would extend beyond the boundaries of traditional policing efforts, providing links to websites that offer information on social, educational, health, and public safety services. Residents could be linked to other city services as well as services provided by local, state, and federal agencies. For active citizens who want to expand their knowledge of community crime prevention and police practices, the page could provide links to other criminal justice sites, locally and worldwide.

The Web and the Future of Community Policing

As citizens become aware of the multiple purposes of Web-based communication—incident reporting, citizen monitoring, neighborhood profiling, enhanced police–community relations, and public service links—they will begin to access resources that can contribute to the empowerment of both the individual and the community, thereby enhancing public safety. Neighborhoods may be better equipped to organize local residents via the Internet and strengthen informal social controls, thus having less need for police intervention. In sum, the proposed Web-based initiative, by facilitating the exchange of new and timely information and intelligence, promises to foster the goals of community policing.

Organizational Implications of Web-Based Communication

When a police department invites the public to participate in a reporting program of this nature, it inevitably creates new expectations. The agency is expected to manage the database, provide certain reports to the public, and function as a more open, transparent organization. To meet both internal and external expectations, the police organization will need to restructure itself. Some police administrators and supervisors may become information managers, with responsibility for handing specific functions (such as responding to email inquiries, facilitating virtual beat meetings, analyzing survey data patterns, mapping perceptions and incidents, and preparing accountability reports). Each agency will need to make personnel adjustments as the demands for specific types of information change. The start-up costs may be substantial, but so too may be the payoffs.

Expanding Web-based services will require allocating additional resources to manage the wealth of new information flowing to and from the organization. The initial challenges include developing the data collection system, field testing it, making modifications, and achieving "buy in" from police personnel and the community. Some community advocates question whether the police should be the repository of this type of community-based information. They argue that an outside, neutral party, such as the university, would be better suited for this task. There is not room to debate this issue here, although it merits discussion.

Obstacles and Challenges

The Web-based survey, a very new methodology for querying the public, must address several obstacles and challenges that lie ahead. The main issues include response rates and generalizability, confidentiality, and technical issues (for example, bandwidth, connection speeds). Because Internet users are not a representative sample of residents in most cities or neighborhoods, local government officials (perhaps in collaboration with the IT private sector) must be willing to invest in closing the digital divide, at least for those who participate in this type of reporting program. Such an investment seems sensible and feasible. As technology costs continue to decline, the digital divide will begin to close on a larger scale, as it did with access to telephones in the twentieth century. Sills and Song (2002) estimate that there will be one billion Internet users worldwide by 2005.

Although the reliability, validity, and security of Web survey data require further study by research methodologists, this modality seems to be the primary choice for the future. The telephone survey has nearly run its course as a method for tapping public sentiment. It has been the primary vehicle for survey research for decades, but with the emergence of Caller ID, privacy managers, cell phones, and telemarketers, response rates have plummeted. Survey research laboratories have shown strong interest in Web surveys as a future methodology for measuring public perceptions, concerns, and behaviors. Web surveys are cost effective, fast, efficient, and convenient for respondents; they are capable of geographic specificity and can handle complex survey questions with skip patterns (James 1999; Perkins 2001; Sills and Song 2002; Tierney 2000).

In sum, community policing can be constrained or facilitated by information technology depending on how it is used. Our ideas about what is important to measure in twenty-first century policing should drive the development of information technology, not the other way around. New community-based data elements must be conceptualized, operationally defined, and systematically collected as possible elements in an official data warehouse. The proper analysis of this information and feedback should create a police organization that is viewed by the public as responsive, legitimate, transparent, professional, and highly effective. Whether these hypotheses are supported by empirical evidence must await the results of future field tests in multiple jurisdictions.

References

Alpert, Geoffrey P., and Mark H. Moore. 1993. "Measuring Police Performance in the New Paradigm of Policing." In G.P. Alpert, and A.R. Piquero, eds., *Community Policing: Contemporary Readings*, 215–232. Prospect Heights, IL: Waveland Press, Inc.

Brown, Maureen. 2000. "Criminal Justice Discovers Information Technology." In LaFree, G., James F. Short, R. J. Bursik Sr., and R. B. Taylor, eds. *Criminal Justice 2000. Vol. 1: The Nature of Crime: Continuity and Change*, 219–259. Washington, D.C.: National Institute of Justice.

Chan, Janet B.L. 1999. "Governing Police Practice: Limits of the New Accountability." *British Journal of Sociology* 50(2): 251–270.

———. 2001. "The Technological Game: How Information Technology is Transforming Police Practice." *Criminal Justice* 1(2): 139–159.

Chan, Janet B.L., David Brereton, Margot Legosz, and Sally Doran. 2001. *E-Policing: The Impact of Information Technology on Police Practices*. Brisbane, Queensland, Australia: Criminal Justice Commission. Available at www.cjc.qld.gov.au.

Cordner, Gary W. 1997. "Community Policing: Elements and Effects." In G.P. Alpert, and A.R. Piquero, eds. *Community Policing: Contemporary Readings*, 45–62. Prospect Heights, IL: Waveland Press, Inc.

Crawford, Adam. 1997. *The Local Governance of Crime: Appeals to Community and Partnerships*. Oxford: Oxford University Press.

Dunworth, Terence. 2000. "Criminal Justice and the IT Revolution." In Horney, J., D. Mackenzie, J. Martin, R. Peterson, and D. P. Rosenbaum, eds. *Criminal Justice 2000. Vol. 3: Policies, Processes and Decisions of the Criminal Justice System*, 371–426. Washington, D.C.: National Institute of Justice.

Dunworth, Terence, Gary Cordner, Jack Greene, Timothy Bynum, Scott Decker, Thomas Rich, Shawn Ward, and Vince Webb. 2000. *Police Department Information Systems Technology Enhancement Project ISTEP*. Washington, D.C.: U.S. Department of Justice, Office of Community Oriented Policing Services.

Eck, John E., and Dennis P. Rosenbaum. 1994. "The New Police Order: Effectiveness, Equity, and Efficiency in Community Policing." In Rosenbaum, D.P., ed. *The Challenge of Community Policing: Testing the Promises*, 3–21. Thousand Oaks, CA: Sage Publications.

Eck, John E., and William Spelman. 1987. *Problem Solving: Problem-Oriented Policing in Newport News*. Washington, D.C.: Police Executive Research Forum.

Fulla, Shelley, and Eric Welch. 2002. *Framing Virtual Interactivity between Government and Citizens: A Study on Feedback Systems in the Chicago Police Department*. Hawaii International Conference on System Sciences, Lectures in Electronic Government, IEEE Computer Society Press.

Goldstein, Herman. 1990. *Problem-Oriented Policing*. New York: McGraw-Hill.

Greene, Jack R. 2000. "Community Policing in America: Changing the Nature, Structure, and Function of the Police." In Horney, J., D. Mackenzie, J. Martin, R. Peterson, and D. P. Rosenbaum, eds. *Criminal Justice 2000. Vol. 3: Policies, Processes, and Decisions of the Criminal Justice System*, 299–368. National Institute of Justice. Washington, D.C.: U.S. Government Printing Office.

James, Dana. 1999. "Precision Decision: Speedy New Standard on Web Research Feeds Accuracy, Privacy, Concerns." *Marketing News* 33(20): 23–25.

Kelling, George L., and Mark H. Moore. 1988. "From Political to Reform to Community: The Evolving Strategy of Police." In J. R. Greene and S. D. Mastrofski, eds. *Community Policing: Rhetoric or Reality?* 3–26. New York: Praeger.

Masterson, Michael F., and Dennis J. Stevens. 2002. "The Value of Measuring Community Policing Performance in Madison, Wisconsin." In Stevens, D.J., ed. *Policing and Community Partnerships*, 202–217. Upper Saddle River, N.J.: Prentice Hall.

Mirzer, M.L. 1996. Policing Supervision in the 21st Century. *FBI Law Enforcement Bulletin* 65, 6–10.

Moore, Mark, with David Thacher, Andrea Dodge, and Tobias Moore. 2002. *Recognizing Value in Policing: The Challenge of Measuring Police Performance.* Washington, D.C.: Police Executive Research Forum.

Morgan, Gareth. 1997. *Images of Organizations*, 2d ed. Thousand Oaks, Calif.: Sage.

Perkins, Gay. 2001. "A Comparison on[a1] Web-based and Paper-and-Pencil Library Satisfaction Survey Results." *College & Research Libraries* 62(4): 369–377.

Rosenbaum, Dennis, P. 1994. ed. *The Challenge of Community Policing: Testing the Promises.* Newbury Park, Calif.: Sage.

———. 2002. "Evaluating Multi-Agency Anti-Crime Partnerships: Theory, Design, and Measurement Issues." *Crime Prevention Studies* 14: 171–225.

Rosenbaum, Dennis P., Arthur J. Lurigio, and Robert C. Davis. 1998. *The Prevention of Crime: Social and Situational Strategies.* Belmont, Calif.: Wadsworth Publishing Co.

Roth, J.A., J.F. Ryan, S.J. Gaffigan, C.S. Koper, M.H. Moore, J.A. Roehl, C.C. Johnson, G.E. Moore, R.M. White, M.E. Buerger, E.A. Langston, and D. Thacher. 2000. *National Evaluation of the COPS Program: Title I of the 1994 Crime Act,* NCJ 183643. Washington, D.C.: U.S. Department of Justice, National Institute of Justice.

Sampson, Robert J. 1998. "What Community Supplies." In Ferguson, R.F., and W.T. Dickens, eds. *Urban Problems and Community Development.* 241–292). Washington, D.C.: Brookings Institute Press.

Scott, Michael S. 2000. *Problem-Oriented Policing: Reflections on the First Twenty Years.* Draft summary report prepared for the Office of Community Oriented Policing Services (COPS). Washington, D.C.: Office of Community Oriented Policing Services.

Sills, S., and C. Song, 2002. "Innovations in Survey Research: An Application of Web-Based Surveys." *Social Science Computer Review* 20(1): 22–30.

Skogan, Wesley G. 1990. *Disorder and Decline: Crime and the Spiral of Decay in American Neighborhoods.* New York: Free Press.

————. 2002. Luncheon address at Police Executive Research Forum conference on Information Technology. Chicago, Ill., July.

Skogan, Wesley G., and Susan M. Hartnett. 1997. *Community Policing, Chicago Style.* New York: Oxford University Press.

Skogan, Wesley G., Susan M. Hartnett, Jill DuBois, J. Comey, K. Twedt-Ball[a2], and J.E. Gudell. 2000. *Public Involvement: Community Policing in Chicago,* National Institute of Justice, NCJ 179557. Washington, D.C.: U.S. Government Printing Office.

Tierney, P. 2000. "Internet-based Evaluation of Tourism Web Site Effectiveness: Methodological Issues and Survey Results." *Journal of Travel Research* 39(2): 212–219.

U. S. Department of Commerce. 2000. *Falling through the Net: Toward Digital Inclusion.* Washington, D.C.: Author. Available at: http://search.ntia.doc.gov/pdf/fttn00.pdf

————. 2002. A Nation Online: How Americans Are Expanding Their Use of the Internet. Washington, D.C.: Author. Available at: http://www.ntia.doc.gov/ntiahome/dn/anationonline2.pdf.

Weitzer, Ronald. 2002. "Incidents of Police Misconduct and Public Opinion." *Journal of Criminal Justice* 30(5), 397–408.

9

Taking Community Policing to the Next Level: Adopting Technology Lessons Learned from the Corporate Sector

by Barbara McDonald, Deputy Superintendent, and Ron Huberman, Assistant Deputy Superintendent, Chicago Police Department

I n early 1993 the Chicago Police Department (CPD) began to change the way it provided police service with the introduction of the Chicago Alternative Policing Strategy (CAPS). The goal was to move from a largely centralized, incident-driven, crime suppression agency to a more decentralized, customer-driven organization dedicated to solving problems and preventing crime. The implementation of CAPS has been a long and arduous journey, and there are still "miles to go before we sleep." However, the original vision, outlined in *Together We Can: A Strategic Plan for Reinventing the Chicago Police Department* (Chicago Police Department 1993), is still robust. New ideas and opportunities have emerged that show promise for further strengthening CAPS and other community-oriented policing models. Key among these is the use of technology to advance our community policing goals.

In the 1990s, America's corporate sector underwent a transformation stimulated by the widespread use of technology to reduce costs, increase the effective use of resources, and increase the capacity to meet customer needs. This effort proved so successful that many of the world's largest companies restructured their framework to take advantage of these powerful new capabilities. And while the widespread implementation of community-oriented policing models during this last decade has also changed the way many law enforcement agencies do business, they may well reach their full potential if they take a page from the corporate experience and embrace technology. This chapter will examine some of the use-of-technology lessons learned from the private sector and delineate their relevance to community policing.

The Chicago Approach: Information-Driven Policing

In 2000 Chicago Police Superintendent Terry G. Hillard challenged his command staff to take the Chicago Alternative Policing Strategy to the next level. Largely successful for almost a decade, CAPS needed new momentum to keep the strategy fresh, effective, and responsive to emerging needs. The superintendent's call to action led to an evaluation of what elements of the model were working and where change was needed. One product of this examination was the development of a new paradigm dubbed "information-driven policing," defined as "the use of real-time, relational information[1] to drive operations, inform policy decisions and strengthen partnerships." Information-driven policing does not replace the philosophy, mission, or guiding principles of CAPS. Instead, it dictates a different way of operating that will enhance the logic and structure of CAPS by integrating private sector "lessons learned" into law enforcement business practices.

CAPS: Making a Difference

Early in the development of the information-driven policing paradigm, it became obvious that an enterprise information system was needed to integrate and manage all of the information needs of the organization. Therefore, in 2000 the Chicago Police Department conceptualized and began developing a technology tool to support the folding of information-driven

---

1. Relational information refers to the comparison of any one data point or points with any other data point or points.

policing practices into Chicago's community policing strategy. This enterprise information system was named Citizen and Law Enforcement Analysis and Reporting (CLEAR). Although CLEAR has not been fully implemented, the department has already seen significant changes (see Box 9-1). Some of these include substantial time savings from eliminating redundant data entry, the ability to solve crimes that were previously unsolvable, increased intra- and interdepartmental communication, and real-time data sharing with 132 suburban law enforcement agencies.

Lessons Learned—Adopting Private Sector Technology

Believing that technology will drive the community-oriented policing revolution, the Chicago Police Department gleaned six relevant lessons from the private sector to apply to CAPS:

Lesson 1: Customers drive and must be active participants in product development.

Lesson 2: Accurate and complete information is needed for effective decision making.

Lesson 3: Real-time information enables proactive responses.

Lesson 4: Effective performance measures result in continually evolving strategies.

Lesson 5: In the absence of process re-engineering, technology implementation will not result in efficiency gains.

Lesson 6: Information sharing leads to win–win scenarios.

A closer look at the department's application of these lessons from the private sector can illustrate how technology could take community policing to the next level.

Lesson 1: The customer drives and must be an active participant in product development.

The advent of the Internet provided the business world with the ability to directly communicate with the majority of its customers. This enabled businesses to better incorporate consumers' needs and desires into product development. While the new policing models of the 1990s emphasized the importance of law enforcement personnel partnering with their customers—the community—law enforcement has failed to take advantage of technology to optimize communication with them.

Box 9-1. *Recent Changes in the Chicago Police Department*

The impetus for the Chicago Police Department's information system, Citizen and Law Enforcement Analysis and Reporting (CLEAR), was the department's community policing strategy—CAPS. In implementing the Chicago Alternative Policing Strategy, the department recognized that to fully realize the potential of its new policing model, it needed to change its business practices. CLEAR and its related business and information-sharing practices reflect a major step forward in the department's implementation of community policing.

The resulting changes in the Chicago Police Department over the past decade have been the subject of one of the most rigorous long-term evaluations in recent history of any police agency or policing model. The department used as a benchmark the components of change outlined in *Together We Can: A Strategic Plan for Reinventing the Chicago Police Department* (Chicago Police Department 1993). The CPD then succeeded in accomplishing many of the objectives set out in its stated vision:

- The department's mission statement and philosophy of policing have been stated in concrete terms in widely distributed documents.
- Roles, responsibilities, and procedures have been delineated for the department's Beat, District, Area, and Citywide Management Teams.
- An around-the-clock team of officers is assigned to serve each of the city's 280 beats.

The Internet has the capacity to transform police and community interaction. To date, most law enforcement departments provide only one-way communication via the Internet, presenting the community with descriptions of services, prevention tips, and basic crime statistics, but not allowing for community input. The true potential of the Internet is two-way communication. It can be used to exchange ideas and report findings and other information that can shape strategies, and it can facilitate as many adjustments as necessary to overcome a problem.

The department is designing CLEAR with the community to ensure that residents are integrated into the system via the Internet. This dynamic and accessible communication link will provide an open exchange of ideas and information that will be the cornerstone for information sharing in the future.

- Beat officers meet monthly with the community to prioritize, analyze, and strategize chronic crime and neighborhood disorder problems that exist on the beat.
- CAPS community organizers mobilize community members and organizations to participate in problem solving.
- Essential city services are provided on a fast-track basis for problems the police and the community identified. (This process is now fully automated and accessed via the city's 311 system.)
- Supervisors and command members are held accountable for crime and disorder strategies through an Office of Management Accountability.
- Several interagency task-force initiatives address a variety of code violations—targeting locations that are the subject of ongoing criminal activity (for example, gang and drug houses and problem taverns), addressing abandoned buildings, eliminating graffiti, etc.
- The Chicago Alternative Policing Strategy is marketed through regular television, radio, and print media venues, including a half-hour television show that airs several times a week at various times to tell success stories resulting from CAPS.
- Point-and-click crime analysis is available to officers with a special version for the community on the department's Internet website.

Lesson 2: Accurate and complete information is needed for effective decision making.

Competition during the 1980s and 1990s forced corporate America to invest billions in information systems to enable accurate decision making based on sound, quantitative data. Likewise, community policing is based on the premise that the police and community will have enough information to attack a problem at its root. All too often, the information needed to address a problem is not available. Therefore, decisions are often made based on limited information, leading to strategies that prove to be only partially effective, at best.

Through the use of information technology, problems can be analyzed in greater depth—identifying patterns of crime, specific offenders, victims, incident locations, and more. CLEAR enables CPD members to use a wide range of real-time, accurate information in their decision making. The department has now centralized all information into one relational database so that it can be easily queried. To make it readily accessible, information is now available through a Web-based interface that is as simple to use as surfing the Internet. The availability of large amounts of data is proving invaluable. Queried more than 10,000 times a day, the relational database has significantly increased and improved the department's decision-making capacity, leading to reduced crime and increased community satisfaction.

Lesson 3: Real-time information enables proactive responses.

Microsoft guru Bill Gates coined the term "business at the speed of thought" to describe a new paradigm in the business world. Technology has provided access to real-time information, allowing corporations to immediately react to changing market conditions. This flexibility, in large part, was responsible for America's booming economy in the 1990s. It is now incumbent on law enforcement to make use of this same technology to "solve crime at the speed of thought."

Real-time information can greatly influence how officers work. Let's imagine an officer responding to a call for service using real-time information; he or she is now armed not only with a gun, but also with a virtual arsenal of automated information. The technology instantly makes available relevant data about the caller, the address, the type of call, and its association with community-identified problems. With this new "big picture" view, the call is no longer treated as just another service call, but rather as an event that is associated with the larger crime and disorder problems the police and community are attempting to address.

CLEAR has been designed to provide department members with real-time information to guide their actions in three ways. It makes possible differential response, information links, and predictive analyses.

- **Differential response.** Chicago, like many other communities, is made up of multiple diverse neighborhoods. Therefore, a "one-size-fits-all" approach to service cannot be applied to community priorities. For CAPS to be effective, officers must be able to analyze and properly identify the community's priorities on their beats. While in some high-crime areas, street drug-dealing is the priority, in other neighborhoods the concern may be panhandlers. CLEAR alerts officers as new information about a specific problem enters the system. This information may come from a 311 or 911 call, a case report, an investigator's supplementary report, a community member's information update via the Internet, or one of many other sources identified as relevant to the problem. The officer is then ready to begin immediate collective action with his or her community partners, adjusting problem strategies when appropriate.

- **Information links.** If police departments had good information about every incident they investigated (call-for-service, offender, witness, victim, and crime scene information, etc.), most criminal acts would result in an arrest or other appropriate disposition. Very often, however, vital information is missing. Frequently, a police department's capacity to solve and address crime and disorder problems is dependent on its ability to link and associate disparate elements from multiple cases. The effectiveness of CLEAR is based on its capacity to conduct, in real time, analyses using every piece of information in the system. This linking provides immediate feedback to investigating officers and places them in a better position to ask questions and follow tips likely to point them to an offender. Without technology, making these links is a cumbersome and often inaccurate process that rarely informs officers of relevant information as incidents are occurring.

- **Predictive analyses.** In uncertain economic times one of the greatest challenges law enforcement personnel face is combating crime and disorder with ever-shrinking resources. Improving the capacity of police to reduce crime will require using real-time data to deploy officers when and where they are most needed. A weather forecaster predicts the weather with a certain degree of accuracy based on certain climatic conditions; Chicago's analysis work suggests that crime can be predicted in much the same way. Historically, predicting crime has not been attempted. There are three possible reasons for this: the necessary data never existed in one relational database; the data were not real time, and technology had not caught up with the processing needs required to run the necessary algorithms.

As part of the CPD strategy, CLEAR is being designed with a predictive analysis component. This technology tool will automatically assess data from the computer-aided dispatch system, incident system, offender database, and more than 200 other data sources to proactively identify hot spots. It will alert officers of emerging crime patterns and of crimes that are statistically likely to occur. Integrating this analysis with resource availability will provide managers with the information necessary to make decisions about police response. Initial statistical analysis of this concept shows a great deal of promise. In the near future, the CPD will be deploying personnel using real-time data to identify where officers will have the greatest impact in reducing crime.

Lesson 4: Effective performance measures
result in continually evolving strategies.

During the 1970s and 1980s, many large American manufacturers lost valuable business to foreign competition. This occurred for a variety of reasons, including competitive wages from abroad. Business was lost, however, because these corporations did not have the appropriate performance measures to identify their competitive advantages. For many corporations, the sole measures were product output, costs, labor, and overhead. The missing measures of performance often included predicting customers' future requirements and identifying those areas in which domestic manufacturing could overcome foreign competition.

These lessons have significance for law enforcement. Policing has yet to evolve from basic performance measures (levels of reported crime, clearance rates, operational costs, etc.) that do not inform our strategic thinking.[2] A new focus on developing performance measures to assess the community's satisfaction with our "products," our effectiveness, and our strategies is needed. While some departments have implemented phone and on-line surveys, using technology to truly capture effective real-time feedback is still missing.

The department is currently working to develop performance measures to judge the effectiveness of strategies, policies, and daily operations, as well as their impact on the community. To garner input from the community, a series of Internet access points are being created (for example, terminals in public facilities). As the "digital divide" in some of Chicago's most troubled neighborhoods persists, new partnerships are being formed with the corporate community to ensure that all residents are connected.

---

2. For more detailed discussions on effective performance measures, see Langworthy (1999) and Moore et al. (2002).

Lesson 5: In the absence of process re-engineering, technology implementation will not result in efficiency gains.

Using the power of technology, many Fortune 500 companies have introduced new business practices that have saved them hundreds of millions of dollars in operating costs. Key to corporations' ability to add value to their operations has been process re-engineering. This entails an in-depth analysis of business processes. Waste, duplication of effort, and other coordination problems or breakdowns in the flow of information are identified. The analysis leads to a new technology-driven workflow in which only those functions that add value remain. A streamlined process of completing tasks is then adopted. This results in a more efficient work force, greater productivity, and increased profit.[3]

Such progressive re-engineering has not been evident in most police agencies, however. They still attempt to develop technology to fit the way they do business today. Although most police departments have changed the focus of their policing strategies (community interaction, problem identification, partnerships, etc.), they have failed to change the core functions of information collection and analysis. For community policing to reach its full potential, departments must change the way they do business by incorporating technology. All aspects of police operations must be examined—from incident reporting, to prioritizing calls for service, to deploying resources, to streamlining information flow to other agencies and the community. New, flexible, and powerful technology systems will also enable law enforcement to quickly adapt to arising concerns, problems, and strategies. This proactive response represents the essence of effective community policing.

To change the way it does business, the Chicago Police Department is throwing out its cumbersome, half-century old case-reporting system. The twelve paper forms currently used to capture all criminal incidents are being replaced by one electronic application that "guides" officers through the preliminary investigative process—exposing them only to those questions that have bearing on the case they are investigating. This re-engineering will result in more accurate and timely data that will link information to solve more crimes and strengthen our partnerships.

The bedrock of community policing is a trusting relationship between

---

3. On Chicago's early efforts and the process mapping experiment, see Fraser et al. (1998).

the police and the community. Nothing erodes trust more quickly than an officer's inappropriate or unlawful action. Therefore, the CPD is in the process of reforming its personnel systems to improve its capacity to deal with problem employees, to reward outstanding performers, and to manage discipline fairly and impartially.

Lesson 6: Information sharing leads to win–win scenarios.

While law enforcement was developing stronger community and government partnerships throughout the 1990s, the corporate world was also building partnerships. There were technology-based, information-sharing partnerships to reduce costs, leverage customer relationships, and build industrywide information for long-term strategic planning. Large corporations invested in information systems that integrated their different supply chains—reducing costs by using information to limit inventories, purchase exact quantities of necessary goods, and reduce the administrative overhead associated with manual job functions.

Integrating systems in the criminal justice community has the potential to achieve the same savings and increase effectiveness. To take advantage of the private sector lessons learned, the CPD approached its information-sharing strategy as though it were a supply chain—a criminal justice supply chain. Two supply chain failures were identified during the process re-engineering phase of CLEAR. The first failure was internal—no tools existed for the meaningful exchange of information among department divisions. The second failure was external—no mechanism existed to share information with the department's partners (other law enforcement agencies, courts, corrections, community members, and others).

To address the internal problem, CLEAR was developed to manage all of the department's activities from start to finish. This enables smooth handoffs between divisions and the sharing of critical information. To address the external problem, the department adopted multiple strategies. It is common knowledge that criminals don't respect jurisdictional boundaries; CLEAR integrates arrest information from 132 suburban agencies into one database that is updated in real time. This enables any officer from any agency to track the activities of an offender regardless of jurisdictional borders. In the near future the system will expand to include information from federal and state agencies, as well as other agencies throughout Illinois.

To improve the department's records and the efficiency of information exchange among non-law enforcement agencies (courts, corrections, other city departments, and others), the CPD designed CLEAR as an information clearinghouse. While CLEAR will not become the records management system for other partners, it will integrate their information so that any agency can track an offender from the front end to the back end of the process. This will not only result in better information; it also will greatly reduce administrative overhead. In 2001 and 2002 the CPD reduced its civilian clerical staff by more than 250 through the efficiencies gained from CLEAR. In addition, base-line studies of officer productivity have revealed a 20 percent increase in efficiency, as measured by the time it takes to complete tasks.

Conclusion

Although the use of technology is only one element in a sound community policing strategy, it is clear that its potential impact can be significant. The private sector's successes and failures using technology should serve as a case study from which the criminal justice system can benefit. While Chicago's community policing strategy has proven successful, the implementation of a strong technology infrastructure will ensure that CAPS remains vital and effective.

References

Chicago Police Department. 1993. *Together We Can: A Strategic Plan for Reinventing the Chicago Police Department.* Available: http://egov.cityofchicago.org/webportal/COCWebPortal/COC-EDITORIAL/TWC.pdf

Fraser, Craig B., Michael Scott, John Heisey, and Robert Wasserman. 1998. *Challenge to Change: The 21st Century Policing Project.* Washington, D.C.: Police Executive Research Forum.

Langworthy, Robert, ed. 1999. *Measuring What Matters: Proceedings from the Policing Research Institute Meetings,* NCJ 170610. Washington, D.C.: National Institute of Justice and the Office of Community Oriented Policing Services.

Moore, Mark, H., with David Thacher, Andrea Dodge, and Tobias Moore. 2002. *Recognizing Value in Policing: The Challenge of Measuring Police Performance.* Washington, D.C.: Police Executive Research Forum.

10

Reflections from the Field on Needed Changes in Community Policing

by Nancy McPherson, Director of Services,
Portland Police Bureau

The "basics" of American policing have changed drastically since September 11, 2001. Decisions regarding individual rights in the context of local and national security are shaping the role of police in all of our cities. Today Department of Homeland Security dollars are allocated to shore up the local response to terrorism and emergency preparedness. Intelligence units search for terrorist connections in local communities as the country debates the merits of war against its enemies. In the past, officers in riot gear provoked thoughts of the police as occupying forces in the community. Today officers are deployed in personal protective gear as standard equipment to deal with groups of individuals bent on using violent, unlawful behavior in crowd situations.[1]

Citizens and police alike are re-examining the question "Is community policing still relevant?" Community policing—which includes solving

---

1. The protesters at the World Trade Organization conference in Seattle are one example.

problems, improving social connectedness in neighborhoods, and forming police–community partnerships—is more relevant than ever in a profession that was unable to fire a single shot to stop the events of 9–11.

The question from the field in this new era is "Are we focusing on the right things?" If we are, what are the challenges to moving community policing forward? In spite of a resistant police culture, community policing progressed during the past two decades. From this practitioner's perspective, the following issues must be addressed to ensure continued progress in community policing:

- developing front-line professionals' leadership abilities,
- conducting problem-solving research and employing technology effectively,
- strengthening core systems that reinforce community policing values,
  - generalist problem solving
  - crime analysis that is accessible to the beat officer
  - performance evaluations premised on clear expectations, ongoing coaching, and acknowledgment of the value of community problem solving
  - structured and meaningful community involvement
  - adult learning and values-integrated training
  - field training programs
- ensuring ethical competence, and
- working with police unions.

Developing Front-Line Professionals' Leadership Abilities

One has only to observe the musical chairs at the top of the law enforcement profession and the brevity of new chiefs' honeymoon periods to realize that however important top cop leadership is—and it is—it is not the leadership that has staying power inside the culture. Several years ago an officer patrolling a beach community in southern California was asked if his sergeant was supportive of the department's five-year-old problem-oriented policing initiative. He said, "My sergeant said this has been around about five years. That's about the average life of a program in our department. You just hang on and we'll ride this one out, too." There are "fence sitters" in every organization who know that change can be outwaited.

Efforts to reform policing have been based on the assumption that change at the top levels of police leadership would result in change throughout the police system. While some of the progress visible today is a result of committed and visionary police leaders, it is also true that "progress" is redefined each time a new leader steps into the role. Line-level officers know this. Every new chief wants to leave his or her imprint on the organization.

An internal look at innovation in the law enforcement profession reveals that much of the visible progress is the result of pragmatic and innovative front-line practitioners—the "leaders in the field"—who put their credibility on the line to try something new or to blaze a trail on their own. It is the "street cop culture" that remains constant, while police chiefs pass through revolving doors, federal consent decrees mandate change, crime rates go up and down, elected officials are seated and unseated, and critical incidents occur regularly that exacerbate racial tensions and other societal problems.

Men and women on the front line who have earned respect and credibility through bravery and competence in the performance of their duties have great influence, often informally, inside the police culture. They are the ones with access to the locker room, the inner sanctum of a patrol car, informal meetings in the field, or off-duty socializing. It is in these settings that the most powerful learning about the organization and what is expected of officers takes place. Many officers will not choose formal leadership during their police careers, while a number will advance to the rank of sergeant—a formal leadership role considered "untainted" by politics. Yet the influence of these officers in the field will be much greater than that of the "higher ups" who are occasionally seen at a roll call, a reward ceremony, a disciplinary hearing, or a social event.

Front-line officers, the backbone of police operations, are the messengers to the American public about police authority, actions, and attitudes. Their "routine" contacts with individuals in the performance of their duties shape community members' feelings about the police role and the feelings and attitudes of those with whom they share their experiences. If one can unleash the potential of these informal leaders to inspire the changes still needed in the police profession, the future of community policing will be ensured.

Are we currently preparing informal leaders in the rank-and-file for future leadership on the front line or as they advance through the ranks? Review the training budgets of most police departments. Note who attends training outside the organization. It is not the officers who do the work everyday. Truthfully, most police departments struggling to maintain minimum staffing levels in the field and to keep overtime costs down cannot afford to have patrol officers gone from their daily responsibilities. Yet to perform effectively in their informal or formal leadership roles, police officers need to reflect on how policing affects them and how their policing affects others. The potential for looking internally to rank-and-file officers as "agents of change" is enormous. The means to develop them must come from resources outside of their own organizations. There is a compelling case for creating a national leadership institute to pull officers out of their agency culture and to expose them to ideas outside their own organizations so that they understand the larger context of policing.

Conducting Problem-Solving Research and Employing Technology Effectively

The strategies of community policing have been overlaid on the traditional model of policing in which a police presence, rapid response, and follow-up criminal investigations are still the priority for patrol operations. Problem solving (that is, addressing the underlying conditions that create crime and disorder) is still difficult to fathom for harried patrol supervisors and their officers who are tasked with responding to community members and elected officials who demand an immediate response to recurring incidents. Yet spending time on understanding a problem before responding to it is critical if a long-lasting solution is to be reached. "Just tell me what you want me to do," a comment often heard in the field, suggests that a guidebook on problem solving would be helpful to these practitioners.

Research on Best Practices

The Office of Community Oriented Policing Services (COPS) in the U.S. Department of Justice has published *Problem-Oriented Guides for Police Series* by a group of highly respected researchers.[2] This body of knowledge

---

2. According to the COPS Office website (www.cops.usdoj.gov), in spring 2004 nineteen problem-oriented guidebooks in this series were available for immediate download: *Acquaintance Rape of College Students; Assaults in and around Bars;; Bullying in Schools; Burglary of Retail Establishments; Burglary of Single-Family Houses; Clandestine Drug Labs; Disorderly Youth in Public Places; Drug Dealing in Privately Owned Apartment Complexes; False Burglar Alarms; Graffiti; Loud Car Stereos; Misuse and Abuse of 911; Panhandling; Rave Parties; Robbery at ATM Machines; Shoplifting; Speeding in Residential Areas; Street Prostitution; and Theft of and from Cars in Parking Facilities.* Also available is a companion guidebook that focuses on assessing and measuring response strategies. It is entitled *Assessing Responses to Problems: An Introductory Guide for Police Problem-Solvers.*

regarding problem-solving efforts is one of the most encouraging developments in the field. These COPS publications provide a wealth of information for detectives and patrol officers on current practices and innovations
to deal with old and new problems. A continued commitment to research-
ing current problems such as identification theft and computer crimes will
support patrol efforts to respond effectively to community concerns and
will engage reluctant investigators in problem-solving strategies.

For fourteen years the Police Executive Research Forum held an *International Problem Oriented Policing Conference*. At this tenured learning lab,
practitioners and researchers met to discuss the latest problem-solving
research and tools. Herman Goldstein Awards for Problem Solving were
given at the conference. A credible panel of evaluators for the awards
helped to define problem solving and set standards of excellence for aspiring professionals. Although the analysis of problems is still minimized in
the real world of everyday policing, the evaluation standards from this
panel of experts have demystified the analysis step of the problem-solving
model for field practitioners. PERF's publication of case studies from the
conference and the work of the award winners are valuable contributions
to local training efforts. Research and opportunities for dialogue of this caliber are vital to maintaining a commitment to problem solving. Agencies
should take advantage of these existing resources to boost their officers'
efforts to do quality work in the field. Although there is a new federal focus
on emergency preparedness and terrorism, there is still hope that funding
will continue from the U.S. Department of Justice for organizational development. This funding has been instrumental in shoring up local community policing efforts.

Technology

Officers' ability to solve problems in the future will be aided with the availability of mug shots, crime analysis information, hot spot notification, and
e-communications on their mobile data computers. Performance evaluations that link satisfactory performance to the application of these data to
field work are essential. Federal grants supporting technology advances,
which are not tied to the redeployment of officers, will also ensure the
availability of these new and exciting tools that encourage patrol problem
solving. With an infusion of new grant dollars, a number of model agencies
could pilot technology projects that might be replicated by others. Technology advances could address safety concerns as well as the analysis of

crime and disorder problems. The National Institute of Justice's Technology Centers are well-positioned to provide support for such efforts.

Strengthening Core Systems that Reinforce Community Policing Values

Structures inside each organization are needed that reinforce the "philosophy" of community policing. One area of great frustration to those involved in implementing community policing is the lack of core system development. The thoughtful design and development of such structures require a change in the way business is done and a change in spending priorities; yet no long lasting changes occur without them. Structural changes guide the most recalcitrant practitioner toward behaviors that support the values and strategies of community policing. Which systems should be developed? The answer lies in answering two questions: (1) "What do we want our officers to do?" and (2) "What is hindering or supporting them in doing that?" While cost is a concern, the internal talent inside most agencies is abundant. When this talent is harnessed and directed, there is no limit to what it can accomplish.

Generalist Problem Solving

During the past decade, local police departments have received substantial federal funding to hire and train specialized "community policing officers." While this was a gain for police departments and for communities, it increased the gulf between these specialist officers and the men and women who perform the daily routines of uniformed police work in the more than 17,000 police and sheriffs' departments in the United States. The result is unfortunate—"community policing" is still seen by most officers as what they do when not doing "real police work." Many agencies are encouraging all officers to engage in problem solving. Such encouragement, however, must be structured through systems that ensure that "real police work" includes engaging with the community to find long-term solutions to problems.

Accessible Crime Analysis

Many patrol officers are well-educated and self-motivated individuals who are innovative and critical thinkers. Yet there remains a barrier to their problem-solving efforts. This barrier is the inaccessibility to crime analysis information in the field in most cities. In some cities, crime analysis is available only to management, specialized units, or supervisors. The average patrol supervisor, who has little discretion to use overtime and worries each shift about fielding the minimum number of officers to ensure officer safety, cares little about the analysis of problems. Patrol officers need a bridge over this barrier, a bridge that links officers to information.

One such bridge would involve decentralizing crime analysts to precincts or area stations where informal conversations about crime problems could occur, and data were available to answer officers' questions about problem locations and crime patterns and trends. With timely information and accessible crime analysts, officers can begin to understand the conditions that create crime and disorder problems in their geographic areas of responsibility. The research shows that one effect of community policing is an increase in officers' job satisfaction. Providing resources to encourage the analysis of patrol problem-solving efforts will result in more effective problem solving, and more satisfied officers.

Performance Evaluation Reforms

Accountability for problem solving must be part of meaningful performance evaluations. For performance evaluations to be meaningful, they must be linked to select assignments and promotions. The relevance of any performance evaluation system is still debated by a profession plagued with paperwork. Supervisors who attempt to hold employees accountable in a performance review and then have their evaluations disregarded or overturned view the process, not surprisingly, as a waste of time.

A good performance evaluation system is not merely an annual review of an employee's performance. It starts with clear expectations, and it is reinforced by ongoing coaching and support. The culmination is a written evaluation containing no surprises for the rater or the employee. Ask participants in any training class how many were told of expectations concerning the job they currently have. Ask how many were given regular feedback on their performance. Ask how many of their departments have credible performance evaluation systems. Few raise their hands.

PERF has developed a supervisors' problem-solving course that introduces the first step in a solid performance evaluation system—expressing to officers clear expectations concerning problem solving and the use of discretionary time. PERF's work, however, has yet to make its way into most agencies. Officers and those who are accountable for their performance will not take community policing seriously until a meaningful system of performance evaluation is firmly in place to reward, recognize, or correct inadequate performance. Agencies need to implement performance evaluation systems that recognize competencies supportive of community policing (for example, ethics, problem solving, leadership, and interpersonal, technical, and communication skills).

Community Involvement

In light of recent concerns about national security, citizens are again being asked to be the "eyes and ears" of federal, state, and local law enforcement. For agencies committed to community policing, this phrase is disturbing. It seems to signal a return to the past and a failure to recognize the progress made in expanding the role of the community in policing. The image of neighbors peeking out from behind their curtains to identify suspicious activity is an image that does not capture the meaningful actions occurring today. Residents are taking ownership of the problems in their neighborhoods and are inviting the police to be partners in the solutions to these problems.

An important lesson from the case studies in problem solving is that there are no long-lasting solutions to crime and disorder problems when the community's role is passive and reliant on police presence. Even with the federal funding for 100,000 new community policing officers during the past decade, the net gain in actual staffing locally is minimal due to retirements and other attrition. The likelihood of having a police officer on every corner now is no greater than when neighborhoods reclaimed their streets from gangs in the late 1980s and early 1990s. Many of the gang members who were incarcerated then are now being released back into the community. The community must keep a proactive role in partnership with the police to prevent fear and crime problems from recurring.

With new immigrant populations and their diverse languages, customs, and concerns, social connections in neighborhoods and positive relationships between police and community members are more important than ever. Many immigrants bring with them a fear of police officers because of personal experiences with corrupt and brutal police regimes in their former countries. At a time in U.S. history when fear of differences has upsurged, the police must work harder than ever to connect with all community residents.

In fifteen American cities, the COPS Office's Value-Based Initiative is strengthening linkages between communities and the police. In Portland, for example, a model for dialogue developed at the Massachusetts Institute of Technology is being used to link police and members of diverse faith organizations. They are engaging in conversations about individual rights in a time of heightened national security. Community members who have not interacted with the police are volunteering to participate in these dialogues. Local corporations in most cities, and some newly formed local police foundations, are also interested in lending a hand to ensure these positive relationships continue. It is incumbent upon police leaders to identify new stakeholders, and to engage faithful ones, to support these connections.

Adult Learning and Values-Integrated Training

A few departments have accepted the challenge of adopting new training methods that encourage adult learners to take responsibility for their own learning. As noted earlier, problem solving and community partnerships require competencies such as creative thinking, innovation, ethics, and leadership. Although there are protests to the contrary, traditional learning is still the method of choice in most state police training academies and in-service training courses. This is a source of great frustration to enlightened police executives. Many changed their recruitment and selection processes to identify thoughtful, innovative candidates only to have the basic state training reinforce a "group think" and "just enforce the law" approach to policing. To counter this, one police chief sends a clear message to all new recruits, "We didn't hire you to come along for the ride. You're here because you have the leadership to do the right thing no matter what anyone else is doing." This admonition is backed by a new performance evaluation system that recognizes leadership as a core competency for every police officer in the organization, from the patrol officer to the chief of police.

Police training should incorporate the values of the organization, and community policing, into every module of training curricula. Stand-alone training for cultural competency, ethics, problem solving, and community partnerships is passé. Values such as respect, compassion, integrity, excellence, problem solving, and service must be integrated into every aspect of police work. Attractive posters on agency walls that espouse the corporate values are meaningless to officers when they are engaged in a routine or deadly encounter. Their focus is on being mentally and physically alert and relying instinctively on their training to carry them safely through the encounter. When training integrates the organizational values into every practicum or scenario, the officers will be better prepared to withstand the scrutiny of their actions once the Monday morning quarterbacking begins. Training of this caliber requires courage to challenge the sacred cows in training units, but it has been developed in some agencies and should serve as a model for others to follow.

Field Training

In most agencies, community policing is not integrated into field training where the most powerful learning for new recruits takes place. "Skip what you learned in the academy; I'll show you how it's really done" is the mantra police commanders most dread when releasing new recruits into the field to their field training officers (FTOs). Accountability is increasing with such tools as daily on-line evaluations of trainees through all phases of field training and evaluations of FTOs by trainees once their phase training is complete. The changes needed to support community policing in field training programs may be just around the corner. A model program and curriculum have been developed by the Reno Police Department and PERF with funding from the COPS Office. The role of field training officers is pivotal as these rank-and-file leaders acculturate new cops into the profession. Agencies must closely examine their FTO programs, and leaders, to see if community policing efforts are undermined or supported by this influential structure.

Ensuring Ethical Competence

Starting with the hiring process, police departments make a valiant attempt to screen for candidates with the highest integrity. In the basic academy and throughout field training, raters are on the alert for any sign of aberrant behavior from the trainees. An assumption is made once the trainee becomes a tenured officer that the individual's integrity has been thoroughly checked for flaws.

A single event can destroy the reputation the idealistic young officer intended to earn. Media images and newspapers highlight these critical points in an officer's life, and in the life of the organization he or she represents. Dramatic accounts of police misconduct in cities across our nation abound. Why do these destructive incidents occur? Was something overlooked in the screening process? If only it were that simple.

The complexities of the world in which police officers work put good people to the test every day. The ethical dilemmas that they will face cannot be understood by rookie police officers. Only with time and experience under their belts can officers gain a deeper understanding of the significance of their authority and power, and the complexity of their role. Only then can officers make informed choices about how policing will affect them and how their policing will affect others.

Officers need opportunities to build ethical competence. What does that entail? Work is under way in the field, not just in the classroom, to design a model for developing ethical competence, just as one develops tactical or interpersonal competencies. This work is challenging but exciting. It can help officers understand that community policing is not just a job but a call to service. The call requires that officers comprehend how to perform their role, how to predict the harm that could occur from wrong choices, and how to inoculate themselves to ensure wellness in the profession.

Fostering ethical competence among police professionals does not mean sending agency personnel to an ethics seminar. It involves daily lessons in ethics, utilizing learning moments that occur in the course of everyday work. Opportunities for reflection and discussion of ethical dilemmas are needed. Ethical competence also involves structured accountability. One idea is an annual audit for work units in which police managers are required to engage the people they supervise in an inventory of their workplace behaviors, attitudes, and environment. It is sensitive work because it touches the core of a proud and committed culture. The return on investment, however, is high. Good people will not be lost from our profession because they were unprepared to make appropriate decisions when they were under pressure.

The relationship between the community and the police is a fragile one and one that must be carefully nurtured. An organization made up of individuals who are ethically competent is an organization that will work effectively with its communities through the most difficult of times.

Working with Police Unions

There is no single formula for ensuring successful relationships between management and labor unions. The role of police unions or associations varies greatly from state to state. When these relationships are successful, it is a result of hard work by two committed and value-based leaders—the police chief and the union president. These successes are rare. Advances in the labor–management relationship found in some industries (advances characterized by interest-based bargaining) have not found their way into most police organizations. City officials, not police executives, set the limits for labor negotiations. The labor–management relationship is still based on position bargaining, which is win–lose in nature and is combined with processes that further exacerbate the conflict inherent in such relationships. The current framework for the police labor–management relationship runs counter to community policing strategies that emphasize teamwork, problem solving, collaboration, creativity, and innovation.

Police administrators with progressive agendas often find them crushed by labor leaders' priorities that focus on pay and working conditions. Progressive labor leaders who promote ethical decision making and community partnerships often find their tenure in office as short as those of the top cops. Labor represents an internal culture that is powerful, resilient, and accustomed to outlasting incumbent chiefs. Those inside see firsthand what happens when progressive chiefs who are committed to the highest ideals of democratic policing leave their agencies after short tenures. Business-as-usual returns in short order.

Union leaders must be treated as police professionals. Indeed, union leaders have an interest in contributing to the dialogue about the evolving nature of police work, as well as in developing appropriate strategies to best meet their communities' expectations. A respectful relationship between police management and labor leaders, even when disagreement is inevitable, is in the best interest of the police and the community. As a union president from Arizona said, "If the community likes what we're doing, they'll be supportive of my officers when it's time to discuss pay increases."

Summary

A patrol sergeant in the Los Angeles Police Department told me recently,

> I have seen many issues surface, and many changes occur, as a result of scandals, uses of force, or political agendas. Many of these issues have risen to the surface due to the traditional style of police work and management, both reactive in nature. If law enforcement would adopt more proactive styles of policing and managing such as those used in community or problem-oriented policing, many of our problems—the result of our own tactics—would be minimized or eliminated.

A crossroads for community policing is imminent. One road will lead to greater tension with all communities over individual rights, police authority, and the exercise of discretion. The other road will give police the opportunity to engage communities in dialogue about individual rights in the context of national security and about ways to work together to identify and solve crime and disorder problems of mutual interest. We must choose this second path. It is our responsibility as a profession and as a society to advocate for the additional support needed from government at all levels. Police and community leaders must ensure that the progress made to implement community policing continues.

11

The Merits of Community Policing in the Twenty-First Century: The View from the Street

by Jerry Flynn, National Vice President/Executive Director,
International Brotherhood of Police Officers, SEIU, AFL-CIO

A lthough the future of community policing is uncertain, the achieve-ments of this nationwide philosophy and organizational strategy are undeniably a success.[1] As the executive director and national vice president of the International Brotherhood of Police Officers (IBPO), I hear from thousands of police officers who have known traditional policing and believe it can be enhanced by community-oriented efforts.[2] Police officers know that it is frustrating and fruitless to respond to the same calls for service over and over again without addressing the cause or the concern of the citizen's initial call. As an original member of the community policing

---

1. The uncertainty is largely due to threats to federal funding of community polic-ing officers and efforts.

2. The International Brotherhood of Police Officers represents federal, state, and local officers across the country. The IBPO, an affiliate of the Service Employees Inter-national Union (SEIU), is the largest police union in the AFL-CIO. The IBPO is a full-service public employees union representing 55,000 police officers nationwide.

unit of the Lowell, Massachusetts, police department, I saw firsthand community policing benefits: the dramatic decrease in crime, the overall improvement of a neighborhood, and the renewed quality of life of residents. Perhaps the most remarkable transformation was not the neighborhood we protected nor the citizens we served but the change in police officers themselves and their renewed commitment to performance.

To assess the future of policing, we must look to where we have been to understand where we are going—by evaluating both our successes and our failures. Community policing will continue to change as communities change: it is from within those communities that real or perceived problems will evolve.

Traditional Policing

Traditional policing generated calls for service that were continuously repeated. Street-line police officers were often subjected to unwarranted stress because of their inability to curb the problem or reach real, long-term solutions. With a rising crime rate came more calls for service. Street-line police officers could do little more than respond to the call, quickly assess the scene, make a decision based on information collected and observations, and then proceed to the next call. In fact, the officer gave little thought to the problem-solving process because he or she was given little latitude, short of making an arrest.

Under the traditional policing model, a community member's only interaction with a police officer was likely to be as a victim, witness, or suspect of a crime, traffic violation, or accident, or as the recipient of news about a loved one. Regardless of the incident, the interaction was probably not a pleasant experience for the community member, and for the police officer it was probably just another call for service. Unfortunately, the memory of the incident may have forever tainted the community member's image of police. This attitude and demeanor toward police are brought into focus when contrasted with the same community member's interactions with the other arm of public safety—firefighters.

A firefighter is often perceived as the person who rescues tenants from burning buildings or frees people trapped in their automobiles. A firefighter may have given your child a tour of the firehouse or, as part of a community program, wrapped holiday gifts or put together kids' bikes. Firefighters were the first to speak to our children in schools about fire safety. Their well-publicized "stop, drop, and roll" program explained what to do if your clothes caught on fire. The other well-known public safety message was to "pick a spot to meet" in the event family members escaped from a fire at home.

Firefighters have been in the forefront when it comes to community involvement and public safety programs, and police can learn a lot from the way they have been working at public relations. They have been involving the community for a longer period of time and have had a tremendous amount of success.

Public Perceptions

Public perceptions of the police can make or break law enforcement efforts. The community's perception will dictate citizens' reception of policing efforts and their demands for service. If citizens trust and respect police, they are more likely to help identify and solve problems that lead to crime. If they believe that crime and disorder are out of control, their fear levels will dictate what kind of police services they want, and their fears will limit how much they are willing to be out in the community to thwart disorder from progressing.

The Lowell, Massachusetts, police department has received national attention for its community policing initiatives. The following mission statement reflects the understanding that public perceptions are critical to policing efforts: "The mission of the Lowell Police Department is to work with the community to reduce crime, the fear of crime, and improve the quality of life in the City of Lowell." The *fear of crime,* especially elderly and school-age citizens' fear, is as compelling as actual crime. One only has to remember the fear that permeated the Washington, D.C., area during the sniper case in 2002 to understand the impact of the fear of crime. Entire cities were paralyzed by the threat of shootings in their area. Isolated criminal acts generate debilitating fear that can wreak havoc in an entire community. Fear is one premise of terrorism, and it is unfortunately very effective.

An Example of Community Policing

The initial success of the city of Lowell's community policing program was based on two critical factors:

1. The citizens of this crime-ridden community wanted the police officers there.

2. The police officers assigned to the community policing unit wanted to be there.

Several other factors were of importance, yet none was more essential than the community's direct involvement and its support of this new and aggressive initiative. Residents, the school district, the business community, politicians, and the local newspaper played a part. The two elements listed above are crucial to community policing in any city. Lowell's program was not without problems, including union issues and political considerations, and cities committed to community policing should be aware of issues that can affect their new community-oriented initiatives.

A section of Lowell was selected by the administration for the police department's first community policing efforts. The area was approximately one square mile, and it was chosen for several reasons. Although this part of Lowell had an extremely high crime rate, it included both a business district and a densely populated residential community. There were several schools and places of worship, and the area was a main artery in and out of the city. It was overrun with prostitutes and drug dealers who worked the street corners day and night. The area also was selected because residents came together to take back their working-class community from the criminals. Finally, the level of agreement between management and labor to work in this area is noteworthy.[3] The union made a commitment to the initial program and became an integral player in the community policing philosophy. In fact, union leaders often spoke of the successes of this program as it grew and became a national model of community policing. For community policing to succeed anywhere, there must be union–management collaboration from the beginning.

The initial selection of Lowell's community policing officers was a process not without political ramifications. In the end, six police officers and one supervisor were assigned to a storefront precinct in the middle of the community, within the same impoverished business district the unit was designed to improve. The final unit selections were as diverse as the community itself. In the beginning, the community policing unit was deridingly called by other officers the "Grin and Wave Squad" because of the unit members' friendly demeanor toward the public and their limited

---

3. Richard Johnson, the former city manager, promised additional personnel as well as additional resources and equipment through grants and other funding sources, in exchange for concessions on several contractual provisions.

role in response to calls for service, even calls in their assigned area. Although those assigned to the unit could have developed an elitist type of mentality, community policing actually became the kind of policing method most of the other police officers loathed. Police officers are creatures of habit, and community policing was a foreign method of policing designed to change their way of thinking. It would be several years before most police officers in Lowell understood and believed in the positive ramifications of community policing; some, however, would never endorse it.

Perhaps the greatest obstacle facing management was a contractual benefit that allowed police officers to select their assigned position every two years. The administration's lack of understanding regarding the strength of the union's position with respect to a seniority provision and the assignment of positions contributed greatly to the negative aspect of many union members' positions. Furthermore, management's perception that some police officers were better suited for a specific geographic area or position based on ethnicity or prior police experience—their idea of placing "round pegs in round holes" with respect to assignments—created a backlash of a "good-ole-boy" mentality among the union loyalists. This management style led many union members to wonder whether community policing was just a disguised attempt to take away a long-standing contractual provision. Some viewed with skepticism management's claim to be matching assignments to officers' characteristics.

As the unit rid the community of drug dealers and prostitutes, it became involved in community policing-based initiatives such as after-school basketball clinics, business community activities, and forms of assistance to the elderly. Officers promoted these programs while continuing to work with citizens and other partners to address the problem individuals who lived in the community's abandoned houses or worked the streets. The team concept of partnering with other city departments (including building and inspectional services and the parks department) quickly rid the area of disruptive and criminal actors. It also ensured a long-term commitment to the community by addressing the problem of absentee landlords. A Neighborhood Watch program as well as beautification of the business district continued the transformation of this part of Lowell.

As George Kelling and Catherine Coles (1996) observed in *Fixing Broken Windows*, since the 1970s, "we have known that 6 percent of the youths who commit crimes in the United States account for more than 50 percent of all crimes committed." Yet police continue to concentrate on ways to combat the 6 percent problematic minority and refuse to focus on the overwhelming 94 percent majority. Our customer base, not unlike Wal-Mart's, is multifaceted, and we need to address the needs of those customers, not just the problematic side of business. In fact, our approach to business has been effectively spending the majority of our time and resources on what I like to call the "shoplifting approach" to policing, while ignoring the "customer service" portion of the job. If the CEO of any corporate 500 company spent 94 percent of his or her time addressing shoplifters and only 6 percent of the time addressing customer service, the only thing the person would be the head of would be the unemployment line. However, this is exactly what administrators and police chiefs across America not engaged in true community policing have been doing regarding the issue of crime and policing in general.

Agencies nationwide have numerous community policing programs, often started by inspired and dedicated officers who solve community problems affecting repeat calls for police service. These officers, frequently on their own initiative, create meaningful responses to crime and disorder problems. In my agency an officer implemented a program to deal with graffiti, a problem in many communities because of related clean-up expenses and because it invites additional disorder. Graffiti signals to residents and criminals that an area is ripe for criminal activity.

Members of the business community, frustrated with the "tagging" of their property, demanded police action from my agency. An officer who responded to numerous calls regarding graffiti noted that the business community was spending an obscene amount of money "cleaning up" their graffiti-laced buildings. The officer began a campaign to rid the business community of this unsightly graffiti and to assist taggers in a way that would direct their talents to a more constructive outlet. He devised a plan, with funds and donations from the community, to provide a competitive forum for these youths. He provided the artists with paper, paint, and supplies, and he secured the corporate sponsors who provided food and soft drinks. The competition was professionally judged by members of the culturally diverse artistic community, including several well-known and respected artists.[4]

---

4. Officer Michael Miles called the effort the "Off-Street Art Program." He later became a finalist for the national Herman Goldstein Award for Excellence in Problem Oriented Policing.

In order to participate in this competition, each of the aspiring artists was required to participate in a class on the new laws and penalties pertaining to "tagging." They also had to sign a contract saying they would not participate in any future tagging in the city. As a result of this program, the two-time winner of this competition was awarded a full four-year scholarship to the esteemed Philadelphia School of Art. But perhaps the greatest change was not recognition for the magnitude of the taggers' talent, but the difference in their attitudes toward the officer who once arrested them.

Changing Our Ways

Our ideas and concepts of community policing may have evolved, but we have lost our focus along the way. Like many corporate businesses, we need to get back to basics. The remarks of newly appointed Los Angeles Police Chief William Bratton underscored the importance of community. He stated, "There is no police department in America that needs the community more than this Police Department." Perhaps the need to regain the community's trust may be more compelling in Los Angeles than in some other jurisdictions, but it is critical for any other city or town in this country committed to progressive policing.

Since September 11, 2001, the approach of the law enforcement profession to crime has changed as well. No longer can we address local problems only, and state and federal agencies can no longer operate without us. Local law enforcement is best positioned to collect and understand locally generated information and intelligence. We must integrate our community policing principles to meet the demands of our work in an antiterrorism context.

Failure to ensure that community policing principles permeate homeland security efforts will hurt not only our communities but also ourselves. We must work together to guarantee the survival of this important and vital initiative. Those in leadership, whether management or labor, must realize that differences of opinion are something to be built on and that diverse perspectives can address mutual concerns and provide a positive outcome. If community policing is going to survive, management must learn that the unions are an integral and necessary component; the unions must realize that any change in management's anti-union philosophy is predicated on the mutual success of labor and management. If police are truly the keepers of the peace, they cannot be distracted by personal agendas or they will be overcome by internal conflict.

Obstacles to Community Policing

As Tom Ridge, the Secretary of the Department of Homeland Security, continuously states across this country, "If we keep the hometown secure; the homeland will be secure." Yet there are a number of obstacles to the future success of community policing, and the following are just a few of them:

- possible elimination of the COPS program because of a lack of funding;
- the administration's decision to have federal grants for first-responders dispersed to governors, not individual police departments; and
- overall cuts to police funding at the federal level and reorganization of the oversight function to entities without experience in overseeing local policing issues.

Community policing is a complex and unique dynamic. Numerous entities with different ideas and concerns act together as a cohesive unit for the betterment of the community. Community policing is a long-standing commitment, not a political aberration. We must resist the notion that any change is good or that we must change for change's sake. To obtain the information we will need in the fight against terrorism, we must seek proper support for community policing. In fact, information received because of improved relations between police and citizens achieved through community policing may be vital.

The COPS program has been highly successful. It placed more than 100,000 police officers on the streets across this county, and it has thrived within the Department of Justice. This program should remain fully funded and under the same domain. Proposals to change the control and very existence of this successful program should be opposed.

Budgetary threats and reorganization plans are not the only threats to community policing's survival. At least three principles relevant to police–management relations should be addressed:

1. Police managers and executives need to include officers in decision making regarding community policing plans. Rank-and-file officers are the ones who will realize the vision of police leaders or even provide them with a vision that will serve the community and the department best. Community policing depends on officers using good decisions based on discretion. Make sure there is an environment where risk taking in efforts to solve problems is encouraged and officers are supported.

2. Police managers and executives need to ensure that there is a reward system that matches the department's goals. Officers should be rewarded for their community policing efforts.
3. Police managers and executives should not underestimate the union. Unions can be an agency's best asset or biggest obstacle to change. Including the union in early discussions about community policing plans can thwart many later problems. Decisions about assignments, promotions, and performance evaluations are going to be top union concerns. Therefore, address them up front by making the union part of the solution rather than part of the problem.

Management and labor should effectively coordinate their efforts for the betterment of citizens and police.

Conclusion

It is ironic that the professional security and support that we found so important in the days immediately following September 11, 2001, have become political rhetoric. The law enforcement community still struggles today with the same problems. Hopefully, the blueprint for success with community policing will be ensured with future accomplishments, not hindered by past failures or the refusal to address the basic needs of the police community. Although the uncertainty of our times and the power struggles from within will undoubtedly continue, those of us policing America will continue to serve those we are sworn to protect and protect those we are sworn to serve.

Reference

Kelling, George, and Catherine Coles. 1996. *Fixing Broken Windows: Restoring Order and Reducing Crime in our Communities.* New York: Free Press..

12

Community Policing During a Budget Crisis: The Need for Interdisciplinary Cooperation, Not Competition

*by Ellen T. Hanson, Chief of Police, Lenexa,
Kansas Police Department*

W hen I speak with fellow law enforcement executives, several topics come up with great regularity. One is how community policing is working in our departments as well as in our communities. Another is how this approach to serving the community affects officers. Police executives are concerned that the resources necessary to run their operations are at an all-time low, and that leads to the final topic: Where do we cut?

This chapter focuses on the resource issues. I believe the current fiscal state for public entities has reached a crisis point. Because the budget crisis is so profound, it touches every operational factor of policing and perhaps even a number of philosophical ones. This fiscal downturn will impact not only public safety agencies but also public schools, mental health providers, and many other social service agencies and the communities they serve.

Resources in all service fields are shrinking at alarming rates, creating strong interdisciplinary competition for available funding. The law enforcement consensus is that this phenomenon will get worse before it gets better. It follows that the continuation of many of our community-oriented enterprises and the morale of community policing officers will be challenged by these circumstances. New and expanded partnerships between public entities are certainly the key to minimizing the negative impact of these budget constraints. Better planned coordination of resources is paramount to ensuring the continued success of community policing. The real challenge is to determine where community partnerships can be used to share resources more efficiently. Ideally, these partnerships will minimize the negative impact created by the lack of funding for programs and personnel.

The Fiscal Downturn since September 11

The 2002 survey by the Police Executive Research Forum (see Chapter 4) asked agency respondents to what extent they believed the events of September 11, 2001, would impact the agency's community policing efforts. As indicated in Figure 4-8, 69 percent of agencies surveyed reported that 9-11 would impact their community policing efforts "to some extent." The major negative effect was the resultant reassignment of personnel and resources, while the significant positive effect was the community's renewed trust in and respect for public safety personnel. The greatest impact, which will have repercussions for all police agencies, is the fiscal downturn since the terrorist attacks.

The financial challenge to community policing is exacerbated because all public agencies are feeling the budget squeezes. Therefore, there is no possibility of one discipline bailing out another for the short term, as we have done for each other in the past. The well is drying up on all fronts.

A September 2002 measure of state revenue in Kansas was $59.6 million below estimates made in March. As a result, the governor ordered state agencies to cut budgets by $41 million. Among the hardest hit was education and mental health services and other social services (including prevention, drug, and alcohol programs, and law enforcement-related initiatives). Municipalities are naturally experiencing a large reduction in state transfers and have already earmarked the programs to be cut. Community policing efforts are considered to be outside of the core "essential" law enforcement responsibilities, and many are in jeopardy. Kansas City, Missouri, at the time this chapter was written, faced a shortfall of more than $50 million. This put "nonessential" law enforcement initiatives on the chopping block. The following scenario is being played out an untold number of times across this country.

In Kansas school districts, school counselors, nurses, and police-related programs are slated to be cut. State law enforcement agencies like the highway patrol will not be able to add or replace personnel, and some of their functions will fall back on municipal law enforcement. This is happening at a time when city revenues are flat, and the extra load is very difficult to bear.

All public entities are under the gun fiscally. In order to avoid a serious denigration of services, including community policing programs, interdisciplinary cooperation and resource sharing must be improved.

Law Enforcement Partnerships

PERF'S 2002 data indicate significantly improved citizen cooperation, involvement, and attitudes toward police as well as increases in volunteer activities and information received from citizens (see Figure 4-3). These very significant benefits are also being jeopardized due to fiscal challenges. The success of community policing and community partnerships in the years ahead depends on all stakeholders exploring ways to collaborate and share resources. Working partnerships between law enforcement and schools, mental health services, and justice programs are essential.

Schools

School funding across the country is at a crisis point. Counselors, nurses, and early intervention programs are prime targets. This leaves the at-risk children in need of community-oriented school policing projects more than ever. Officers who demonstrate the ethic of caring promoted in community policing should be filling some of the voids left by the elimination of school support staff. However, police departments are feeling the financial strain, and unfortunately some of the community policing positions become the most expendable. This happens even in the most proactive community policing departments when police administrators are pressed to choose between "essential" services (answering emergency calls for service or responding to a terrorist alert) and school programs. I was recently at a meeting of police executives where the future of school programs was at issue. In the face of military call-ups after the terrorist attacks and budget cuts that necessitated personnel reductions, some of these police executives had decided to remove all of their school-based officers; others had reduced the numbers significantly. "Cops in Schools" grants have helped mitigate some reductions, but it is obvious that a stronger initiative in support of the country's school-age population must be a high priority to secure the future of community policing. School administrators and law enforcement leaders will need to explore more flexible and responsive ways to deliver cooperative services to students.

Mental Health Facilities

Mental health facilities and resources funded through state and local governments cannot keep pace with the growing demands and shrinking budgets. Following the de-institutionalization of several decades ago, community mental health initiatives were established to assist individuals who were removed from in-patient care. Yet these individuals ended up having increased contact with public safety personnel because they were placed in situations requiring them to interact closely with members of their communities. The problems resulting from these contacts provided the rationale for myriad outpatient clinics, mobile crisis intervention teams, crisis hot-lines, emergency commitment facilities, and other services for people with mental illnesses. Now as budget cuts slash state, county, and municipal entities, many of these programs have been reduced or eliminated, leaving this vulnerable population without necessary support and removing many first-line resources for police officers.

Creative efforts should be made to form partnerships that will help *prevent* problem behaviors that result in law enforcement contact. These contacts are draining critical police resources that do not benefit the person with mental illness. One example of an effective partnership is the New Haven Child Development Community Policing Partnership in New Haven, Connecticut. This is a cooperative initiative between the Yale Child Student Center and the New Haven Police Department. It is designed to understand and mitigate the impact of violence on children who have been exposed to it. Programs such as this may take a comparatively small up-front investment from two diverse disciplines and prevent untold costly demands for service far into the future. The citizens' improved quality of life is justification alone for these initiatives.[1]

---

1. For a comprehensive resource on the criminal justice response—including extensive guidance for law enforcement—see Council of State Governments et al. (2002).

The Justice System

As in the mental health field, practitioners in the justice system with a commitment to helping their communities realized that, operationally, they were able to afford only stopgap measures. There were few opportunities to have a positive and long-term impact on the offender's behaviors and to improve the environment for the affected community. Traditional justice systems also provided little or no support for families of offenders or for victims.

Community-oriented programs have paired police officers with probation officers to increase both professions' understanding and effectiveness. Law enforcement and probation personnel can team up to use techniques (such as GIS mapping) to determine the most effective locations from which offenders can be monitored and served. If offenders live and work in a certain area, it stands to reason that placing probation officers in that area, rather than across town, will increase successful contact, which should lead to more effective reentry and improved living conditions for many.

Restorative justice initiatives help offenders re-enter society as productive citizens. These community-oriented partnerships also work constructively with many who have connections to the offenders. Working together they attempt to break the cycle of criminal activity within families and neighborhoods.

As the financial support for such community-oriented programs dries up, the fall back position will be traditional treatment for offenders. Officers will once again see only one way to approach the offender; probation and parole staffs will be restricted to rote monitoring. Few changes will occur, and all of society will lose.

The Impact of Community Policing on Officers' Job Satisfaction

The PERF 2002 survey indicates that one of the effects of community policing is officers' increased job satisfaction (Chapter 4, Figure 4-3). In fact, the data show that more than 80 percent of the respondents reported that officers had increased job satisfaction to some extent; just over 10 percent reported a great increase in job satisfaction; and only about 5 percent indicated no increase in officer job satisfaction. These findings have dual significance for the future of community policing. First, as the fiscal constraints become tighter, the positive elements of an officer's job (sources of

job satisfaction)—compensation such as pay and benefits as well as training opportunities and equipment—will likely be reduced. Second, as community policing programs lose fiscal support and programs are eliminated,
the source of job satisfaction that comes from working closely with the
community will also be lost. Officers may resent being deprived of this
important source of job satisfaction. We hope that they will retain at least
some of the community contacts, improved feedback and outlook, and
other benefits they have gained. But when officers know what they are
missing, the loss may be a significant demotivator.

The results of the 1992, 1997, and 2002 surveys discussed in Chapter 4
make clear that community policing has positively affected community
members' regard for, and relationship with, law enforcement. It has given
many citizens the chance to share their ideas for a safer community and to
contribute to making it a reality. Community policing has also provided an
opportunity for officers to become collaborators with citizens rather than
simply reactors to their behavior. Police have learned not only to recognize
problems but also to form the necessary partnerships within the community to solve many of them.

There is not much any of us can do to stop the fiscal free-fall that we are
experiencing in this country. However, to ensure the future of community
policing, we need to recognize the threats that may arise from shrinking
resources. Instead of an exhaustive list of solutions, I offer the suggestion
that those in the appropriate positions pull representatives from various
disciplines together to work on this challenge at the community level. Mayors or city and county administrators should conduct focus groups and
plan a series of workshops in which agency staff and agency heads can set
responsive goals and priorities aimed at preserving service levels for the
community. Then this information could be used as the framework for
subsequent work sessions to determine what each agency can do to coordinate efforts, eliminate redundancy, and share resources.

Those responsible for organizing these workshops need to demonstrate
how community policing enhances the overall quality of life for those living where it is practiced. These efforts are truly successful only when the
programs include interdisciplinary partnerships and establish very clear
goals that minimize the usual competing interests.

Another opportunity to realize efficiencies would be to formalize the
process and raise issues at regularly held strategic planning sessions and
annual meetings attended by representatives of the many disciplines that
need to be involved. Most of these meetings would have sessions dealing

with the allocation of resources and fiscal challenges. Many of the people in positions to explore the advantages of interdisciplinary partnerships would participate.

The leaders in law enforcement, schools systems, mental health services, social programs, and justice systems must recognize the dangers in competing with each other for the limited available public funds. And they must be challenged to explore the best ways to motivate and satisfy their personnel, the most effective ways to pool resources, and the most workable means to form strong and sustaining partnerships. It is these interdisciplinary partnerships that can see us through the fiscal challenges and carry us forward to the successful future of community policing.

Reference

Council of State Governments, Police Executive Research Forum, Pretrial Services Resource Center, Association of State Correctional Administrators, Bazelon Center for Mental Health Law, and the Center for Behavioral Health, Justice, and Public Policy. 2002. *Criminal Justice/Mental Health Consensus Project*. New York: Council of State Governments.

13

Community Policing: Common Impediments to Success

by Wesley G. Skogan, Professor of Political Science and a Faculty Fellow at the Institute for Policy Research, Northwestern University

According to the first survey finding reported in Chapter 4, community policing is very popular. So popular is the concept with politicians, city managers, and the general public that few police chiefs want to be caught without adopting something they can call community policing. The 1997 survey of police departments indicated that 85 percent had reported adopting community policing or were in the process of doing so (see Table 4-1). The biggest reason for not doing so was that it was "not practical" in the community at this time. The departments not engaged in community policing were mostly small, with only a few officers. Cities with populations greater than 100,000 all claimed in the 1997 survey to have adopted community policing—half by 1991and the other half between 1992 and 1997. This group included urban giants as well as places like Akron, Ohio; Richmond, Virginia; Mobile, Alabama; and Jersey City, New Jersey.

There are reasons to be skeptical of these claims, for I have learned that adopting community policing is hard work, and the political risks it entails are considerable. What do cities that claim they are doing community policing actually do? Many claim to have adopted a long list of projects or tactics (see Chapter 4). Some of the "community policing" departments I have visited patrol on foot or perhaps on horses and bicycles. Some train civilians in citizen police academies, open small neighborhood offices, conduct surveys to measure community satisfaction, publish newsletters, conduct drug education projects, and work with municipal agencies to enforce health and safety regulations.

Community policing, however, is not defined by these kinds of projects. Projects, programs, and tactics come and go as conditions change. Community policing is not a set of specific programs. Rather, it is a way of changing decision-making processes and creating new cultures within police departments. It is an organizational strategy that redefines the goals of policing but leaves the means of achieving those goals to citizens and the police who serve in their neighborhoods. Community policing is a process rather than a product.

General Principles of Community Policing

Four general principles define community policing: community engagement, problem solving, organizational transformation, and crime prevention by citizens and police working together.

First, community policing requires that police respond to the public when they set priorities and develop their tactics. Effective community policing requires responsiveness to citizen input concerning both the needs of the community and the best ways by which the police can help meet those needs. It takes seriously the public's definition of its own problems. This is one reason why community policing is an organizational strategy, not a set of specific programs. How it looks in practice should vary considerably from place to place in response to unique local situations and circumstances. Better listening to the community can produce different policing priorities. Officers involved in neighborhood policing quickly learn that many residents are deeply concerned about problems that previously did not come to the attention of police. The public often focuses on threatening and fear-provoking *conditions* rather than discrete and legally defined *incidents*. They often are concerned about casual social disorder and the physical decay of their community rather than traditionally defined "serious crimes." The police, however, are organized to respond to the latter under the traditional model of policing.

The second principle is that community policing assumes a commitment to broadly focused, problem-oriented policing. Problem-oriented policing encourages officers to respond creatively to problems that they encounter, or to refer them to public and private agencies that can help. More importantly, it stresses the importance of discovering the situations that produce calls for police assistance. Police need to identify the causes that lie behind the calls and design tactics to deal with these causes. Officers must be trained in methods of identifying and analyzing problems. Police work traditionally has consisted of responding sequentially to individual events; problem solving calls for recognizing patterns of incidents. Helpful in this identification are computer analyses of "hot spots": places where numerous complaints and calls for service arise. Problem-oriented policing recognizes that the solutions to patterns of incidents may involve other agencies and may be "nonpolice" in character; in traditional departments, this would be cause for ignoring these problems.

Third, community policing involves organizational decentralization and a reorientation of patrol in order to facilitate communication between police and the public. Line officers are expected to work more autonomously at investigating situations, resolving problems, and educating the public. They are being asked to discover and set their own goals and sometimes to manage their work schedules. Decentralization facilitates the development of local solutions to local problems and discourages the automatic application of central-office policies. The police are not independent of the rest of society, in which large organizations have learned that decentralization often allows flexibility in decision making at the customer-contact level. Accordingly, many departments that adopt a serious community policing stance strip a layer or two from their rank structures to shorten lines of communication within the agency.

Finally, community policing involves helping neighborhoods solve crime problems on their own, through community organizations and crime prevention programs. The idea that the police and the public are "coproducers" of safety, and that they cannot claim a monopoly over fighting crime, predates the current rhetoric of community policing. In fact, the community crime prevention movement in American policing during the 1970s was an important precursor to community policing. It promoted the idea that crime was not solely the responsibility of the police. The police were quick to endorse the claim that they could not solve crime problems without community support and assistance, for it helped share the blame for rising crime rates at the time. Now police find that they are expected to lead this effort. They are being called upon to take the lead in mobilizing individuals and organizations around crime prevention. These efforts include neighborhood watch, citizen patrols, and education programs stressing household target-hardening, and rapid crime reporting.

Implementing Community Policing "On the Cheap"

Adhering to the preceding principles of community policing is difficult, and it is risky to undertake the kinds of hard organizational changes that have been described. Therefore, many departments are tempted to try and adopt community policing "on the cheap" instead. Unfortunately, they have adopted community policing programs that feature shortcuts. A few of the most common shortcuts are described below.

Make Community Policing an Overtime Program

For years, many departments paid volunteer officers some extra money for conducting community-oriented projects. The officers were to do community policing *after* their day of "real" police work. Not only were they tired, but the officers, it seems, were unlikely to do things differently during that extra two hours. I once studied a narcotics team in a large southern city that was paid to do "community-oriented narcotics policing" for an extra three hours, four days each week. There was a lot of federal money for the program, but I found the officers did not have the slightest idea how to do "community-oriented narcotics policing." They all worked undercover, dressed like pirates, and could not reveal themselves to the community!

Form a Special Community Policing Unit

Community policing units are usually volunteer units as well. Often working outside of the regular chain of command, they are directed by the chief's office, or they are part of a special bureau separated from the main patrol division. The special unit strategy means that the department does not have to address difficult issues of supervision, performance evaluation, or resistance to the project among officers. Officers with community assignments may appear to have easy lives. They are frequently in the media and get invited to attend conferences in other cities. Sometimes they are free to choose their own work hours, and somehow they always seem to decide that they are really needed on their beat from 9 to 5, Mondays through Fridays. Officers who serve in these units may be seen as not "real police." What they do gets labeled "social work," the job of "empty holster guys" and not of "real police officers." Morale flounders, and some of the best officers will try to transfer out. In a large southwestern city, community officers get flexible shifts, carry a cell phone, and take a patrol car home every night. When I asked an officer what the rest of the department thought of members of the community policing unit, she replied, "They really hate us."

Shortchange the Infrastructure

One important organizational function that often gets shortchanged is training. Training is expensive, and officers have to be removed from the line—or paid overtime—to attend. During the early 1980s, a large southwestern agency tried to run a program with no training at all; they hoped that officers (who were doing it as an overtime assignment) would guess what to do from the name of the project. More recently, in a large West Coast jurisdiction, officers received one day of training; in another major agency, it was two. This is for a project that is supposed to revolutionize policing.

Why Community Policing Efforts Fail

Departments are tempted to take these shortcuts because adopting community policing is risky. There are good reasons to be nervous about undertaking the hard and expensive organizational reforms community policing requires. Community policing efforts can fail for many reasons. The wise police administrator should have a defensive plan to counter the reasons for failure listed below. The list is a depressingly long one. Once I wrote it down, I wondered how anyone could be optimistic. But thankfully there are those who are.

Resistance in the Ranks

Efforts to implement community policing can flounder in the face of resistance by rank-and-file officers. Public officials' and community activists' enthusiasm for neighborhood-oriented policing encourages its detractors within the police to dismiss it as "just politics" or another passing civilian fad. Some police are skeptical about programs invented by civilians—persons, they are convinced, who cannot possibly understand their job. They are particularly hostile to programs that threaten to involve civilians in setting standards or evaluating their performance. They also do not like civilians influencing their operational priorities. Volunteer units or overtime programs are obviously attractive in this environment. No one *has* to do community policing, and sometimes there is extra money for doing it.

Resistance by Police Managers

Resistance to community policing does not come only from the bottom of the organization. Mid-level management revolts have sunk community policing in several cities. These managers see authority taken from them and pushed to lower levels in the organization. Supervisors typically are command-and-control oriented, and they feel most comfortable when everything is done by the book. Their own opportunities for promotion may be limited by shrinking management layers and the flattening of the formal rank structure that goes along with many efforts to decentralize in accord with the community policing model. Discussions of community policing often feature management buzz words like "empowerment" and "trust," and it makes these mid-level managers nervous. Top management worries about corruption and inefficiency. This is one reason why special community policing units are often run from the chief's office. Or, to avoid entrenched bureaucracy, the department may decide to house the units in a special new bureau.

Resistance by Police Unions

Unions' response to community policing is variable. In Chicago the major police union has endorsed community policing, but in many cities unions have decided to attack the program. In a West Coast city, the union protested strongly against the community policing program (giving it the familiar "social work" label) and threatened to keep officers from appearing at training at all. A week's planned training became a day, as a compromise. In many cities the contract that the union has with the city binds the department to work rules, performance standards, and personnel allocations that run counter to the organizational changes required by community policing. For example, in Chicago, officers' work in the city is decided by seniority, and it is impossible to put officers where you want them (based on their language capabilities, for example) or to keep them assigned to a beat if they want to leave.

Resistance by Special Units

In my experience, special units (like detectives) often are threatened by department-wide community policing programs that require them to change their ways (for example, to exchange information with uniformed officers and the general public, and to open to debate their effectiveness). Often special units have special relationships with politicians who will move to protect them. I described one city's detectives as "the biggest, toughest, and best-armed gang in town" (although in truth there are four bigger and better armed gangs—street gangs). These detectives proved very difficult to integrate into the city's community policing program.

Competing Demands and Expectations

Police managers and city executives also have to find the officers required to staff the program. Community policing is labor intensive and may require more officers. Finding the money to hire more officers to staff community policing assignments is hard, so departments may try to reduce existing projects. This can bring conflict with powerful police executives and politicians who support current arrangements. Community policing advocates also face the 911 problem. Police commitment to respond to 911 calls as quickly as possible dominates the resource expenditures of most departments. Community policing has encountered heavy political resistance when the perception has arisen (encouraged by its opponents) that resources previously devoted to responding to emergency calls were being diverted to this untried social experiment.

Lack of Interagency Cooperation

Adopting community policing inevitably means accepting a widely expanded definition of the responsibilities of police. When the public becomes involved in setting priorities, issues previously outside the police mandate will be included high on the agenda. Police can note that trash-filled vacant lots are a high-priority problem, but they have to turn to other city agencies to get them cleaned up. For a long list of familiar bureaucratic and political reasons, those agencies may think that community policing is the police department's program—not theirs—and resist bending their own professional and budget-constrained priorities. Making this kind of inter-organizational cooperation work turns out to be one of the most difficult problems facing innovative departments. When the police chief in an East Coast city was new, he told me that he could handle things in his department. His biggest fear was that his mayor might not handle the city's other agencies and that they would not provide the kind of support that community policing requires. Here is a rule: If community policing is the police department's program, it will fail. Community policing must be the city's program.

Problems Evaluating Performance

The problem-solving component of community policing shifts the unit of work from individual incidents to clustered problems, and those are harder to count. It is also hard to evaluate whether problem solving is effective and whether individual officers are doing a good or a bad job at it. The public often wants action on things that department information systems do not count at all. As a result, both individual and unit performance is hard to measure or reward. However, the thrust of CompStat and other new "accountability processes" in police departments is that measured activities get attention and unmeasured accomplishments do not, even if the measured activities do not matter very much.

An Unresponsive Public

Ironically, it is difficult to sustain community involvement in community policing. The community and the police may not have a history of getting along in poor neighborhoods. Organizations representing the interests of community members may not have a track record of cooperating with police, and poor and high-crime areas often are not well endowed with an infrastructure of organizations ready to get involved. Fear of retaliation by gangs and drug dealers can undermine public involvement. Finally, there may be no reason for residents of crime-ridden neighborhoods to think that community policing will turn out to be anything but another broken promise. Residents may be accustomed to seeing programs come and go in response to political and budgetary cycles that are out of their control.

Nasty Misconduct

The investment that police make in community policing is always at risk. When use of excessive force or killings by police becomes a public issue, years of progress in police–community relations can disappear. Similarly, revelations of widespread or deep corruption by police can undo past gains. Nasty misconduct can undermine community policing because it can cause department and city leaders to lose their focus on managing innovation. The mayor of one major city once remarked to me that he had to think about his police department every day. He hated that, but he knew that managing change in large organizations requires focus. Nasty misconduct causes city and department leaders to lose that focus, and it diverts the attention of the media.

Leadership Transitions

When new police chiefs and mayors come into office, they want to do new things. They want to make their own mark. They often have little interest in picking up the unfinished projects of the people they replaced. The old chief in one town I know struggled for a decade to build a new community-policing program. But when he retired, his replacement (who came from out of town) had no interest in the program at all, and it was gone overnight. If community policing is to persist, it must be the city's program, not just the police department's program.

Conclusion

In light of these daunting problems, it is surprising that policing has responded as much as it has to the popular and political forces pushing it toward community policing. Astute executives can overcome the problems; the most important thing they can do is ensure that community policing *is* the city's program, not just their program. That can give them staying power with the city council when budgets are tight and resources are hard to come by for training and community outreach. Political support and deep support from the community are also tools for quelling internal dissent. Building capital with the community can pay dividends when things go unfortunately wrong, because the promise that it won't happen again will have some credibility. Involving other city agencies in community policing can give them visible results, while the less visible things they hope for have a chance to take hold. Finally, if community policing is the city's program, maybe even the chief's successor will think it is a good idea, or at least one that he or she must promise to get behind in order to get the job.

14

What Future(s) Do We Want for Community Policing?

by Richard Myers, Chief of the Appleton, Wisconsin, Police Department, member and past president of the Society of Police Futurists, and a member of the FBI's Futures Working Group

Futurists, whether they are police or other professionals, attempt to envision as many *possible futures* as they can using forecasts and trend analysis. They then try to project the most *preferable futures* and focus on how to get there. Since 1991, the Society of Police Futurists International (PFI), a small but dynamic membership of practitioners and academics, has discussed possible and preferable futures and their implications for policing.

In 2002 PFI signed an extraordinary memorandum of understanding with the Federal Bureau of Investigation to form the Futures Working Group (FWG). This group and PFI members have discussed the future of community policing, one of the topics high on their agenda. This chapter reflects ideas generated by PFI and FWG, the May 2002 PERF focus group on the future of community policing,[1] and personal experiences.

---

1. As part of the project that produced this document, the Police Executive Research Forum brought together practitioners and academic experts to review the survey results presented in Chapter 4 and to discuss key themes related to the future of community policing.

Several factors account for the slow and less-than-full implementation of community policing in this country. I begin with an explanation of these factors as well as general factors that will influence the speed and quality of implementation in the future. I then present a list of possible and preferred futures for community policing. They range from the relatively mundane to the seemingly bizarre. The latter scenarios merit prompt consideration. In fact, the scenarios that appear outrageous reflect likely future technologies that could greatly enhance law enforcement capacities. Before the technologies emerge, however, we need to begin discussing whether or how they should be applied and their "costs" with regard to individual autonomy and privacy. This chapter is meant to facilitate this discussion.

In many police agencies the movement to community-oriented, problem-solving policing (COP/POP) has been more evolutionary than revolutionary. COP/POP activities that most mirror longstanding, "traditional" police practices are implemented frequently (see Chapter 4, Figure 4-4). The community policing activities that have been implemented with the lowest frequency are those that reflect a deep penetration of citizen participation into the most "sacred" police operations, such as developing policy, reviewing complaints, and measuring officers' performance. Few agencies in the 1992, 1997, and 2002 surveys reported significant structural changes to implement community policing, and the common practice of establishing specialized units devoted to doing community policing increased markedly. This specialization ignores the vision of community policing as an organization-wide philosophy. Community policing is not merely a program or a set of specific services. The civilianization of certain police functions has somewhat changed the paramilitary nature of police agencies. However, departments that have civilianized some detective positions and privatized crime-scene perimeter control (the Lakewood, Colorado, police department, for example) are still viewed as revolutionary.

Challenges that Hamper the Vision of Community Policing

Limiting the broad and full implementation of COP/POP around the nation are

- lack of buy-in by personnel,
- insufficient training in COP/POP,
- lack of leadership and climates that do not support risk taking,
- fiscal constraints, and
- challenges to defining "community."

No matter how committed leadership may be, how well-structured an organization may be, and how unlimited the fiscal and technological resources may be, the success of community policing will ultimately come down to the buy-in and skill set of the field problem solvers. Police officers and supporting personnel who are not a good fit for the COP/POP philosophy will always find ways to circumvent policy, eschew public partnerships, or (worse yet) damage relations between police and the public. Tom Frazier, former director of the Office of Community Oriented Policing Services in the U.S. Department of Justice (hereafter referred to as the COPS Office), often described the need for police agencies to hire for the "spirit of service" instead of the "spirit of adventure." Despite years of COP/POP marketing for this contemporary policing philosophy, many departments continue to use traditional recruiting criteria, including requiring academic backgrounds in criminal justice and police certification pre-hiring (although some departments do not require any college credits for entry-level positions). Some of the most popular "list servs" for police on the Internet reflect a vocal movement of police officers who reject COP/POP as ineffective and "politically correct" and who favor an alternative model of policing that is best described as "combat policing." Written and psychological tests, as well as hiring standards and expectations, that have not been significantly modified to reflect community policing values will yield the same undesired results that have perpetuated traditional police cultures.

After police are recruited, training helps shape their skills and mindset. Some popular survival training for police officers emphasizes one thing: getting home at the end of a shift. The combat policing model is strengthened when survival is the *sole* police mission, and devotion to community is excluded. While officer safety is the highest priority, it need not be attained at the expense of innovative policing and community partnerships. This realization is reflected in a growing number of police agencies. The 2002 survey described in Chapter 4 indicated that 75 percent of the self-identified community policing agencies provide academy and/or in-service training on community policing concepts. Sixty-five percent of the responding agencies indicated that recruits are trained in problem solving, and 74 percent provide problem-solving training to in-service officers. Likewise, 62 percent of these agencies provided recruit training in community interactions. In my state, Wisconsin, the basic academy curriculum is expanding to increase the training of core skills essential to community policing (such as interpersonal communication), while maintaining training in safety, defense, and firearms tactics.

According to the 2002 survey, in-service training for existing officers reflects similar prioritization. In-service training would provide added value with greater emphasis on core community policing skills such as problem solving and effective communication. But perhaps the most profound learning experience for police officers is their Field Training Officer (FTO) mentoring. It is a unique time when their life skills and acquired academy training are translated into the organizational culture of their employing agency. FTOs teach officers "how we do things around here." The survey numbers suggest an impediment to the further evolution of community policing: FTO programs are emphasizing traditional police culture as much or more than they are advancing the COP/POP philosophy.[2]

Police leaders can facilitate or impede the advancement of COP/POP within an organization. The element of empowerment that provides line officers with an increased sense of autonomy can be thwarted by supervisors, from the chief on down. Ego and power struggles within organizations, while not unique to policing, quickly squelch risk taking by individuals. Retribution also can be severe in organizations that retain a paramilitary structure. In the business world, risk taking is encouraged as a learning exercise. In policing, recruits are taught from the first day to *not* take risks due to officer-safety and liability concerns. There is no distinction in policing between *tactical* risk taking (officer safety) and *strategic and relational* risk-taking (learning and growth). The first should be discouraged and the latter supported. Another popular business strategy is leadership succession planning, which is also rarely practiced in policing. Leadership succession in policing usually depends on factors such as seniority or local politics, and not all CEOs agree with training several emerging leaders for assuming their role. Turnover at the top in policing can be abrupt, with inadequate time to purposefully plan for the continuity of leadership.

Fiscal constraints also provide both legitimate and contrived challenges to community policing. Early in its development as a model for policing, COP/POP was criticized by many departments as being difficult to implement because of a lack of additional personnel. Over time, however, it was demonstrated that existing personnel with a new orientation could practice

---

2. The new Police Training Officer (PTO) program developed by the Reno Police Department and the Police Executive Research Forum, with support from the COPS Office, serves as an alternative to these traditional programs. It incorporates COP/POP in a field training program based on problem-based learning. More information about the PTO program is available on the PERF website at www.policeforum.org.

the philosophy; significantly increasing staff was not needed. But the decline in the American economy coupled with the post-September 11 reprioritization of government resources have placed legitimate fiscal constraints on many local communities. In several states, the sharp decline in state tax revenues has led to actual or threatened reduction of revenue sharing in local communities. Some communities are reacting by questioning the efficiency of decentralized police operations characteristic of COP/POP. Efforts to consolidate small agencies into larger, regional agencies may destabilize the decentralized and neighborhood-focused style of policing.

Another challenge to COP/POP is defining what "community" means in the twenty-first century. At the local level, the changing face of America has diversified many previously homogeneous cities. Today *community* means a collection of many *communities* representing different special interest groups, cultures, races, and religions. At the global level, satellite telephones and CNN have contributed to the phenomenon of a "world neighborhood." Geopolitical boundaries that define arbitrary jurisdictions have little relevance to the desired outcomes of policing. High-speed Internet has created the cyber-neighborhood, facilitating relationships that span continents and crimes that defy political jurisdictions. In the cyber-community, jurisdictional disputes and inadequate expertise in computer-based crimes highlight police deficiencies.[3] If increasing the partnership with the community is a core element of COP/POP, determining how to strengthen the police relationship with the cyber-community and other constituencies will be a growing challenge.

Factors Affecting the Future of Community Policing

The post-September 11 era of policing is not yet fully defined, but clearly the role of the first responder to disasters and crises is a high priority for

---

3. Problem solving and community partnerships require that police understand the communities they serve. Defining the cyber-community poses a significant challenge to the COP/POP philosophy. The World Wide Web isn't a place; it isn't a time; it's ubiquitous. Regulations and international laws may shape the virtual community in the future, but managing the explosive growth in the dissemination of information (both factual and fraudulent) will affect all aspects of policing. The pre-eminence of the virtual community is one aspect of the technology age that will largely determine future models of policing. Although policing will likely remain an order-maintenance function focusing on people, technology will influence the nature of crime and the delivery of police services.

American police departments. The national surveys described earlier found that police executives perceived potentially positive and negative effects on community policing of the terrorist attacks.

The immediate public reaction to seeing brave public safety personnel perish while trying to save lives brought communities closer to their police. Police departments that appeal directly to citizens to help achieve a more secure community are finding a more receptive audience. The public apathy that prevents Neighborhood Watch from functioning in low-crime areas also may diminish in the aftermath of the September 11 attacks. Engaging people to more closely monitor suspicious activity has a beneficial impact on typical anticrime programs involving community residents, a staple for departments practicing community policing. Such departments view citizens' increased appetite for information as an opportunity to increase public participation in the overall mission of police.

Many survey respondents, however, reported that they needed to divert resources away from community policing activities and toward basic security functions. In cities with critical infrastructure that demands labor-intensive scrutiny, this removes staff who may have been engaging in problem solving and proactive measures. The mobilization of National Guard and Reserve members of the military also disproportionately hits the staffs of police departments, leading to vacancies that cannot be filled.[4]

The "homeland security" function of police may have even more profound effects on policing. Just as the military has assisted police in the fight against drugs, the police may be called upon to assist the federal government's intelligence and military functions. Prior to September 11, the decline in military spending led to the transfer of many weapons and tools to civilian policing that were long the sole domain of the military. In some communities, police officers are being much more heavily armed, and they are adopting more physically aggressive styles of policing consistent with the combat policing model. These factors may result in an abandonment of COP/POP, ongoing clashes between the two philosophies of community policing and combat policing, or perhaps a blending of both.

In 1970 futurist Alvin Toffler described the human and social impact of an ever-accelerating pace of changing technologies. Toffler's book *Future*

---

4. Preliminary survey results from a U.S. Justice Department, National Institute of Justice-funded study on recruiting/police personnel issues included a single question on military call-ups. Of 976 law enforcement agencies surveyed by PERF in 2002, 43.8 percent reported that they had personnel take leave for military call-ups.

Shock has been around for years, but society is only now realizing the conditions he envisaged. Technology changes have stimulated tremendous increases in the quantity of information available, and they have affected the quality and timeliness of that information. People's ability to assimilate and process knowledge has already been challenged. The increasing use of technology by police to better analyze the seemingly endless information flow will influence a new trend of intelligence-led policing efforts. Nanotechnology, biometrics, and Augmented Reality (AR)[5] may have little meaning for the average person, but these developments will change society in ways that inevitably will change policing.

Possible Futures in Community Policing

As noted at the beginning of this chapter, futurists forecast a wide range of *possible* futures before considering which *preferred* outcomes are desired. By studying a wide range of possible futures, decision makers can understand which factors or conditions are valued that, together, reflect a preferable future. Listed and rated below are several possible futures. Some of these futures are possible in the near future; many elements for those scenarios exist today. Other futures are possible only in the coming few decades because concepts currently being researched have yet to move into the development phase; the rating given to these future scenarios is based on the author's experiences with the applications of new technologies as well as their current use and proposed development. The latter scenarios listed in this section—however fantastic they now may seem—should be considered and discussed. Technology is advancing at an unprecedented rate, and the law enforcement field needs to be ready to evaluate not only the benefits but also the costs of these developments.

- Building on the increasingly collaborative model of problem solving, local communities that have embraced COP/POP further develop this model into *community-oriented government.* Police beats become government service areas where interdisciplinary teams representing local government services work together with residents to identify

---

5. Augmented Reality is a technology in which a user's view of the real world is enhanced or augmented with additional information generated from a computer model. For more information on AR applications for law enforcement, see Cowper and Buerger (2003).

problems and develop solutions. Both government and private sector organizations provide expertise in keeping with an overall focus on community residents' quality of life. Any member of the local government team may trigger a problem-solving effort, but police officers, given the nature of their 24-hour deployment, are the primary gatekeepers for local government services, and they remain invaluable sources of information. This model of community-oriented government relies on integrated databases and other means for sharing information across government agencies. The model is likely to decrease reliance on sworn police officers and to increase demand for civilian police employees and citizen volunteers. (Rated: *Mostly possible*)

- In 2002 the number of *private* police already exceeded *public* police officers. In the future, policing in some wealthy neighborhoods may well be provided exclusively by private police forces.[6] Public police may be relegated to serve only economically depressed, high-crime areas that are undesirable for business opportunities. Those public police departments will need to fight the trend toward engaging more in combat policing than in community policing. They are likely to be strapped for resources for responding to even urgent calls for service. Private sector computer experts or forensics experts may conduct sophisticated investigations of high-tech crimes and then team up with police investigators to build criminal cases for prosecution. The private–public partnerships could fit into the scheme described in the previous model of community-oriented government. (Rated: *Mostly possible*)

- Police officers will be asked to engage the community in a full partnership, yet they will be required to conduct combat policing during certain critical incidents. This is not a model in which community policing permeates the entire department. A *proactive* or quality-of-life division and a *reactive* or crisis division may co-exist within a single department. Employees will be selected and trained for one of the divisions based on their skills and philosophy. The COP/POP staff, tasked with building community relationships, may rely on a blend of sworn and civilian staff. The reactive staff will be more military

---

6. The following links provide statistics for public law enforcement officers/deputies and for private security officers: http://www.bls.gov/oes/2002/oes333051.htm and http://www.bls.gov/oes/2002/oes339032.htm.

oriented. They will still need interpersonal skills, but much more emphasis will be placed on physical fitness and specialized tactics. Whenever the reactive, crisis units respond the COP/POP staff will be deployed to ensure that community relationships can be preserved in the event of the use of force. (Rated: *Mostly possible*)

- Policing the World Wide Web will evolve into an even more complex system. International standards for conducting e-commerce will have addressed jurisdictional concerns, and specialized investigators located around the globe will have formed a cooperative network that supervises prosecutions in a virtual court system. A network of specialized investigators and virtual courts will also manage enforcement of privacy laws and combat hacking. Because most large financial crimes occur electronically, virtual police, many of whom will be employed by companies or international units of government, may outnumber street police. The strategic alliance of international virtual police (public and private) will extend the community partnership of COP/POP to the global cyber-community. Sanctions against virtual criminals could include virtual prison in which offenders are prohibited from using the Web's vast electronic resources. Hackers have always found ways to overcome security measures. This model emphasizes finding ways to effectively block their access.

Police officers who are not engaged in virtual policing will still heavily rely on the Web as a tactical tool. SWAT commanders on prolonged critical-incident call-outs will log into expert chat rooms to develop strategic plans with peer mentors. Criminal investigators will exchange forensic evidence and suspect information globally and instantly through open-architecture data systems. Virtual Neighborhood Watch networks will allow local police officers to provide prevention and crime analysis information to residents. These networks also will allow citizens to provide immediate information to the police. The COP/POP philosophy, driven by enhanced problem solving, will draw on a vast array of information management tools. Web-based models will allow officers to plug-in geographic criteria and possible factors to enjoy automated SARA-type problem solving.[7] Preventive and emergency alerts will be programmed for calls for service involving specific addresses or individuals. Computer and

---

7. This is problem solving that involves scanning, analysis, response, and assessment (SARA).

communication technologies will ensure that police and civilians are never out of touch with relevant sources of information. (Rated: *Some possible, some conceptual*)

- Web-based technologies facilitate communications that will result in police reforms. Other, less-visible technologies also could significantly influence policing, however. Augmented Reality (AR), defined in footnote 5, could turn prototypical ideas from Hollywood fantasy into pragmatic applications. Police officers may one day train using a blend of virtual reality (VR) and AR to sharpen their physical skills and weapon proficiency. AR-fitted officers could carry infrared vision and acute listening devices. As the AR technology becomes more accessible, an officer could compare the faces he or she observes with the database of known criminals and terrorists. Officer safety issues and citizen interactions would be easy to address, as the images the officer in the field sees are recorded back at the station and systematically analyzed by intelligent systems that flag incidents for supervisory review. Privacy advocates raise concerns about the application of these new technologies by police; continual legislative and judicial review is required. Severe criminal and civil sanctions address abuse of privacy rights.

  Officers carry more debilitating devices that dramatically reduce their need for deadly force. As in the rest of society, however, the emphasis on new technologies may surpass the emphasis on basic interpersonal skills. Like other members of society, the well-equipped police officer on the street may have little personal contact with the community he or she serves, even while exchanging more information with more people than in the past. The COP/POP philosophy may well be embodied by police officers who tailor the format for community access to problem solving to the format (electronic or person-to-person) that is most accommodating to or preferred by constituents. (Rated: *Some possible, mostly conceptual*)

- The complexities of modern society create a need for constant training of police personnel. Rote practice of basic physical skills (such as shooting, driving, and defensive tactics) are enhanced by AR and VR (see earlier discussion). More training time is spent on developing enhanced interpersonal skills using adult learning and organizational learning models. Networking with similar agencies facilitates organizational learning through regular critiques of critical incidents and common problem-solving challenges. Theory is buttressed by research knowledge about "best practices." Thanks to biometrics and other technologies, much less time is needed to study law and policy; more time is available for practicing interpersonal skills. Imagine, for example, officers being able to access text-book-level information on laws or procedures that can be immediately retrievable when needed. Multilingual officers are common, and translation technologies facilitate cross-cultural communication between the police and the diverse public. With the COP/POP emphasis on keeping the peace and enhancing quality of life, officers participate in dialogues and roundtables on integrity and ethics, understanding cultures, and effective communication techniques. As multiracial families become more prevalent, police officers represent an increasingly broad range of ethnic, racial, and cultural backgrounds. Police agencies employ analysts who review social trends as well as crime trends, and futures research drives organizational planning and learning. (Rated: *Some possible, some conceptual*)

- Police responses to disturbances and violence are largely the work of robotic devices. Nearly all public places and most private places are under video surveillance that is monitored by computers for patterns of problem behaviors. Observed behaviors are analyzed remotely by field technicians who can combine the video feed with firsthand observation and intelligence generated by both computers and people. Criminals who attempt to mask behaviors trigger the attention of police monitors, and a well-educated public increases police personnel's ability to identify offenders. Video replay of criminal behaviors is standard fare on prime-time television, and the first viewers to identify offenders are rewarded with prizes. Computers, telephones, and television have merged into wireless information systems that are always "on" and available. Civil libertarians and others concerned about privacy and individual rights engage in heated debates with the police on whether citizens should be constantly tracked using personal information systems. Electronic fingerprints coupled with personal communication devices facilitate quick identification of all individuals in the area of a crime. Rapid analysis of crime scenes by automated evidence detection systems minimizes human involvement, and the resulting evidence can be linked to all known evidentiary databases.

The largest role for humans in policing is in investigating crime, educating the public, and organizing community responses to situations that diminish quality of life. Police–public partnerships focus on increasing public trust and support for the largely automated technologies that drive policing, and on resolving conflicts between police organizations and segments of the community. Conflict resolution, police accountability, and prioritizing resource allocations reflect the vestiges of COP/POP. Because so much routine service is automated, the human resources in policing can devote significant time to relational aspects of policing. COP/POP provides the "high touch" to balance the "high tech." (Rated: *Very conceptual*)

Preferable Futures in Community Policing

The possible futures projected above include outcomes and forecasts that are independent and may never come together as described. Each possible future, however, contains elements that exist, are under development, or are conceivable today. Nearly every aspect of these projections is technologically probable within twenty years and possible within seven to fifteen years. Therefore, we now have an opportunity to consider these elements and the directions that may lead to the most preferred outcomes. Futures research that focuses on the most likely social conditions, crime trends, and technologies can identify the current elements of COP/POP that have great potential, and the police reforms needed to stay effective and relevant. It is not enough to promote community policing because it feels good today or because we guess it is what we need in the years ahead. Strategic thinking, rather than sentiment and guesswork, is required.

Strategies for Change

Although this chapter will not attempt to discern the most preferable futures for COP/POP or for policing in general, key strategies to address the most common themes for needed change will be described. First, the entire process of recruiting, selecting, and training police officers must be grounded in the principles of COP/POP. The future generations of police must be mission driven, adaptable, and committed to the kind of integrity critical to their position. The core elements of COP/POP must become second nature to police employees. Second, organizational structures need to change radically. The trends toward flattening police hierarchies may be only the beginning of major structural change in law enforcement organizations. It is unclear how police will handle the highly specialized demands of managing emerging technologies, addressing violence, and ensuring officers employ advanced interpersonal skills. A balance is needed between highly effective decentralized service delivery and highly efficient centralized resource management.

The opportunity for the criminal justice system to deal with legal, social, moral, and ethical questions on emerging technologies has a window that gets narrower every year because of the pace of such advancements. The medical community is scrambling to consider the ramifications of rapidly evolving experiments, such as those on cloned body parts, stem cells, and artificial organ replacements. The police should be facilitating a similar dialogue within the justice community on the impact of biometrics, accountability for cybercrime, and the potential consequences of intruding deeper into the space and minds of the public. The police are the segment of the justice system that most often pioneers the application of new technologies in the field and stimulates enabling legislation. Being proactive on these concerns will engender public trust that is necessary for the current COP/POP model to evolve. If police fail to engage the community in such a dialogue, proactive efforts to shape the future of policing may end. Indeed, police may be forced to wait for case law to determine the course of American policing. A wait-and-see strategy could result in piecemeal acceptance and rejection of key police technologies. Both the credibility and effectiveness of the police would be eroded.

Some critics feel that it was an error for the police to take on the many non-law-enforcement responsibilities that characterize full implementation of COP/POP. No other public or private entities jumped in as police did to take on the challenges and approaches described by Wilson and Kelling (1982) in their work on "broken windows" and by Goldstein (1990) on problem solving. Discussion by community stakeholders, representatives from government agencies, and others about their capacities to meet these challenges may help determine the appropriate allocation of resources. Departments that have both a COP/POP orientation and the capacity to provide combat policing when necessary may possess the flexibility to police effectively in the future.

COP/POP has been fueled by research and academic theories since its inception. To move toward preferable futures, the connection between academia and policing should be strengthened. We must ensure that the theoretical and the practical work reveal the innovative research that can be translated into best practices. Collaboration between universities and police departments on models that can rapidly adapt to change will help overcome the bureaucratic sluggishness of many government agencies. Increased collaboration with the business community can also provide police with lessons from that sector. At least in the private sector, resources will continue to flow toward organizations that are efficient and deliver desired and creative outcomes. Outmoded and ineffective organizations will be left behind. The belief that police departments are monopolistic "sacred cows" may prove to be a false assumption; the growing rate of private police may already signal some shifting of resources away from the public sector.

Within the past few years numerous organizations have called for a new Presidential Commission on Policing or even a commission on the entire criminal justice system. Bureaucratic government commissions may not provide the flexible, adaptable, decentralized, and risk-taking style needed for determining the shape of the future. Only now are some of the ideas generated by the Presidential Commission on Policing of the 1960s being implemented. Perhaps a national debate, supported by research and conducted among diverse participants, *could* challenge conventional wisdom on policing. American policing is designed to be locally focused. An appropriate federal role may be simply to coordinate local research and dialogue that could set the future agenda of policing. Absent a strategic plan to identify preferable futures, COP/POP has an uncertain fate.

References

Cowper, Thomas J., and Michael E. Buerger. 2003. *Improving Our View of the World: Police and Augmented Reality Technology*. Washington, D.C.: Federal Bureau of Investigation. Available at http://www.fbi.gov/publications/realitytech/realitytech.pdf.

Goldstein, Herman. 1990. *Problem Oriented Policing*. New York: McGraw-Hill.

Toffler, Alvin. 1970. *Future Shock*. New York: Random House.

Wilson, James Q., and George Kelling. 1982. "Broken Windows: The Police and Neighborhood Safety." *Atlantic Monthly* 249: 29–38.

15

The Impact of September 11 on Community Policing

by Ellen Scrivner, former Deputy Director for Community Policing Development of the Office of Community Oriented Policing Services in the U.S. Department of Justice, former Senior Associate, FBI Office of Law Enforcement Coordination and currently Deputy Superintendent, Bureau of Administrative Services, Chicago Police Department

Community policing has been acknowledged as one of the most significant reforms in the history of American policing. Driven by police leaders seeking more effective ways to control crime, and supported by an unprecedented level of federal resources to help them meet their mission, community policing became the darling of the 1990s. But the events of just one day dramatically changed the context in which law enforcement operates. Now police are called on to meet the new service demands associated with combating terrorism in addition to meeting the traditional demands for service. Can community policing maintain its pre-9-11 identity as a significant crime control reform, even as it meets the challenges associated with the terrorist threat environment? This chapter will explore this question that is so integral to the future of policing in America.

Policing before September 11

In examining law enforcement's ability to meet what now could be considered its dual mission, we will consider how community policing became a change agent for the profession. Community policing has presented a unifying framework that has represented progressive law enforcement. It has incorporated competing and diverse approaches—such as proactive problem solving and computer-tracked accountability for crime patterns— under one umbrella. As law enforcement coalesced around community policing, a new level of creativity was unleashed, and this tradition-clad profession began to break out of the mold of reactive approaches to policing that were insufficient to control pervasive crime. Moreover, community policing created a national dialogue and gave law enforcement leaders a voice at the criminal justice policy table as community policing was incorporated into other criminal justice initiatives. Various programs (such as Weed & Seed[1] and re-entry, drug court, juvenile justice, domestic violence, and mental health initiatives) adapted community policing as the law enforcement method-of-choice to help them meet their respective missions. Through this work, police developed a renewed appreciation for civil liberties and constitutional rights.

Community policing seems to be working. Zhao, Scheider, and Thurman (2002) have linked funding for community policing to decreases in violent and nonviolent offenses in cities with populations greater than 10,000. They have found a relationship between community policing hiring and innovative grants, on the one hand, and lower crime rates in these cities, on the other. The finding that more community police officers are engaging in innovative activities comports with the survey data presented in Chapter 4 on the implementation of community policing. The data provide indirect evidence that community policing today is far more than a department philosophy: it has fundamentally changed how police do their business. These data are supported by the Law Enforcement Management and Statistics survey (LEMAS) conducted by the U.S. Department of Justice, Bureau of Justice Statistics (2000). This national survey of state and local law enforcement agencies examined the change in community policing efforts by local law enforcement from 1997 to 1999. The number of community policing officers in state and local law enforcement agencies increased from 21,000 in 1997 to 113,000 in 1999; full-time officers

---

1. Weed and Seed is a strategy to reclaim and rejuvenate embattled neighborhoods and communities. Weed and Seed uses a neighborhood-focused, two-part strategy to control crime and provide social and economic support to communities where high crime and social ills are prevalent (U.S. Attorney's Office, Western District of New York website).

engaged in community policing served 62 percent of all residents in 1997 compared to 86 percent in 1999.

The Office of Community Oriented Policing Services (COPS) examined the effects of COPS grants from 1995 to 1998 (U.S. Department of Justice, National Institute of Justice 2000). The study provided a wide array of findings on the effectiveness of the COPS Office in meeting its goals, as well as on changes in policing practices. Among the agencies surveyed, problem-solving partnerships and prevention efforts were commonplace, but the form and visibility varied widely. These results confirmed that community policing was expanding across the country and that it was not a "one-size-fits-all" approach to policing.

In addition to the PERF survey results, the two other independent data collections show that in police departments nationwide community policing has advanced beyond being a fad or set of platitudes and has actually changed how the police interact with and respond to the communities they serve. Police are thinking differently about solving crime and disorder problems, and they are behaving differently by collaborating with citizens and asking for their help in controlling crime. Arrests, once viewed as the only way to address crime, are now just one option. Larger policing agendas and priorities are being influenced by community input derived from surveys and citizen contacts. Operational changes have included more police walking their beats, engaging in problem-solving partnership projects in their neighborhoods, and meeting with community groups. Moreover, about two-thirds of the departments in the LEMAS survey reported having community policing plans in place, sharing information, and relying on citizen input to assess their performance. The last is unprecedented in the police culture.

Today, as law enforcement is called upon to meet the post-9–11 demands to secure the homeland, will departments retain the advances that came with implementing community policing? Can those processes used so successfully to fight crime also be applied to terrorism? Or does the new imperative to safeguard the country require a change in strategy that will cause us to revisit past practices that were not necessarily the *best* practices?

Policing after September 11

Harbingers for how police may address a dual mission emerge in positions such as those posited by Stephens and Hartmann (2002). Writing in a report of the Harvard Executive Session on Domestic Preparedness, they detail policing challenges and discuss how applying community policing skills can prevent and prepare for acts of terror. They cite the value of developing relationships with stakeholder groups that are potential targets of terrorist acts while also engaging citizens in activities that deter criminal acts and decrease fear. These relationships evolve from a foundation of problem-solving partnerships that have been the life-blood of community policing's prevention orientation. Stephens and Hartmann make eight recommendations to help police departments rethink the threat of terrorism and what that threat means for law enforcement. One recommendation is for law enforcement agencies to use community policing skills. Stephens and Hartmann also stress the value of partnerships, particularly as applied to a large-scale, coordinated, multiagency response to manage community catastrophes (All-Hazards Plan). That plan will clearly test relationships, as it defines expectations for police and provides direction on how all agencies will share information and resources as they work to achieve a common goal. The Stephens and Hartmann recommendations achieve a balance between prevention and response that reflects the required balance between community policing and homeland security.

Another forum that touched on terrorism's effects on community policing was the Summit on Criminal Intelligence Sharing that was sponsored by the International Association of Chiefs of Police. The summit report (IACP 2002) presents a national strategy for improved intelligence sharing. It discusses how community policing initiatives can aid in the gathering of locally driven intelligence. Line officers, closer to the community and with more immediate access to information than others, can help gather the intelligence data needed to disrupt terrorists' preparations. The summit report discusses how thousands of community policing officers have been building close and productive relationships with citizens—relationships directly related to information and intelligence sharing. Consequently, rather than undermining community policing, the current and urgent need for timely and accurate threat information becomes a natural integrator by taking advantage of mechanisms already in place. These assets include communication based on problem solving, familiarity with community, and strong partnerships based on trust. In this way police can contribute to developing reliable intelligence while still observing constitutional rights.

At the more anecdotal level, police chiefs across the country report that citizens still want their neighborhoods to be safe havens and that they continue to expect the police to control the type of crime that affects their quality of life. Many argue that after the initial shock of September 11, things have not really changed in their communities. People still use drugs, steal cars, and beat up on their families. ATMs continue to present opportunities for crime, people continue to drive while drunk, and women continue to be raped. While potential terrorist attacks are of great concern, it is local crime that remains the growth industry, and citizens are concerned about their safety. These anecdotal reports are supported by a December 2002 survey by the National League of Cities. City officials' report that citizens are more concerned about traditional types of crime than they are about terrorism.

Some police chiefs report that their relationships with immigrant communities have improved and that they are engaging in more viable working partnerships with other local government entities. They also state that greater interagency cooperation, in contrast to turf battles, can result in better preparedness for emergencies. Ongoing communication networks are critical to managing in the threat environment. Serial sniper attacks in the Washington, D.C., suburbs demonstrated the importance of interagency teamwork. Also revealed during the shooting spree was the changing face of public leadership and the need for local government officials to fulfill unfamiliar roles such as calming widespread, crisis-induced fear. These are elements of community government long believed to be the logical outgrowth of community policing.

Prior to September 11, the U.S. Conference of Mayors (2001) conducted a survey of 281 member cities. Seventy-six percent of the respondents indicated that the community-oriented approach used in their police department had influenced or altered service delivery by other city agencies and by the city government overall. It is possible to apply those same community policing skills across local government agencies and to take advantage of existing partnerships to enhance community preparedness for responding to terrorist acts. Conversely, in communities where local partnerships have not yet been welded, the need to respond to the terrorism threat may build alliances that will provide the basis for buttressing community policing efforts. In other words, rather than derailing community policing as we know it, the current crisis could help actualize community government.

Terrorism and the New Realities

The realities imposed by September 11, however, cannot be ignored. The new mission of homeland security has altered priorities, while budget crises in a soft economy strain services. New federal laws, new federal agencies, and proposed federal programs have created a certain level of disarray. During the 1990s, law enforcement leaders helped to determine how resources should be directed to continue the fight against crime, and they had a strong voice at the federal funding table. Now they struggle to find where the table is located. Despite a strong level of congressional support for community policing, new and substantial funding streams for first-responders are not clearly focused on law enforcement. Moreover, there is no one at the federal level taking on the convener–facilitator role that brought law enforcement together to plan and strategize the best way to take on these issues. Consequently, police leaders question whether law enforcement interests will be fully represented in what is now a competition for resources. These events cannot help but influence the future of community policing as local agencies modify operations to position their agencies to receive homeland security funds.

The unified strategy of community policing now faces the risk of fragmentation. The philosophies, strategies, and practices endemic to community policing could be at risk of becoming another area of specialization, or they could fall victim to split-force thinking. This threat is particularly compelling given the potential for law enforcement to revert back to a paramilitary orientation during crises. This scenario is supported by the plethora of training offered to help police learn how to respond to terrorism and by the expanded role for the military in ensuring domestic security. A military presence is clearly needed to provide a national preparedness strategy, especially for responding to large-scale catastrophes. However, we need to ensure that mission creep does not occur, that boundaries are maintained, and that community policing retains its identity as a problem-solving approach—not a problem-reacting orientation.

Suggested Strategies for Law Enforcement Executives

How do law enforcement executives go about retaining community policing while still responding to urgent new demands related to homeland security? What follows are suggestions that can help maintain the balance between community policing and combating terrorism.

- Keep the core business of policing—crime control—front and center. The primary mission of law enforcement is maintaining public safety, not going to war. It is possible to avoid war rhetoric and still maintain the array of public safety activities that have implications for counterterrorism. They include intelligence gathering, domestic counterterrorism, infrastructure protection, defense against community catastrophes, and emergency preparedness across agencies.

- Reinforce the fact that the gathering and sharing of timely and accurate information depend on strong partnerships between community residents and police. Defeating criminals and defeating terrorists is not an either–or situation.
- Apply the lessons learned from history related to safeguarding citizens' rights. An analysis of urban crises of past eras can help prevent the repetition of some of the more egregious mistakes and abuses of criminal justice (for example, the internment of citizens based on their ethnicity, the formation of "red squads," and episodes of widespread violence resulting from abuse of authority, such as the abuse of Rodney King in Los Angeles). Understanding these lessons is essential to avoiding a repetition of past mistakes.
- Since law enforcement currently has a less prominent voice at the federal table, this is clearly a time for law enforcement associations to assert leadership. Law enforcement articulated the need for the Violent Crime Control and Law Enforcement Act of 1994 and helped craft the federal legislation that endorsed a specific form of policing. Similarly, leadership is needed today to provide the blueprint for accessing homeland security resources.
- Exercise caution in expanding the definition of community policing to include approaches that might be considered draconian under other circumstances. An example of such an approach is an overemphasis on zero tolerance. Conversely, avoid labeling anything and everything "community policing." A corollary suggestion is to maintain the organizational structure that supports community policing. Although wide-scale mobilization may require centralized, top-down decision making, there is a need to establish boundaries so that this mode of functioning does not merge into other activities and change the nature of the organization. In particular, crisis functioning does not absorb ongoing management activities and change a decentralized organization.
- Learn from the past and enlist rank-and-file officers and middle managers in decision making on how the balance between community policing and homeland security will play out. Failure to involve them in decision making has been identified as a strong impediment

to implementing community policing. There is an opportunity for us all to do it right this time.

- If pressured to create specialized tactical teams, take steps to build in safeguards so that the teams do not become elite groups. In law enforcement agencies, such groups can quickly escape institutional norms and cross the line to abusive behavior.
- Finally, count on the wisdom of police leaders to do the right thing. Law enforcement CEOs today are well educated and informed by research. They have demonstrated the capacity to respond with thoughtful and creative approaches that have worked well in many jurisdictions.

In summary, September 11 and the resulting homeland security demands have had a strong impact on the implementation of community policing. It is still too soon to know just how community policing will fare in this post-9-11 threat environment, but the prior successes of this model of policing and new realizations as to how it can enhance neighborhood security suggest that community policing can hold its own. The key to the future of community policing is in the hands of law enforcement officers, chiefs and sheriffs, and deputies and line officers on the street. They understand police accountability in the community better than anyone, and they can draw on a reservoir of partnerships that have helped them do their jobs. Moreover, citizens are looking at officers and deputies with a new awareness of the difficult challenges they face. Renewed respect is a powerful incentive to keep the community safe from both criminals and terrorists, and it can serve as a basis for closer police–citizen interaction. In the end, it is officers and citizens, working together, who will maintain the prevention–reaction balance that needs to be achieved between community policing and homeland security.

References

IACP (International Association of Chiefs of Police). 2002. *Criminal Intelligence Sharing: A National Plan for Intelligence-Led Policing at the Local, State and Federal Levels: Recommendations from the IACP Intelligence Summit.* Alexandria, Virginia. August.

Stephens, Darrel W., and Francis X. Hartmann. 2002. "The Policing Challenge." In *Beyond the Beltway: Focusing on Hometown Security. Recommendations for State and Local Domestic Preparedness Planning a Year after 9–11,* 15–22. John Fitzgerald Kennedy School of Government, Harvard University. September.

U.S. Conference of Mayors. 2001. *The Influence of Community Policing in City Governments: A 281 City Survey.* Washington, D.C. April.

U.S. Department of Justice, Bureau of Justice Statistics. 2000. *Law Enforcement Management and Administrative Statistics, 2000.* NCJ 196002.

———. 2001. *Special Report: Community Policing in Local Police Departments, 1997 and 1999.* NCJ 184794. February.

U.S. Department of Justice, National Institute of Justice. 2000. *National Evaluation of the COPS Program—Title I of the 1994 Crime Act. Research Report.* NCJ 183643. August.

Zhao, J., M.C. Scheider, and Q. Thurman. 2002. "Funding Community Policing to Reduce Crime: Have COPS Grants Made a Difference?" *Criminology and Public Policy* 2:201–26.

16

The Challenges to the Future of Community Policing

by Darrel Stephens, Chief,
Charlotte-Mecklenburg Police Department

Policing in America has changed significantly in the past thirty years. It is not the same institution that was chronicled in the presidential commission reports on crime and the administration of justice in the late 1960s and early 1970s. It is much better. Innovation has been driven by a growing body of knowledge and thoughtful experimentation. We know a great deal more about the impact of the fundamental strategies that police have used for many years to address crime problems. We know more about the limitations of the police and how they might be more effective.[1] Police departments are more diverse, police officers are better educated, and both citizen oversight and community engagement are stronger.

Over the past two decades, two policing concepts have been advanced— community-oriented policing and problem-solving policing—as new ways

---

1. Research on random preventive patrol, rapid response, and criminal investigations has helped police understand the limitations of these strategies and provided opportunities to improve the use and effectiveness of police resources. See, for example, Kelling et al. (1974); Kansas City Police Department (1977); Greenwood, Chaiken, and Petersilia (1977); Spelman and Brown (1982); and Pate et al. (1986).

of delivering police services to the community. Yet as these two ideas have developed (and merged into one policing framework in many cities), a competing approach called "CompStat" has emerged. As a crime-reduction strategy, CompStat has had enormous appeal to police executives and local political leaders.[2]

By 1997, 85 percent of police departments reported they had implemented community policing or were in the process of implementing it—a significant increase from 1992, when 51 percent of the agencies reported implementation.[3] This increase tracks the creation and work of the U.S. Department of Justice Office of Community Oriented Policing Services (COPS). This office managed the infusion of an unprecedented federal government investment that leveraged local dollars. The equivalent of 100,000 additional police officers was put on the street to engage in community policing.[4]

The impact of the COPS Office on the community policing movement should not be underestimated when considering both positive and negative effects. As a positive influence, the COPS Office directed an unprecedented influx of federal dollars to provide officers, technology, training, and technical assistance. Equally significant (perhaps even more so) was the national political consensus that emerged with the creation of the office and its mandate. Not only had the federal government become more involved in local policing than ever before, political leaders—from the president to local mayors—publicly embraced the idea of community policing. Prior national efforts to improve policing and address crime concerns accepted the basic premise on which the police and criminal justice system rested: We need only to conduct traditional police duties but do

---

2. "CompStat (Computer Statistics) was first developed by the New York City Police Department in 1994. It is primarily used as a forum to discuss computer-generated statistics that assist with the effective and timely development of resources to prevent and suppress criminal activity or quality of life issues" (Lowell Police Department website, www.lowellpolice.com/crime_safety/compstat/compstat.htm).

3. See Chapter 4, Figure 4-1.

4. For most communities, the federal contribution paid about 50 percent of the annual cost of a police officer for three years. Other funding for technology was aimed at producing efficiencies that could enable officers to spend more time engaged in community policing. "The COPS Making Officer Redeployment Effective (MORE) program expands the amount of time current law enforcement officers can spend on community policing by funding technology, equipment, and support staff, including civilian personnel" (Office of Community Oriented Policing Services website, www.cops.usdoj.gov/default.asp?Item=55).

more of it and better. Before community policing took hold, most decision makers thought the best way to deal with crime was to increase the number of police; improve training and equipment; develop systems to reduce response time; create more prison beds; impose harsher sentences; and federalize those crimes that historically had been the responsibility of the states and local governments.

The COPS initiative was strikingly different. To be sure, the legislation responded to national concerns about crime, but it reflected a wide-ranging consensus that community policing was the most promising approach. The legislation called for fundamental changes in the way the police related to citizens and stakeholders. Increasingly, citizens have been considered more than the "eyes and ears" of the police, simply providing information to the criminal justice apparatus. They have come to be viewed as partners in community policing who have ideas, resources, and the ability to help prevent crime, as well as solve it. The COPS initiative made it clear that police would be expected to use problem-solving techniques to gain deeper insight into the issues they were called on to address, and to develop solutions that reflected that enhanced understanding. Moreover, these solutions would not be confined to a *law enforcement* response. The response might be aimed at prevention or at engaging other community or government resources better positioned than the police to deal with the problem.

The value and accomplishments of community-oriented policing have been the subject of great discussion. This is not to say that there have been no negative challenges for police. But challenges to the future of community policing must be understood within the proper context. Accordingly, this chapter will describe the key components of community policing and then detail obstacles to their implementation and acceptance.

What is Community Problem-Oriented Policing?

The term "community problem-oriented policing" (CPOP) more aptly describes the type of policing that is the focus of this commentary.[5] CPOP is a problem-solving partnership with the community. It engages the police

---

5 An ongoing criticism of community policing has been that it has not been clearly defined. It is true that community policing looks very different from one jurisdiction to another. Therefore, it is important to provide a definition that provides a common backdrop for discussing law enforcement's challenges in advancing community policing. The definition offered here is essentially the definition offered by the Police Executive Research Forum in a Bureau of Justice Assistance publication in the early 1990s.

and stakeholders (neighborhoods, businesses, and government agencies) in a collaborative effort to understand the conditions that contribute to problems and develop tailored solutions to address them. The basic idea is one of building relationships and partnerships with a view toward addressing some issue or problem that is of concern to the community and appropriate for the police to address.

Too often community policing has been framed as just improving relationships with the community, and the approaches that police take to do that (for example, bicycle patrols, foot patrols, storefront substations, etc.). Although positive relationships are important, if they do not progress toward collaborative efforts aimed at solving problems, they lose their potential value for dealing with crime. Stronger community relationships provide the means for citizens to gain greater access to police services, but if the problems they raise are thought to be the responsibility of *only* the police, they will not be satisfactorily resolved.

The Foundation of Community Problem-Oriented Policing

Community problem-oriented policing has at its foundation a base of research and experience that clearly suggests it is a viable and effective approach to policing. It has its roots in early work by the Police Foundation, the Police Executive Research Forum, and the National Institute of Justice on preventive patrol and response time. Not only did this research raise questions about these traditional law enforcement strategies; it also prompted police professionals and academics to realize that there were opportunities to improve how police resources are used. The door was opened to looking at how noncommitted patrol time and improved call-management approaches could be used more effectively. Directed patrol and improved preliminary investigations were the first to address the need, but these efforts were soon followed by attempts to address citizens' fears and to develop closer ties with the community through foot patrol, neighborhood watch, and similar initiatives.[6]

Problem-oriented policing was introduced by Herman Goldstein in 1979.[7] Research followed on several problems in concert with the Madison

---

6. See, for example, research cited in footnote 1 of this chapter.

 ' ' be noted that Goldstein espoused problem-solving concepts well before
       'n-oriented policing" was coined. His work in *Policing a Free Society*
              'erican Bar Association (ABA) Standards of the early 1970s called for

Police Department. Promising work in Baltimore County, Maryland, and Newport News, Virginia, reinforced the idea, and it emerged as a competitor to "community policing" as a new direction for the police.[8] At the same time, work in situational crime analysis, crime prevention through environmental design (CPTED), and efforts on specific problems like domestic violence reinforced the value of the focus on problem solving.

By the COPS era, the debate over the relative value of community policing and problem-oriented policing had subsided as the police became more comfortable merging the approaches to embrace partnerships with stakeholders to solve problems. The debate, however, was itself important to the evolutionary process. The debate focused police, citizens, stakeholders, and policy makers on understanding the substance of what "community policing" actually meant. Through the 1980s, it looked to many people like one of those "feel good" programs that was more of a public relations gimmick than an approach that actually contributed to improving policing. "Community policing" advocates argued that problem-oriented policing was police-centric and left the *community* out in defining the problem. These debates continued from the early 1980s through the mid-1990s and both arguments had merit. For many, the answer was to build on community policing partnerships to strengthen the problem-solving collaborations as a sensible and effective way to police the community—much the way we police today.

Challenges Facing Community Problem-Oriented Policing

In many ways, aspects of CPOP are very much a part of the daily fabric of policing in America. There are numerous examples of successful problem solving. Perhaps the best indicator is the large attendance since 1990 at the (previously hosted by PERF) Problem-Oriented Policing Conference in San Diego and the presentation at each conference of successful problem-solving efforts nationwide. There are many examples as well of strong

---

a focus on substantive problems, rather than tinkering with internal administrative issues in the hope (or belief) that it would make a difference in the things the police were supposed to do.

8. See, for example, Eck and Spelman (1987), an account of work in Newport News funded by the National Institute of Justice. The work demonstrated that officers whose primary responsibility was handling calls could also effectively engage in problem solving. Herman Goldstein's 1990 book *Problem-Oriented Policing* captured the essence of this idea and chronicled the progress across American since his seminal article in 1979.

relationships that police have developed with their neighborhoods. In some cases, residents have become very protective and possessive of officers assigned to their neighborhoods, thus complicating transfers and promotions. In spite of the progress and success, however, significant challenges lie ahead for the police and communities that may limit further progress or even cause backward movement in community problem-oriented policing.

The COPS Office and its Effects

The significant contributions that the COPS Office made can bring the profession only so far. Momentous challenges still face the police and communities that want to see their investments in community policing survive and progress. Numerous police agencies have simply overlaid community policing on their traditional policing approaches by creating special units or dedicating full-time patrol officers to that task, while the majority of officers continue with business as usual. The addition of 100,000 police officers[9] allowed many departments to continue doing "business as usual" while dipping their toes into new approaches to policing. Fundamental changes in the way they approached their work were not made.

This situation presents at least two challenges for those departments. First, they are engaged in CPOP with a relatively small number of officers, while the majority of patrol resources are devoted to responding to calls or doing "real police work," as it is described by some still steeped in entrenched approaches. In these departments, traditional criminal justice–focused policing remains the dominant culture. Second, the cost of maintaining the COPS-funded officers falls on local governments that may not be in a position to sustain the increases in staffing beyond the mandatory requirements. Even if they can sustain the staffing levels, there are no guarantees the officers will remain devoted to community policing over the long haul. In fact, a number of police departments have laid off officers because they did not have the funds to continue their employment.

The Transition to Departmentwide Involvement

An enormous challenge for the police is to fully engage all employees in community problem-oriented policing while continuing to perform traditional duties that remain a necessary part of police responses. At the same

---

9. This references both officers and officer equivalents obtained through hiring grants and MORE grants.

time officers are expected to work with the community in a problem-solving partnership, they must respond to calls for service, conduct follow-up investigations, make arrests, prepare for court, and be visible. Citizens and businesses are not likely to stop calling the police even if there is a successful community problem-oriented policing philosophy in place. Effective problem solving should ultimately result in a reduced call load. Community expectations are very difficult to meet, even with the additional officers funded by the COPS Office. This is particularly true when the expectations include visibility and immediate response to calls that are not emergencies.

The police departments making the most progress are those that manage workload and resources in ways that allow for all employees to play a role in community problem-solving partnerships. This applies to the special units (such as traffic, narcotics, and investigations) as well as the patrol function. In patrol, departments are creating teams that have 24/7 responsibility for specific geographic areas. Some departments are integrating investigators and other specialists into these teams. Supervisors and managers have the flexibility and mandate to use their resources to engage in problem solving while handling calls. Police departments that are not able to manage their resources in a way that allows a broad base of employees to be involved in their community policing initiatives are likely to gradually abandon those initiatives.

Homeland Security and the Economy

Following the tragic events of September 11, 2001, homeland security has emerged as a top national priority. Federal resources are rapidly shifting in that direction.

The sagging economy has reduced revenue streams at every level of government and has further depleted funding for criminal justice. Very few states do not have significant deficits that require increased taxes, reductions in expenditures, or both. These conditions create additional challenges to sustaining community problem-oriented policing. The police face added demands to support homeland security efforts but without concomitant resources.[10] A number of cities are making significant reductions to balance budgets and to meet increased homeland security demands. In

---

10. According to Figure 4-8 (see Chapter 4), 69 percent of the departments surveyed in 2002 reported that the events of September 11, 2001, had an impact "to some extent" or "to a great extent" on their community policing efforts.

that type of environment, nonessential programs suffer. CPOP is most vulnerable in cities where it is viewed as a *program* rather than as a *fundamental way of policing* the community.

Crime and Politics

As crime dramatically declined through the 1990s, it moved lower on the national and local political agendas. Even though the decreases have leveled off and there are signs that crime may be increasing, priorities have changed. Crime is simply not the hot-button political issue it was through the 1980s and early 1990s. As public interest in violence, drug abuse, and disorder has waned, resources have been directed toward other issues. From the mid-1980s through most of the 1990s, crime and drug abuse were always in the top five issues of greatest concern in national polls. That is no longer the case. After several decades of national political interest, crime was not a factor in the 2000 presidential election, and it is not a factor in the 2004 presidential election either. The challenge for police will be to address crime problems while competing for the resources and public attention needed to maintain the partnerships that are critical to community policing.

Expanding the Base of Community Involvement

The growth and further development of community problem-oriented policing depend on the active involvement of a sufficient base of citizens. In most neighborhoods only a small number of people are energetically engaged in community activities directed toward safety. Several factors contribute to this environment.[11]

One of the most significant is that many people simply do not have the time or inclination to take part in neighborhood activities. Today in many families both parents work. If there are children in the family, parents'

---

11. Robert Putnam (2000) makes a very strong case that civic disengagement by people throughout America has increased over the past thirty years. Mark Correia (2000) also notes that members of a community must be organized into a social network—in which neighbors know and rely on one another and government officials—to advance community policing effectively. Without a cohesive social network, community policing efforts may be ineffective. He contends that police need to pay as much attention to how communities mobilize and develop bonds of trust, as they do to innovative policing principles.

leisure time is often consumed with child-related activities. Another factor relates to the difficulty of sustaining citizens' interest. In a neighborhood crisis, residents will respond and focus on the problem for a short period of time. In some cases, the focus is limited to putting pressure on the police for increased visibility or investigative activity. In other cases, community members will engage in specific activities; they may leave lights on, escort people in the neighborhood, or conduct vigils or marches to address a particular problem. Sustaining community activity that may help the neighborhood avoid future problems is more difficult once the crisis has abated. Accordingly, ongoing police contact may be all that is required in most cases to rapidly engage the community in some appropriate response, but it is sustained involvement that just might prevent the next crisis from occurring.

The real challenge, then, is sustaining a level of community engagement when there is no crisis. It is difficult to identify activities that citizens are willing to do for an extended period of time. Addressing the elements that contribute to neighborhood decline (ill-maintained yards and homes, litter, broken or poorly situated street lights, absentee landlords, etc.) requires a neighborhood effort—whether to enforce association covenants or to pressure codes inspectors and public works agencies enough to make neighborhood revival a priority. In many cities, police officers have assumed these "citizen" roles in inner-city and transitional neighborhoods where residents have not come forward.

Today, as crime increases and resources decline, some cities are beginning to struggle again with questions about the appropriate role for police officers. Should officers become neighborhood advocates? Should they track code complaints, assist landlords with the eviction process, publish newsletters, coordinate clean-ups, and arrange meetings? To the extent that these activities contribute to the real or perceived safety of neighborhoods, the questions may not have to be fully examined. In communities where the economy has taken its toll and federal assistance has been redirected to other priorities, hard choices must be made about what police officers should be doing.

Drug Abuse and Neighborhood Safety

Although drug abuse has reportedly declined, it continues to be a major contributing factor to neighborhood crime and violence. Arrestee Drug Abuse Monitoring (ADAM) data indicate that 65 percent of those arrested have the presence of one or more illegal drugs in their system (Taylor et al. 2001). Drug dealing continues to generate many complaints from inner-city neighborhoods, and the police spend considerable time addressing these problems. Although enforcement continues to be the primary strategy for addressing the drug problem, some believe education and treatment should receive equal emphasis. That would require either a greater investment in overall resources devoted to drug abuse or a shift away from the emphasis on enforcement as the primary strategy.

The challenge for community problem-oriented policing is for officers to continue handling drug abuse problems in a manner that is helpful and responds to neighborhood concerns, even while priorities and resources are shifting away from the department. The more successful efforts seem to combine enforcement initiatives with strategies aimed at changing the environment. Some departments have been able to work effectively with landlords in developing lease agreements that prohibit drug sales or in conducting criminal history checks to screen out potential problem tenants. Other departments have applied nuisance abatement strategies to change the environment. Still others have implemented drug courts that use the authority of the courts to place individuals in treatment programs.

CompStat

Although the architects of CompStat probably did not have this outcome in mind, CompStat has emerged as a competing policing strategy to community problem-oriented policing. It has a great deal of appeal because it has been credited with achieving enormous reductions in reported crime in New York City and a number of other cities that have adopted this approach. The New York CompStat model is based on five principles (McDonald 2002):

1. specific objectives,
2. timely and accurate intelligence,
3. effective strategies and tactics,
4. rapid deployment of personnel and resources, and
5. relentless follow-up and assessment.

The New York Police Department believes the enormous reductions in crime in the city were the result of police application of these principles. In sharp contrast to departments that had come to believe the most effective means of crime prevention was to build community problem-solving partnerships, the NYPD relied almost exclusively on traditional strategies and tactics. Of the eleven strategies and tactics noted in McDonald's book on CompStat in New York, only two—nuisance abatement and working with landlords to evict illegal businesses—could be described as nontraditional and within the framework of a CPOP response.

How can the principles of CompStat be applied in a way that embraces community problem-solving partnerships? Answering this question is one important challenge facing CPOP in the future. A second challenge is presented by the wrong idea that police alone can control crime. The way CompStat has been portrayed in the news media is that the police can control crime through the application of these principles. While the police can make significant contributions to reductions in crime, the process requires more than rapid redeployment of police officers based on up-to-date crime statistics.

The Bottom Line

Community problem-oriented policing must demonstrate that this approach makes a difference in dealing with crime and the myriad issues that the police are expected to address. This is not a new challenge for the police. It has always been difficult to show there is a relationship between what police do and the outcomes.

Crime, as measured by the Part 1 category (most serious crimes) of the FBI Uniform Crime Report, has once again become the bottom line for measuring police effectiveness. To be sure, it is an important outcome measurement for the police, but there remains a wide gap that precludes linking crime-fighting strategies and tactics to the outcome of a reduction in crime. Many other factors (for example, a strong economy, low unemployment, higher levels of incarceration, and restoration of neighborhoods and center city areas) were in play during the 1990s that may have contributed to the decline in crime at that time.

A significant challenge for the police, government, and communities is to remain focused on the importance of other responsibilities (traffic, order maintenance, illegal drugs, etc.) and to identify appropriate measurements to gauge police effectiveness in those areas. These are important duties, and they are consistently among the reasons people call the police for help. And how important is community residents' fear of crime to the bottom line? A reduction in reported crime does not necessarily translate to an enhanced sense of safety. Police effectiveness will surely be measured, at least in part, by residents' perceptions of their safety, regardless of how closely those perceptions parallel actual reported crime.

There are many potential measurement systems one could use to assess the effectiveness of various aspects of policing (Moore et al. 2002). Some are better than others. The bottom line for community problem-oriented policing must be more clearly defined and articulated if this approach is to survive in the future.

Conclusion

The future of community problem-oriented policing lies in how well individual communities and the field as a whole address these challenges. The national political consensus on CPOP may fade as new priorities force attention elsewhere.

The leadership for CPOP *and advocacy* will have to come from the police. They must continue to make the case for how problem-solving partnerships can have a more lasting impact on creating safe neighborhoods and communities than traditional approaches to policing. They must demonstrate that solutions tailored to specific problems (such as taking neighborhood action, changing a business practice, or conducting after-school programs, for example) can be more effective (and efficient) than solutions reached by police acting alone without the assistance of the community.

If the future can be determined by the past, CPOP will continue to develop in those communities that have had solid leadership and a good policing history. Policing in America has developed at an uneven pace throughout its history. Some cities and some areas of the country have historically set the pace for research and innovation. Some have remained essentially the same in their fundamental approaches to delivering police services. Although that is likely to be the pattern of the future, it does not have to be that way.

It is indeed within the power of the police and communities to change the future by what they do today. The fundamental principles of CPOP can help law enforcement meet the challenges of homeland security and reductions in resources caused by the economy and redirected federal support. Community problem-solving partnerships can produce better ideas and a broader base of resources than efforts by police to resolve problems on their own. Those partnerships might serve as the broad base of authority required to establish new priorities and discard old activities that undermine efforts to deal with future challenges. The police agencies that have made the most progress with community policing using the additional resources from the COPS Office are those that were committed to the philosophy before the COPS Office was created in the U.S. Department of Justice. They have already demonstrated that positive change can occur and a great deal can be accomplished in difficult times. The challenges in the early twenty-first century may be no more difficult than those of the late 1980s and 1990s. They simply present our current and emerging leaders with new opportunities to enhance the delivery of police services to all our communities.

References

Correia, Mark. 2000. *Citizen Involvement: How Community Factors Affect Progressive Policing.* Washington, D.C.: Police Executive Research Forum.

Eck, John E., and William Spelman. 1987. *Problem-Solving: Problem-Oriented Policing in Newport News.* Washington, D.C.: Police Executive Research Forum.

Goldstein, Herman. 1977. *Policing a Free Society.* Cambridge, Mass.: Ballinger.

Goldstein, Herman. 1990. *Problem-Oriented Policing.* New York: McGraw-Hill.

Greenwood, Peter W., Jan M. Chaiken, and Joan Petersilia. 1977. *The Criminal Investigation Process.* Lexington, Mass.: D.C. Heath.

Kansas City Police Department. 1977. *Response Time Analysis.* Kansas City, Missouri.

Kelling, George L., Tony Pate, Duane Dieckman, and Charles E. Brown. 1974. *Kansas City Preventive Patrol Experiment: A Summary Report.* Washington, D.C.: Police Foundation.

McDonald, Phyllis Parshall. 2002. *Managing Police Operations: Implementing the New York Crime Control Model—CompStat.* New York: Wadsworth.

Moore, Mark, with David Thacher, Andrea Dodge, and Tobias Moore. 2002. *Recognizing Value in Policing: The Challenge of Measuring Police Performance.* Washington, D.C.: Police Executive Research Forum.

Pate, Anthony M., Mary Ann Wycoff, Wesley G. Skogan, and Lawrence W. Sherman. 1986. *Reducing Fear of Crime in Houston and Newark: A Summary Report.* Washington, D.C.: Police Foundation.

Putnam, Robert. 2000. *Bowling Alone: The Collapse and Revival of American Community.* New York: Simon and Schuster.

Spelman, William, and Dale K. Brown. 1982. *Calling the Police.* Washington, D.C.: Police Executive Research Forum.

Taylor, Bruce G., Nora Fitzgerald, Dana Hunt, Judy A. Reardon, and Henry H. Brownstein. 2001. *ADAM Preliminary 2000 Findings on Drug Use and Drug Markets: Adult Male Arrestees.* Washington, D.C.: National Institute of Justice. December.

Part IV

Institutionalization of Community Policing

17

Making Sure Community Policing Is Here to Stay

by Mary Ann Wycoff, Independent Researcher/Consultant

The preceding chapters of this book reflect the rough consensus that the ideal of community policing has captured the attention of police leaders—the vast majority of whom support its basic tenets and believe it is the most effective way to deliver police service. It probably is safe to say that the *idea* of community policing is here to stay. A large majority of police leaders undoubtedly agree with Secretary Ed Flynn[1] that the reality of community policing *should* be here to stay. For Flynn (see Chapter 3), the choice is between futile and effective policing, and obviously no chief would consciously choose futile policing.

Despite widespread belief in the advantages of community policing, its survival is uncertain. The authors of the previous chapters express more hope than consensus that community policing can weather a variety of challenges, either present or probable. Their concern about the future of community policing is justified, especially since there seems to be little recognition that the greatest hazard to the survival and growth of community policing is one barely mentioned in the book. This threat has nothing

---

1. Formerly the chief of the Arlington County, VA Police Department, Ed Flynn is now the secretary of public safety for the Commonwealth of Massachusetts.

to do with budgets, unions, politicians, reticent officers or citizens, drug wars, or terrorism. It is a much less engaging issue than any of these concerns, in part because it is virtually invisible. Even when the culprit is detected, it is hard to make headlines from material as dry as "the failure to complete the implementation process." And yet the failure to institutionalize changes that represent commitments to community policing is a killer as deadly as it is silent. The murder will be committed so stealthily that it will remain undetected long after the corpse of community policing is tossed—without benefit of a memorial service—onto the large bone pile of splendid but decaying new ideas. Chiefs may still proclaim that their organizations are community policing organizations even though the newest officers may have no idea what that means. Unless it is institutionalized, community policing can slip unobserved into history.

The process of developing and implementing a new idea is multistaged. The stages can be identified in a number of different ways, but the simplest model includes at least these six:

1. identification of the new idea/procedure,
2. organizational commitment to the idea,
3. planning for its implementation,
4. implementation,
5. assessment and revision, and
6. institutionalization.

It may be safe to bet that most departments that embrace some form of community policing (or most organizations that embrace any new idea) remain attentive only through the fourth stage of implementation. But the fifth stage—assessment and revision—is critical, both to determine whether the change was actually implemented as planned and to determine whether the implemented change is achieving anticipated outcomes. If not, the original ideas need to be reconsidered, revised, re-implemented, and re-evaluated. While the emphasis in this discussion is on institutionalization, there is something worse than failing to institutionalize a change and that is institutionalizing a *wrong* change. Assessment is critical, and the failure to carry it out can sabotage the finest plans.

Beyond the failure to assess, the greatest stumbling block to the success of the new undertaking is the failure to persevere in the implementation process. No change, however laudatory, is self-sustaining. Until it is woven into the structure and functions of the organization and undergirded with support systems, it is vulnerable to being quietly washed away by the familiar, comfortable ways of doing business. Until community policing becomes the business-as-usual approach to policing—something that probably has been accomplished in relatively few departments—there is the grave possibility that it will vanish, even as it continues to be heralded as a sterling idea. Indeed, to the extent that police managers celebrate the successful implementation of community policing, they may fail to see the need for the next critical steps to ensure the permanence of the implementation. The time and effort required to operationalize the idea to date will have consumed organizational resources and attention to the point that organizational leaders, including even those who may suspect there is more work to be done, will feel compelled to move on to other issues. They will fail to institutionalize the change.

Two types of institutionalization—internal and external—are essential to the survival of community policing.

Internal Institutionalization

Institutionalizing change requires modification of the organizational systems and processes that are linked to the new idea or application. In the case of a department that intends to conduct community policing on a departmentwide basis, almost every organizational system or procedure should be reviewed for its relationship to, and impact on, the new approach. Examples of the issues that might need to be addressed can be categorized as structural, functional, procedural/policy, or support.

Structural Changes

Many community policing departments have redesigned their beat structure so that it conforms to natural neighborhoods. This makes it possible for officers to know and interact with an organic community that can identify itself and define issues of common concern.

If the police organization is large and multilayered, it may be important to reduce the number of layers or create some mechanism for enhancing the flow of information between top and bottom. If a basic tenet of community policing is that the citizen and the officer at street level are critical sources of information about problems and possible solutions, then those managing the organization need ready access to this information. Problem solving often requires more flexible and timely reallocation of resources than routine policing, and this responsive support will be contingent on current information about needs. If information flow cannot be enhanced by removing organizational layers (often a politically hazardous operation), processes can be created to facilitate the exchange of information. Some departments (Madison, Wisconsin, being an early example) have established a chief's advisory council in which representatives of every rank and unit meet for regular discussions with the chief. Some chiefs have institutionalized weekly or monthly meetings with area commanders at which commanders are expected to provide operational information that demonstrates close familiarity with their community and the needs of their officers. In this way managers are prompted to develop communication channels that previously may not have been used. In some departments these meetings are open to personnel of any rank who wish to be included in the discussion of a particular issue or who just have a desire to know what is going on. In Sacramento, California, for example, detectives who sat in on the meetings might hear their bosses talking about a crime issue and then leave the meeting determined to solve the problem before their managers did. The meeting stimulated not only communication but also healthy performance competition.

A realignment of organizational structure might place authority for all police services in the hands of a manager who is responsible for a specific geographic area of the city. Rather than having two separate chains of command for patrol and investigations, the department would have all personnel report to one commander. This unified chain of command may facilitate smoother integration of services to a community and more open and convenient communication among all police personnel serving the area.

A change in structure may literally mean a change in the physical structure (or structures) housing the police department. Many cities (Houston, Texas, and Madison, Wisconsin, being two of the earliest) have built full-service area police stations in several neighborhoods and have designed them to facilitate interaction between the public and the police, and among police personnel. In Fort Worth, Texas, new stations are being designed so that teams serving neighborhoods share the same office space, including space for their sergeants. More commonly (and less expensively), cities develop neighborhood storefront offices from which a few patrol officers and perhaps a supervisor are dispatched from centralized or area headquarters.

Functional Changes

Community policing should mean that the jobs of many employees, including supervisors and managers, change. This will be true in departments where community policing entails more than the designation of a few officers as community policing or problem-solving officers. In the Spokane County Washington Sheriff's Department, for example, property crime detectives have become the department's primary problem solvers. Many of them work out of storefront offices and partner with residents to determine which types of cases are a priority for the neighborhood. It is a dramatic change from the traditional detective's role. Patrol officers in many departments find themselves doing new kinds of work, often in different settings such as schools and neighborhood offices. New functions for first-line employees mean novel kinds of functions for supervisors and managers who need to be able to guide and support employees in their efforts. This commitment is reflected, for example, in the employee performance assessment packet of the Santa Ana, California Police Department. Detailed role definitions were rewritten as a result of the department's adoption of community policing for employees at each organizational level and in each function.

Procedural or Policy Changes

Traditional as well as nontraditional work may be done in new ways. Officers may function in neighborhood teams rather than as pairs or as individuals. Rather than only responding to calls for service, officers may be part of planning groups that work to devise solutions to neighborhood problems. Instead of responding to calls all over the city or in their quadrant or sector of the city, officers may be expected to work as much as possible in the beat or neighborhood to which they are assigned and for which they are responsible. This new role requires a dispatch system that can identify officers with particular beats and assign nonemergency calls to the beat officer rather than to the next available officer. And it requires supervisors who are trained to direct the attention of officers to their neighborhood rather than to the next available action.

Decentralized decision making and command may be needed to allow judgments to be made that are timely and responsive to local needs. Decentralized decision making does not happen by fiat; it requires substantial resocialization and training for both managers and subordinates.

Deployment policies need to be designed to leave officers in their neighborhoods for as much of their shift as possible; deployment policies also need to leave officers on assignment in the same neighborhood so they can become effective there. This may mean at least a one- or two-year commitment to a particular geographic location and a particular shift.

New procedures may include new kinds of paperwork or electronic reporting. In Chicago, for example, officers are expected to develop and share beat profiles and beat plans among officers at team meetings and with citizens at community meetings.

Changes in Human and Technical Support

As noted in this chapter so far, institutionalization of community policing within a police department requires structural, functional, and procedural or policy changes. It also requires changes related to support issues. For our purposes, support can refer either to human resources or to material/technical resources.

Modifications in the management of human resources can take many forms. A department may decide to change how it recruits and hires personnel. Specifically, it may choose to focus on attracting and retaining different kinds of personnel psychologically suited to the broad range of roles community policing entails. Modifying human resources also could include changes to the following: content and training methods for both officers and citizens; content and methods for performance evaluations and corrective measures; criteria for promotion; and promotional processes that include input from citizens. Any one of these adjustments can be vital to the long-range success of community policing, and any one of them is a major undertaking for any police organization.

Material and technical support might include funds for police facilities for those departments that want their structural changes to include decentralized work settings. To exchange information more effectively both internally and externally, departments may seek new communication support. Officers working in decentralized settings need on-line access to information they might formerly have retrieved manually in a centralized setting. Computer systems and software need to be designed to capture and disseminate information at the beat level. In addition, fax machines, scanners, and cell phones become more important. And websites and e-mail need to be created and maintained so citizens can gather and share information easily and efficiently.

Summary of Internal Reforms

The projects, summarized so briefly above, can take months of organizational time and considerable resources to create. If they are addressed—as the outline of the implementation process suggests they should be—as the last step in a strategic plan, the organization is very likely to have run out of gas by the time it gets this far. The change will have been operationalized. It will be time to move on.

Ideally, the changes won't occur in this linear fashion. The systems that must support community policing will have been planned along with the operational components, and work will have been occurring to change structures, functions, procedures, and technologies at the same time organizational behavior is being changed. It's not clear how often this happens. Organizations that led the movement toward community policing often began by experimenting. There was no road map, no proven best way to accomplish community policing or even proof that community policing would be effective. It would not have been wise to totally revamp organizations to support a change that had not yet been evaluated. So, insofar as changes were made to institutionalize community policing in these agencies, they were made after the operational changes had been assessed—after the organization was already weary of change and ready to coast for a while in a recovery phase. It is during this "maintaining" phase that critical gains can slip away.

The list of internal systems and organizational linkages that must be changed or created to support and institutionalize community policing is truly daunting. As Professor Wesley Skogan pointed out in Chapter 13, the task of addressing them can be hazardous to the political health (and even the physical health) of the sturdiest chief. The difficulty of the task is one of the reasons Professor David Bayley reached this conclusion in 1988: "It is probably fair to say that community policing in 1988 is more rhetoric than reality. It is a trendy phrase spread thinly over customary reality. Unless this state of affairs changes, the most likely future for community policing is that it will be remembered as another attempt to put old wine into new bottles" (Bayley 1988, 225–226). Or—given our concerns in this chapter—it may be remembered as an attempt to pour new wine into old bottles that will contaminate and destroy it.

Certainly, there are police executives who understand the need to create the new bottle. In the national surveys that were administered in 1992 and again in 1997 (see Chapter 4), approximately 24 percent of responding chiefs stated that "community policing requires extensive reorganization of police agencies." These numbers seem small unless there were questions in the minds of respondents about the meaning of "extensive" and "reorganization." It is possible that system changes do not translate into reorganization for many executives.[2]

In the same surveys, approximately 44 percent of respondents in each survey period agreed that "community policing requires major changes in organizational policies, goals and mission statements." Other research data also are promising: 89 percent of respondents in 1992 and 93 percent in 1997 agreed that "some form of participatory management is necessary for the successful implementation of community policing." In a follow-up survey in 2002, the Police Executive Research Forum found that 70 percent of respondents reported having in place recruitment and selection procedures that target individuals suited for community policing and 69 percent reported having in place employee evaluations to reinforce community policing and problem solving.

Clearly, there are signs that a sizable number of police leaders recognize the need for organizational changes to support the philosophy of community policing, and this recognition bodes well for the future of those changes that have been implemented. Better data about the nature and extent of these changes would be welcome, but just as important as national-level data will be the data that individual departments collect to monitor the continuing support for the changes.

Internal Monitoring of Change

An invaluable means of institutionalizing community policing is an organizational performance measurement system that assesses both the process of implementation and the effects of community policing. Some departments

---

2. It is also possible that many of these respondents are from departments that are too small to support—or actually to need—the kinds of institutional changes that would be necessary in larger departments and communities. Many communities in this country are no larger than a neighborhood or beat in a large city. Officers already know citizens and the conditions in which they live, and citizens are likely to know all the officers. All that may be required for community policing to take hold in these places is a change of philosophy on the part of chiefs who have sufficient direct contact with officers and the community to make it effective. In these departments, the implementation and institutionalization of community policing may be no more complicated than some training for officers and a commitment by city leaders to replace the current community-oriented chief, whenever necessary, with a similarly oriented chief. Making and keeping change in a medium- to large-size department is a much more complex matter.

(such as Lakeland, Florida, and Colorado Springs, Colorado) already have developed such a measurement system or are developing one. The U.S. Department of Justice's National Institute of Justice is funding a Police Executive Research Forum project to develop a measurement system that could be a model for other agencies.

Ideally, a measurement process designed to support change would reflect the inputs needed to conduct community policing (resources, policies, support systems), outputs (including implementation efforts and community policing activities), and outcomes (measures of the impact of police service).[3] The system or process probably would require multiple levels and methods. Some data would be collected at the organizational level, and other data might be collected at the unit level or the neighborhood level. Some data are "formal" data collected through routinized, computerized formats and processes. Other data are "informal" and may be the result of conversations around the question of "how are we doing on that?" In Lakeland, Florida, for example, everyone at the rank of sergeant and above is required to attend an "action list review." Less senior members of the department also are welcome to attend. On a month-by-month basis, current and upcoming events and issues are identified and discussed. If action is required, someone in the group is assigned to tend to it, and he or she is expected to report back at the next meeting. Whether the method of collection is formal or informal, the data and the issues discussed at every level of the organization relate to the department's strategic plan for community policing. The plan identifies steps to be taken, the target dates for accomplishing them, the particular resources needed, and the performance measures that reflect either progress or impact. With a system like this in place, the implementation of community policing is not going to fall through the cracks—unless forces external to the police department have left a gaping hole.

External Institutionalization

Another safeguard against the demise of community policing is external institutionalization of the approach and its support systems. There are two fronts on which external institutionalization can—and ideally would—occur. One is governmental and the other is communal.

---

3. Readers interested in the complex challenge of measuring police efficacy should see *Recognizing Value in Policing: The Challenge of Measuring Police Performance* (Moore et al. 2002).

From the governmental perspective, community policing could be embraced by politicians and administrators who might, for example, approve the strategic plan, approve a budget designed specifically to support the plan, and require regular accountability about implementation and outcomes from the police department. The mayor or city manager might help inspire the public, other city departments, and private organizations to participate in community policing. He or she might provide training in community policing and problem solving to other departments, organizations, and members of the public. Beyond that, the city administrators might make a commitment to hiring in the future only police chiefs who support the community policing strategic plan, thus helping ensure that a new chief won't toss aside what a predecessor has worked so hard to put in place.

Many chiefs attempting to implement community policing would eye with green envy a department that receives this kind of governmental encouragement. It is not, however, the strongest support a government can provide because it runs the risk of being temporary. As good as this kind of governmental backing is, it is not the ideal. The ouster of a supportive city manager or the election of a new mayor or city council can mean slow erosion of the previous support or even its swift elimination.

The best approach to the institutionalization of community policing is the integration of community policing into community-oriented government (Gates 1999; King and Behr 2003). Community policing then would become an integral part of a broad, citywide approach to government. The expectation from the highest levels of city government would be that all city services would be planned and delivered in a way that focused on problems and took into account the needs and wishes and the problem-solving resources of citizens. Rather than city departments operating independently of one another, city administrators representing geographic areas of the city would coordinate service delivery and problem solving in these areas across departments. Police agencies would no longer carry the load of trying to get other city departments to cooperate with their efforts to improve neighborhoods. Under the guidance of a city administrator, departments would plan together how to deliver services to the community or to a specific area of the community. Measures of accountability would reflect the level of cooperation among the different city entities. A new police chief could not abandon strides toward community-oriented policing without confronting (and being confronted by) the community orientation of the entire city government.

Can community-oriented government disappear as new leaders are chosen? Yes, but its demise would require a highly visible public decision. Indeed, the decision would be much more visible and controversial than a police agency's internal decision would be to abandon community policing.

Community policing also can be institutionalized on a second external front. Not only city government but also the community can play a key role in sustaining community policing. There are chiefs who will say that community policing could not possibly disappear in their community because citizens would not allow it to happen. In these places, the community has come to expect the type of service delivery that community policing provides, and it would not settle for less. While one can hope this is the case elsewhere, it is conceivable that community policing could be eroded or even eliminated before the public noticed and organized to protest the change. This is less likely to happen in places where the public is not merely the recipient of community policing but a full partner.

When citizens are involved in making decisions about which problems to address in their neighborhood and how to address them, community policing will not slip quietly away. When citizens are involved in selecting and evaluating police personnel, community policing will not vanish as a result of budget cuts. When citizens are involved in setting policies about the delivery of police service, they will not awake one day to find that community policing policies have been supplanted by policies that exclude the community in the name of national security or the wars against crime or drugs. The more closely involved the community is with policing, the greater the likelihood that community policing will be here to stay.

New Wine in New Bottles

Police departments, then, can safeguard the future of community policing in a number of ways. Two of the most important are

- the redesign of all internal police systems to support the community policing philosophy, and
- the creation of a performance measurement system to monitor the implementation of community policing and its effects.

Internal institutionalization along these lines is more effective if accompanied by external institutionalization. Three essential developments on the external front are

- support for community policing by the local political authorities,
- integration of community policing into community-oriented government, and
- citizens' involvement in the design and delivery of police services.

With even one of these supports in place, the chances for the survival of community policing increase, and they grow better with the addition of each item on the list. Taken together, they would provide a strong bottle to hold the new wine. One day the label on the bottle may read, not "Community Policing," but simply "Effective Policing."

Next Steps

In the absence of data, one can only opine that few departments currently engaged in community policing enjoy more than one or two of the supports listed above. Significant work remains to be done to convince leaders both inside and outside police departments of the need to institutionalize their hard-won changes in these ways. A conference (or conferences) built around these issues and attended jointly by police, politicians, city administrators, and representatives from the community could raise awareness of the need for completing all six stages of the implementation process described earlier. The sharing of performance measuring systems among police agencies would be extremely helpful. In addition, the publication of case studies of departments/cities that have invested heavily in institutionalizing change would be helpful. Current attention to the need to provide foundations for the change that has been made will give critical support to future efforts to build on that change.

A curriculum and support system should be developed for individuals who will have (or *should* have) the organizational responsibility for monitoring and managing the entire organizational change process. The person in charge might be the chief (in a small organization) or someone appointed by the chief. First, the realization that such a person is vital must be fostered; without someone in charge of the process, change either will not happen or will melt away between organizational cracks. Second, there needs to be training and support for these individuals. Very few police managers are going to acquire (through experience or their own initiative) an understanding of the breadth and complexity of the change process. They need special training, and, beyond training, they need the support of a peer group of change agents from other departments. A national organization could make a powerful investment in community policing by training and facilitating (with classes, meetings, websites, on-line conversations) present and future change agents in police departments.

The implementation and institutionalization of community policing are a long-term undertaking. This process is not complete. Indeed, it probably is still in its infancy in many departments. In others, some of which were the premier community policing departments a few years ago, community policing already has slipped away for precisely the reasons explained in this chapter. There is a lot of work to do to keep this paradigm alive and well. This is the time to take stock of the progress made in community policing and of the work still to be done to sustain and expand it.

References

Bayley, David. 1988. "Community Policing: A Report from the Devil's Advocate." In Greene, Jack R., and Stephen D. Mastrofski, eds. *Community Policing: Rhetoric or Reality*, 225–237. New York: Praeger.

Gates, Christopher. 1999. "Community Governance." *Futures*. 31(5), 519.

King, Richard, and Kelli L. Behr. 2003. "Gladstone Adopts Community-Oriented Government Approach." *Public Management* 85(3): 21–22.

Moore, Mark, with David Thacher, Andrea Dodge, and Tobias Moore. 2002. *Recognizing Value in Policing: The Challenge of Measuring Police Performance*. Washington, D.C.: Police Executive Research Forum.

About the Contributors

Lisa Belsky is a Senior Program Director at the Local Initiatives Support Corporation (LISC). She has been active in community development for more than thirteen years, launching her career as Special Assistant to the President of Local Initiatives Support Corporation, the country's largest community development intermediary, in 1988. She went on to become LISC's first national program officer (1990); and, in 1992, took the lead in designing and structuring LISC's Community Safety Initiative (CSI). An innovative national program that links police departments which have active community policing initiatives with community development corporations (grassroots non-profit development agencies that are LISC's core constituents) in formal, long-term partnerships, the CSI is now active in more than a dozen cities around the country. Ms. Belsky has also been working with police officials across the U.S. through a range of other forums, including the Department of Justice's Community Oriented Policing Board on which she served. Since 1996, she has been working with senior executives at Justice to develop a series of joint ventures between LISC and the Department's myriad safety-targeted programs. Prior to joining LISC, Ms. Belsky worked on the 1988 presidential campaign; and before that, spent a number of years at Harvard University's Institute of Politics, focusing on a range of domestic policy research initiatives. Ms. Belsky holds a Bachelors Degree from Princeton University.

Bonnie Bucqueroux has spent 30 years writing about crime and violence and working to prevent these problems in our society. She won a Detroit Press Club Foundation Award in the 1970s for a series on rural crime in Michigan and earned a National Magazine Award in 1985 for an article on suicide. As Associate Director of the National Center for Community Policing for almost a decade, Bucqueroux co-authored two books on community policing. Bucqueroux now serves as the coordinator for the Victims and the Media Program at the Michigan State University's School of Journalism, a program dedicated to educating journalists about victim issues and as the Executive Director of Crime Victims for a Just Society, an organization that promotes progressive solutions to problems of crime and violence in society. She also consults nationwide on the development and production of online training courses, including courses on community policing and effective media strategies for victim's advocates. She continues to consult with national police organizations and individual police departments through her firm Policing.com

Gary Cordner is Dean of the College of Justice & Safety (formerly the College of Law Enforcement) at Eastern Kentucky University, where he is also a Professor of Police Studies and Director of the Regional Community Policing Institute. He received his doctorate from Michigan State University and served as a police officer and police chief in Maryland. Cordner has co-authored textbooks on police administration and criminal justice planning and co-edited several anthologies on policing. He edited the *American Journal of Police* from 1987 to 1992, co-edited *Police Computer Review* from 1992 to 1995, and now edits *Police Quarterly*. Cordner is past-president of the Academy of Criminal Justice Sciences, the country's largest association of criminal justice educators and researchers, and founder and former chair of that organization's Police Section.

Edward A. Flynn is the Secretary of Public Safety for the Commonwealth of Massachusetts. His early career was spent in the Jersey City Police Department. He has been the chief of police in Braintree, Massachusetts; Chelsea, Massachusetts; and Arlington, Virginia. Chief Flynn is a member of the board of directors for the Police Executive Research Forum and the anti-crime organization, Fight Crime: Invest in Kids. He is a member of the Administration of Justice Advisory Committee at George Mason University. Chief Flynn is a graduate of the FBI National Academy, the National Executive Institute and was a National Institute of Justice Pickett Fellow at Harvard's Kennedy School of Government.

Jerry Flynn is the Executive Director of the International Brotherhood of Police Officers (IBPO), the largest police union in the AFL-CIO. In this capacity, he has testified before Congress on a number of issues including the Columbine School Shooting, Collective Bargaining, Patient's Bill of Rights, The William Deagan Law, and was the keynote speaker at the White House on The Brady Law. Officer Flynn has also appeared as a guest on numerous media shows including Court TV and Chief Darrell Gates National Radio Show. He also serves as the National Vice President of the National Association of Government Employees (NAGE) and is on the Board of Directors for the National Law Enforcement Officers Memorial Fund (NLEOMF) and the Law Enforcement Steering Committee, as well as an adjunct professor of criminal justice at Western New England College in Springfield, MA. He is currently on leave from the Lowell Police Department to focus on his IBPO responsibilities; he has served as an officer with the Lowell (MA) Police Department since 1985. Officer Flynn has a bachelor's degree in Law Enforcement and a Master's degree in Criminal Justice Administration.

Lorie Fridell is the Director of Research at the Police Executive Research Forum (PERF). Prior to joining PERF in August of 1999, Fridell was an Associate Professor of Criminology and Criminal Justice at Florida State University (FSU). She has 20 years of experience conducting research on law enforcement. Her subject areas include police use of deadly force, use of less than lethal weapons, police-minority relations, police pursuits, felonious killings of police and community policing. In addition to articles and chapters on these topics, she published, with Tony Pate, a two-volume report entitled *Police Use of Force: Official Reports, Citizen Complaints and Legal Consequences,* and co-authored with Geoff Alpert a book entitled *Police Vehicles and Firearms: Instruments of Deadly Force.* She is the first author of the PERF book entitled *Racially Biased Policing: A Principled Response,* which guides law enforcement agencies in their response to both racially biased policing and the perceptions of its practice and the author of *By the Numbers: A Guide for Analyzing Race Data From Vehicle Stops.* (Both COPS-Funded documents are available at www.policeforum.org.) Dr. Fridell speaks nationally on the topic of racially biased policing and testified before a subcommittee of the Senate Judiciary Committee on the topic.

Paul Grogan became the President and CEO of the Boston Foundation, one of the nation's oldest and largest community foundations, on July 1, 2001. With an endowment of more than $630 million, the Foundation distributes almost $50 million to nonprofit organizations throughout the Greater Boston community each year. .

Grogan joins the Foundation from Harvard University, where he served as Vice President for Government, Community and Public Affairs from 1999 to 2001. One of five vice presidents of the University, he oversaw all government relations for Harvard, relations with Harvard's host communities of Cambridge and Boston, and the Harvard news office. He was also a Senior Lecturer at the Harvard Business School.

From 1986 through 1998 he was President and CEO of the nonprofit Local Initiatives Support Corporation (LISC), the nation's largest community development intermediary. In Mr. Grogan's term as president, LISC raised and invested more than $3 billion of private capital in inner city revitalization efforts across America, all channeled through local nonprofit community development corporations.

Before joining LISC, Mr. Grogan served Boston Mayors Kevin H. White and Raymond L. Flynn in a variety of staff and line positions. He headed Boston's Neighborhood Development and Employment Agency in the early 80s, where he pioneered a series of public/private ventures that have been widely emulated by other cities.

Mr. Grogan graduated with a degree in American History from Williams College in 1972, and earned a Masters degree in Administration from the Harvard Graduate School of Education in 1979. He is a trustee of Williams College, the John S. and James L. Knight Foundation, and the for profit company, the Community Development Trust, which he chairs. Mr. Grogan is also a fellow at Harvard's Joint Center for Housing.

Mr. Grogan is the author, with Tony Proscio, of the book "Comeback Cities: A Blueprint for Urban Neighborhood Revival," published in October 2000 by Westview Press, which Ron Brownstein of the Los Angeles Times has written is "arguably the most important book about cities in a generation."

Chief Ellen T. Hanson has been with the Lenexa Police Department for 27 years. She began her career as a patrol officer and was later transferred to the Investigations Division where she served as a detective and later as the commander of that unit for 12 years. Before being named Chief of Police in 1991, she served as commander of the Patrol Division and as Deputy Chief.

Chief Hanson is a 1980 graduate of the FBI National Academy and past president of the Johnson County Chiefs and Sheriffs Association and Metropolitan Chiefs and Sheriff's Association. She has served as a board member for the Police Executive Research Forum and currently serves on the Executive Committee of the International Association of Chiefs of Police, the Environmental Crimes Committee of the IACP and the Patrol and Tactical Committee of that organization. She is a peer review consultant for the National Institute of Justice, and is a member of the Department of Justice Community Oriented Policing Resource Board. She also served as an instructor of human relations and communications at the Johnson County Regional Police Academy for 16 years.

Chief Hanson has an undergraduate degree in Political Science from Kansas University and a Masters Degree in Management Science from Baker University.

Ron Huberman has worked for the Chicago Police Department since 1995 in various capacities. Under his leadership, the department has risen as a leader in state of the art policing strategies, effectively lowering crime rates through out the city. As the Assistant Deputy Superintendent for the Office of Information and Strategic Services, Huberman served as the principal architect of the award-winning Citizen and Law Enforcement Analysis and Reporting (CLEAR) system. The system currently shares information with 242 local, state and federal law enforcement and criminal justice agencies and will be expanded to share information in real time with all law enforcement in the state under its new name, I-CLEAR. In addition to the various command positions he has served in, Huberman also has served as a beat and tactical gang team officer with the department. He was recently named the Executive Director for the Office of Emergency Management and Communications (OEMC) where he manages the public safety communications system and coordinates major emergency response. He was awarded the Gary P. Hayes award for Innovation in Policing and most recently accepted CIO Magazine's Enterprise Value Award for CLEAR. Huberman holds a Master of Business Administration and a Master of Social Service Administration from the University of Chicago, where he was both an Albert Schweitzer and a Soros Fellow.

Barbara McDonald is currently a consultant acting as the Senior Advisor to the City of Chicago Office of Emergency Management and Communications. In this capacity she is responsible for the continuation of the development of the CLEAR system, which includes the expansion of I-CLEAR, as a powerful homeland security tool for law enforcement officials in Illinois and other jurisdictions; the ongoing development of the Personnel Suite;

the coordination of interagency plan developments and grant application processes for the City's homeland security efforts; and advising on the development of educational and public awareness campaigns to augment the Department's homeland security and technology initiatives.

Prior to her retirement, she served as Deputy Superintendent of the Bureau of Administrative Services for the Chicago Police Department where she directed activities related to Information and Strategic Services, Financial and Personnel Services, and oversaw five divisions: Personnel, Finance, Information Services, Records Services, and Research and Development Division. In this capacity she headed the design, marketing, funding, and implementation of *Citizen and Law Enforcement Analysis and Reporting*, or CLEAR B the Department's enterprise technology solution. CLEAR is widely recognized as the most advanced law enforcement technology system in the country. Acquired largely by private funding for the $30 million initiative, including an unprecedented $10 million pro-bono partnership with the Oracle Corporation. Recently awarded CIO Magazine's Grand Prize for Enterprise Value in a competition that included organizations such as Dell Computer, Ace Hardware, Continental Airlines, Pfizer, and Procter & Gamble.

Previous to becoming Deputy Superintendent in June of 2000, she served as the Assistant Deputy Superintendent for Research and Planning. In that capacity she directed the activities of the Research and Development Division and also served as the Co-Manager of the department-wide community-oriented policing model—the Chicago Alternative Policing Strategy (CAPS). She joined the Chicago Police Department in 1993 as the Director of the Research and Development Division.

Before coming to the Department, she served as Deputy Executive Director of the Illinois Criminal Justice Information Authority, the state's criminal justice planning agency. Prior to that she was the Director of the Illinois Juvenile Justice Commission and the Associate Director of the Illinois Law Enforcement Commission. Before coming to Illinois in 1978, she taught at the University of Vermont's College of Education and Social Services.

Ms. McDonald holds masters degrees in Planning and Administration and Human Resource Development from the University of Vermont and has done doctoral studies in Education at Boston University. In 1990, she became the first woman president of the National Criminal Justice Association (NCJA), a Washington-based interest group representing state and local governments on issues concerning public safety and criminal justice. She is one of the principal architects of the Chicago Alternative Policing Strategy (CAPS), which has gained national recognition since its inception.

In 1995, she received the Police Executive Research Forum's (PERF) Gary P. Hayes Award for her work with CAPS. She also served for several years as policy staff to the Major Cities Chiefs, an organization of the top law enforcement executives from 57 of the largest urban areas in the United States and Canada. She also serves on the PERF Board of Directors.

In 1988, **Nancy McPherson** was hired by the Police Executive Research Forum (PERF), an association of law enforcement executives in Washington, D.C., to develop and implement Problem Oriented Policing in the San Diego Police Department. From 1990, Nancy worked as the Manager of Neighborhood Policing for the San Diego Police Department, reporting directly to the City Manager and the Police Chief. In 1994, Nancy moved to the Seattle Police Department as the first civilian assistant chief where she worked until 2000. In December 2000, Nancy began as the Director of Services for the Portland Police Bureau, serving as a civilian at the assistant chief level where she is responsible for Training, Police Corp, Personnel, Data Processing, Records, Fiscal, Alarm Administration, and Management Services. Since 1990, Nancy has worked as a consultant assisting cities and leaders in developing a problem oriented approach to city government. She was appointed to the California Attorney General's Advisory Board on Community Policing. She was one of two Americans to serve as an expert advisor to the British Columbia Royal Commission of Inquiry on Policing in 1993. Nancy was also appointed by the LAPD to their Advisory Committee on Community Policing in 1991. In 1990, she co-founded the International Problem Oriented Policing Conference in San Diego now in its 13th year. Nancy is the recipient of a number of awards including PERF's Gary Hayes Leadership Award in 1998 given each year at PERF's annual conference to one police professional in the nation for leadership and inspiration. Nancy has a B.A. in political science from San Diego State University and a MPA from Old Dominion University in Norfolk, Virginia. Nancy is a graduate of LEAD, San Diego, and Leadership Tomorrow, Seattle. She has volunteered as a coach/mentor for youth development programs including Big Sisters, the YWCA, and the Youth Economic Enterprise Zones.

Richard Myers has served as Chief of Police since 1995 for the City of Appleton, Wisconsin. A native of Michigan, he has previously served as the Police Chief in a suburb of Chicago and in two communities in metropolitan Detroit. Prior police experience includes service as a public safety officer, a sheriff's deputy, and a medical examiner investigator. Myers is an active member of numerous professional organizations including PERF and IACP, and is a current member and past president of both the Society of Police Futurists International and the Wisconsin Chiefs of Police Association.

Myers received his Bachelor's and Master's degrees from Michigan State University, where he studied under advocates of Community-Oriented Policing (COP) such as David Carter and the late Robert Trojanowicz. He is a graduate of the FBI National Academy and the FBI LEEDS programs.

Dennis P. Rosenbaum is Professor of Criminal Justice and Psychology and Director of the Center for Research in Law and Justice at the University of Illinois at Chicago. Previously, he served in the positions of institute director, department head, and Dean. Dr. Rosenbaum's research agenda has focused on police, community, and school efforts to prevent violence and drug abuse. In addition to community policing initiatives, he has evaluated community mobilization efforts, comprehensive interagency partnerships, media-based crime prevention, school-based drug education, and crime prevention in public housing. Dr. Rosenbaum has completed eight books and numerous articles. He teaches courses in research methods, evaluation research, organizational behavior, community processes, and policing. His latest research seeks to understand the formation of African American and Hispanic attitudes toward the police in Chicago, the effects of the Internet on police-community relations and community empowerment, and the effects of inter-agency partnerships on youth and gun violence.

Dr. Ellen Scrivner, the Deputy Superintendent, Bureau of Administrative Services at the Chicago Police Department, is the former Deputy Director for Community Policing Development of the Office of Community Oriented Policing Services (COPS). She previously served as Assistant Director of the Training and Technical Assistance Division of the COPS Office where she managed all training and technical assistance initiatives and was instrumental in launching the innovative Regional Community Policing Institutes Program, a nationwide network of community policing training opportunities for police and citizens. She is a national expert on community policing and police integrity and has consulted to some of the larger departments in the country. She has written about community policing, the requisite broad-based changes in training that are needed to institutionalize this type of policing, and the related impact on police integrity. Prior to government service, Dr. Scrivner studied police behavior over a twenty-year career as a police psychologist before being selected as a Visiting Fellow at the National Institute of Justice (NIJ).

Wesley G. Skogan is a Professor of Political Science and a Faculty Fellow at the Institute for Policy Research at Northwestern University. Dr. Skogan, an expert on crime and policing, has conducted research on fear of crime, citizen participation in community crime prevention, and victim responses to crime. He directed the evaluation of Chicago's experimental citywide community policing initiative which resulted in a co-authored book entitled *Community Policing, Chicago Style*. Skogan has written four other books and numerous journal articles, monographs and chapters on police and crime topics.

Darrel Stephens was appointed Charlotte-Mecklenburg Police Chief in September 1999 where he is responsible for an organization of 2000 employees serving a population of 625,000 people. Prior to Charlotte, he was the City Administrator for the City of St. Petersburg for two years and the police chief from December 1992 to June 1997. He came to St. Petersburg after serving for 6.5 years as the Executive Director of the Washington; DC-based association the Police Executive Research Forum (PERF). He began his career in 1968 as a police officer with the Kansas City, Missouri Police Department, which included a 10-month visiting fellowship at the National Institute of Justice in 1972. He was appointed Assistant Police Chief in Lawrence, Kansas in 1976. In 1979 he moved to Largo, Florida where he served as police chief for 3 years. In 1983 he took the Police Chief's position in Newport News, Virginia where that department became nationally recognized for its work with problem oriented policing. He has co-authored several books and published many articles on policing issues. He holds a B.S. degree in the Administration of Justice from the University of Missouri-Kansas City and an MS degree in Public Administration from Central Missouri State University.

Mary Ann Wycoff began conducting research on policing for the Police Foundation in 1972 and, in 1995, with the Police Executive Research Forum. Her first project was a study of the efforts of the Dallas Police Department to reshape the organization and its approach to policing. Thirty years later, very similar efforts would be recognized as the implementation of community policing. It is a development that Ms. Wycoff has observed for thirty years and the movement has been the focus of her research throughout her career.

About The
Annie E. Casey Foundation

The Annie E. Casey Foundation was established in 1948 by Jim Casey, a founder of the United Parcel Service, and his siblings, George, Harry and Marguerite. Named in honor of their mother, the foundation first provided grants to support a camp for disadvantaged young children in Seattle, Washington. When Jim Casey left UPS in the 1960's, he began to meet with experts in the field of child welfare and learned of the many problems facing children growing up in the foster care system.

Casey Family Programs was established in 1966 and now operates as an independent operating foundation in Seattle while the Casey Family Services, headquartered in New Haven, Connecticut, has eight operating divisions and offers an array of foster care and other services throughout the New England area and Maryland.

Drawing on an examination of past investments and the best practices of other private and public institutions, the foundation today works primarily in the areas of family development and community building. The Foundation continues to build upon its original bedrock principles, including supporting social, civic, and faith-based institutions; providing accessible and responsive public services, such as good health care, decent schools, and fair and effective law enforcement.

About PERF

The Police Executive Research Forum (PERF) is a national professional association of chief executives of large city, county and state law enforcement agencies. PERF's objective is to improve the delivery of police services and the effectiveness of crime control through several means:

- the exercise of strong national leadership,
- the public debate of police and criminal issues,
- the development of research and policy, and
- the provision of vital management and leadership services to police agencies.

PERF members are selected on the basis of their commitment to PERF's objectives and principles. PERF operates under the following tenets:

- Research, experimentation and exchange of ideas through public discussion and debate are paths for the development of a comprehensive body of knowledge about policing.
- Substantial and purposeful academic study is a prerequisite for acquiring, understanding and adding to that body of knowledge.
- Maintenance of the highest standards of ethics and integrity is imperative in the improvement of policing.
- The police must, within the limits of the law, be responsible and accountable to citizens as the ultimate source of police authority.
- The principles embodied in the Constitution are the foundation of policing.